Fred Jones

Tools for Teaching

Discipline · Instruction · Motivation

Fredric H. Jones, Ph.D.

with

Patrick Jones and Jo Lynne Jones

Illustrations by Brian T. Jones

Fredric H. Jones & Associates, Inc.

103 Quarry Lane
Santa Cruz, CA 95060
tel: (831) 425-8222   fax: (831) 426-8222
info@fredjones.com   www.fredjones.com

Finalist for the 2002
Association of Educational Publishers
Golden Lamp Award

Finalist for the 2001
Independent Publishers
IPPY Award

Executive Producer: Jo Lynne T. Jones
Production and Web Design: Patrick Jones
Illustrations: Brian T. Jones
Book Design and Cover: CHRW Advertising

ISBN: 0-9650263-0-2
Library of Congress Catalog Control Number: 00-091002

printed in Hong Kong
1st Edition

00 01 02 03 04 05   12 11 10 9 8 7 6 5 4

Contents

iv

Preface

Over ten years ago, I published two books with McGraw-Hill entitled, *Positive Classroom Discipline* and *Positive Classroom Instruction*. I intended for them to be one volume because I considered the skills of classroom management to be totally interdependent. But McGraw-Hill had other ideas. I also thought it should be published under a single cover as a textbook, but McGraw-Hill said, "There is no point in publishing a textbook for a course that no one is offering." I couldn't fault their logic on that point.

A lot has changed over the past decade. Teachers routinely receive courses in classroom management as part of their training. Many young teachers who come to my workshops say things like, "Oh, you're the same Fred Jones that was in my college textbook. I thought you were dead."

I put off writing updated versions of the first two books because, frankly, it is very hard to write books and travel at the same time. I rationalized, "They're not dated. Fundamentals don't change." Actually, that was only a half-truth. Fundamentals don't change, but my understanding of them certainly does.

I have never given a workshop without returning home knowing more than I did when I went out. New insights come from stories that teachers tell me, from discussions over lunch, or perhaps from answering a question that forces me to think on my feet in a new way. And, of course, I read constantly. I may be thinking about some aspect of

body language only to read a journal article about the body language of flirting or the signalling of dominance and submission. Suddenly, a few more pieces of the puzzle fall into place.

I realized how much my understanding of classroom management had grown when I finally sat down to write this book. Discussions of key aspects of classroom management such as meaning business and Responsibility Training are on an entirely different plane from those contained in *Positive Classroom Discipline* and *Positive Classroom Instruction*. They are more thorough and more clear.

In addition, my perspective has changed as I have gotten older. I don't much care about impressing my academic peers any more, and that somehow makes my writing more straightforward. I am writing for teachers now. Most of them are the age of my own children. I just want to describe how the best teachers make success look easy so that the rest of us can do the same. When I read that over a third of new teachers quit before the end of their second year, I feel a deep sense of loss. Most of them would still be teaching if they had been given the skills to succeed without working themselves to death.

This book is the culmination of all that I have learned about managing classrooms. It describes the fundamentals of the job of being a classroom teacher. It is my gift back to the profession.

Acknowledgements

I credit my wife Jo Lynne with much of my interest in classrooms. Throughout my years in graduate school she was a classroom teacher, and every night when she came home from work, we had a 1-hour "debriefing" – like the astronauts have when they return from space. During our debriefings I relived every trauma and gratification of the day, and by Thanksgiving, her students were, for better or for worse, members of the family. After years of debriefings, you either get very interested in classrooms or you get entirely turned off by the whole subject. When I began to do classroom management research, Jo Lynne was a collaborator, and she has been my partner in this endeavor ever since.

Jo Lynne was the kind of teacher who did several hours of work each evening to prepare for the next day. Knowing how hard good teachers work has been a crucial consideration in the development of the classroom management methods contained in this book. It is not enough for a technique to succeed. It must also be affordable on a daily basis in terms of time and energy.

I must also acknowledge a debt to my family. I come from a family of teachers. Both sides of my family come from Lancaster County, Pennsylvania, and they have supplied the area with teachers for four generations. Not only was my mother a teacher, but so also were many aunts and great-aunts. Both of my parents taught me crucial lessons about effective discipline before I ever entered a class-room. One of the most important lessons was that strength and firmness could be both gentle and loving.

When I sit down to write with pen on paper, it always ends up reading like an essay. Workshops have an entirely different character, so spontaneous and conversational. In order to put that feeling into this book, I dictated the manuscript to my older son Patrick. He would type a section as I repeatedly stopped and started, and then we would read it on the computer screen. Patrick was a great help in addition to being very patient. I remember one time dictating a paragraph on verbosity. After we read it over, I said to Patrick, "What do you think?" He said, "Do you really want to know?" I reread it and cracked up before I got halfway through. "A little verbose, huh?"

My son, Brian, did all of the cartoons and graphics for the book. He was finishing at San Francisco Art Institute just as Patrick and I were beginning the manuscript. Brian has cartooning in his blood. The timing was perfect. I said to Brian, "How would you like your first job to be drawing 50 or 60 cartoons for my new book? We are going to do it in full color." It was not a hard sell.

I also want to thank Virginia Rossi, Stephanie Hill, Monique Jones, and Jenny Rosenfeld for keeping the office running during this project and for proofreading. Without their help, we would still be struggling to finish the manuscript.

Beyond the Book

Skill Building

Tools for Teaching describes the skills of classroom management in detail. Any treatment of skills, however, leads to the topic of skill building. To help teachers master *Tools for Teaching*, we provide materials and resources that extend beyond the contents of this book.

Web Site: **www.fredjones.com**

In this age of cyberspace a book can be more than just the pages between a cover. Resources for skill building and staff development are provided for **free** at our web site.

Study Group Activity Guide

The *Study Group Activity Guide* structures twelve 45-minute after school meetings in which teachers share ideas, solve problems, and practice the tools for teaching. It is our hope that the *Study Group Activity Guide* along with *Tools for Teaching* can provide quality staff development for individual teachers and entire faculties regardless of budgetary limitations. Each meeting includes:

- reading assignments with focus questions
- sharing and problem solving
- performance checklists
- skill building activities

Skill building activities include the practice of discrete management skills plus simulations of more complex classroom management scenarios. Coaching skills are described in detail so that participants can help each other "learn by doing." In addition, a Group Problem Solving Process is provided so that participants can develop effective strategies for management dilemmas as they arise.

Sharing

While Study Group meetings include sharing, the web site also provides opportunities for teachers to share their ideas and experiences with colleagues worldwide. Sections of the web site devoted to sharing include a Preferred Activity Bank, applications of Bell Work, tips for substitute teachers, a message board, and a college report page.

Video Toolbox

Any attempt to build skills must rely heavily on the visual modality – the modality most limited in the book as well as the web site. The *Video Toolbox* augments the book and the web site by giving you a front row seat at one of Dr. Jones' workshops in which he explains procedures, models key skills, and demonstrates skill building exercises.

The *Video Toolbox* contains twelve training sessions, one for each meeting in the *Study Group Activity Guide*. In addition, Overview and Coaching tapes are included. The Overview tape shows Dr. Jones presenting highlights of *Tools for Teaching*; The Coaching tape models the steps of each skill building exercise and classroom simulation and provides a demonstration of the Group Problem Solving Process.

Section One

Building a Classroom Management System

Chapter One

Learning from the "Natural" Teachers

Succeeding in the Classroom

Focus on Teachers

This book is for teachers. I want teachers to enjoy teaching.

I know teachers who thrive in the classroom. They are energized by teaching. I have heard them say, "I can't wait until school starts." These teachers, however, are a distinct minority.

Most teachers are exhausted by the end of the day. Over a third of new teachers quit by the end of their second year on the job. Many who stay suffer from burn-out.

Most of the stress of teaching comes from getting students to do things. Managing the behavior of young people is no easy job, as any parent can tell you. Managing a whole classroom full of young people is the subject of this book.

Focus on Students

This book is for the students. For students to learn, they must enjoy learning. They must look forward to entering the classroom in the morning.

Some teachers create just such classrooms. They make learning an adventure. There is excitement in the air.

It is no mystery to the parents who these teachers are. They can see how one teacher causes their child to love school while another teacher causes the same child to

Preview

- All of our efforts to improve education come down to the classroom. Whether or not lessons come alive and students learn depends upon the teacher's skill.

- In some fortunate classrooms, both the teacher and the students look forward to getting to school in the morning. This book describes how to produce such classrooms.

- Many of the lessons in this book were learned in the classrooms of gifted or "natural" teachers. As a result, the procedures described are practical and down to earth.

- Natural teachers do not work themselves to death. Instead, they put the students to work.

- Effective management saves you time and effort. As a result, you have more time for learning and enjoyment in the classroom, and more energy after you get home.

You are on your toes all day long until the bell rings.

complain and fall behind. Parents know that the key to success in the classroom is the teacher.

Focus on Classrooms

All of our efforts to improve education come down to the classroom. National policies and state mandates and district guidelines must be translated into better teaching practices, or they are of no use.

Whether or not lessons come alive and students learn depends upon the teacher's skill. Whether or not the students are even on task depends on the teacher's ability to manage the group.

This book is about classroom management. It is a description of the skills that exceptional teachers use to make classrooms come alive.

Enjoying Learning

Learning by Doing

Students learn by doing. They like being active. Even more, they like being interactive.

Students enjoy learning when the process of instruction engages all of their senses. When the students enjoy learning, teachers enjoy teaching.

Reducing "Goofing Off"

Within the classroom, the main impediment to learning by doing is *not doing*. The many ways of *not doing* are known to us all from experience – whispering to the kid sitting next to us, passing notes, sharpening pencils just to be out of our seats, doodling, dawdling and gazing out the window. We will refer to these pleasures of the flesh collectively as *goofing off*.

Teaching a lesson would not be so hard if the students would just pay attention and get to work. It is the goofing off that wears you down.

Then, you keep working into the evening.

When exasperation mounts, we swing into action. At such times, we sound like a recording of every teacher we ever had.

"Robert, would you please stop talking and get some work done?"

"Sandra, I am sick and tired of looking up to find you out of your seat."

"What are you two playing with? Let me see that."

Working Yourself to Death

How do you get a classroom full of students to do what you want them to do all day long – hand papers in, pass papers out, get into groups, line up, sit down, pay attention, take turns? How about the students who sit helplessly with their hands raised day after day and say, "I don't understand how to do this!"? How about the students who say, "This is stupid!"?

After school you have parent conferences, committee meetings, and paper grading. You are on your toes all day long, and then you keep working into the evening. You can *run yourself ragged.*

But, some of our colleagues find the job *energizing.* These teachers do not work themselves to death. They work *smart,* not hard.

Lessons from Natural Teachers

We Have a Problem

The year was 1969, and I was asked to consult at a private school for emotionally, behaviorally and learning handicapped junior-high-age students. All of them had been "removed" from Los Angeles Unified School District. I had just been given a free ticket to the all-star game of classroom goof-offs.

"Group, I am simply going to wait until you all settle down!"

On my first visit, I observed four classrooms, two in the morning and two in the afternoon. The two I observed in the morning were a shock.

As I approached the first classroom, I could hear yelling. As I entered, I saw only empty chairs. I looked to my left and saw, to my amazement, nine kids crouched *on top* of the coat closet staring at me. I thought, "What an unusual lesson format."

Then, a half-dozen other kids poured out of the coat closet. They were armed with items of clothing with which they began pelting the students above. One student leaped from on top of the coat closet to wrestle a classmate to the floor.

In front of this scene was a male teacher who was donating his body to the betterment of young people – his stomach lining, his dental work, and his circulatory system. With arms folded, teeth clenched and a look of grim desperation he shouted,

"Group!"

This worried me. I am a clinical psychologist by training, and I had spent years working with groups. I knew all about group process, group dynamics, group communication, group problem-solving. I did not see a *group*.

Then, he said,

"I am simply going to *wait* until you *all* settle down!"

I didn't know how long he had been waiting. It was November.

The second classroom I visited that morning was almost as bad. A young female teacher was leading a class discussion. I could tell because everyone was talking. Who do you think was talking louder than any of the students?

"Class, there is absolutely no excuse for all of this noise!"

By the end of the morning, I desperately wanted to leave. But, since I had promised, I stuck it out past lunch.

Observing Two Naturals

After lunch I watched the students who had been on top of the coat closet enter a new teacher's classroom. The teacher greeted them warmly at the door. The students took their seats as they entered, looked at the chalkboard where an assignment was posted, and went to work.

When the bell to begin class rang, no one looked up. The students worked on a math assignment for about twenty minutes. Then, there was a lesson transition. The teacher said,

"I want you to place your papers here on the corner of my desk. If you need to sharpen pencils, now is the time to do it. Get a drink of water if you need to, and return to your seats."

I thought, *This is where chaos sets in.*

However, the students did as the teacher instructed and were back in their seats ready to go in *41 seconds*. The teacher then conducted a group discussion in which the students *took turns.* Since the faculty at UCLA could not do that on the best day of their lives, I was thoroughly impressed. Throughout the

Good Instincts

The natural teachers had no technology of management. They had good instincts.

ten similar results with the refugees from the morning's group discussion. She had her own style, of course, but, with apparent ease, she got respectful behavior and good work.

As far as the management of discipline is concerned, I observed three characteristics of these teachers that I will never forget.

- They were not working hard at discipline management. In fact, they were not working very hard at all.

- They were relaxed.

- They were emotionally warm.

At the very least, I learned that discipline management did not have to be humorless or stressful or time-consuming. You certainly do not have to wait until December to discover the secret. All that I saw were two "old pros" making it look easy.

They Didn't Have a Clue

These two exceptional teachers could not have been more generous in their efforts to help me understand

their teaching methods. Unfortunately, they did not help very much.

They both said, "You have to mean business."

I said, "Right! What does that mean?"

They said, "Well, on the first day of school, the classroom will either belong to you or it will belong to them."

I said, "Right! What do you do?"

They said, "Frankly, a lot of it has to do with expectations. If you do not expect them to learn, they won't."

I said, "Right! How do you get them to do that?"

They said, "Well, a lot of it has to do with the value of learning that you impart to the students."

I said, "*Wait!* Give me credit for good values and good expectations. I want to know *what to do*. Imagine that I am a substitute teacher taking over your class tomorrow morning. You obviously have the students in a groove. I don't want to lose it. What do I do?"

"Oh, yes," they said. "I see. Hmmmm. Well, I can tell you this much. You had better mean business."

On that day I learned something remarkable about these natural teachers. They could not tell me what they were doing if their lives depended on it. They had no technology of management. They had *good instincts*.

Common Sense

My best explanation for the inability of natural teachers to explain their management skills is that they learned them from their *parents*. Before they even went to kindergarten, these teachers had been on the receiving end of effective management thousands of times as their parents taught them to come to the dinner table, pick up their toys, share, and take turns.

class period, these students behaved like any well-mannered group of kids.

I might have written this experience off as a fluke had not the second teacher of the afternoon gotten

But, early childhood learning is not accompanied by a descriptive language. Rather, natural teachers describe it as "common sense." In later life we will call this learning *instinct*.

The down side of instinct is that natural teachers have no way of passing their expertise on to the next generation of teachers. There is no terminology, no scope and sequence of skills, no task analysis.

The lesson to be learned from this is clear. Choose your parents very carefully. They are your primary "methods course."

Making Management Affordable

Management Can Be Expensive

I very much wanted to understand how these natural teachers could get so much good behavior from problem students. I especially wanted to know how they did it without working themselves to death.

At that time, we at the university were in the throes of the "behavior modification revolution." We had learned that consequences govern the rate of behavior; and we were setting up contingency management programs for every behavior problem in the classroom from acting out to social isolation.

The real problem, from my perspective, was *cost*. We were designing individualized management programs for students with problems such as aggression, social isolation, and oppositionalism. Each program was custom-built

and required conferences after school, data collection, specialized contingencies, and constant monitoring.

The good news was that these programs worked. The bad news was that they cost an arm and a leg. I once calculated that teachers who were using one of my "B-Mod" programs had to spend between 30 and 45 minutes a day just to implement it.

To my mind these apparent classroom successes were, in fact, thoroughly impractical. We had just consumed the teacher's planning period to solve one behavior problem. The teacher had a dozen other problems in the same classroom that were just as serious.

A Teacher Perspective on Cost

I came from a family of teachers – my mother, sister, aunts, great aunts, and many cousins. When we get together, it is like a staff development conference.

Growing up in such a family, I absorbed certain lessons about the teaching profession without anyone ever having to explain them to me. Prominent among them are:

- Teachers work twice as hard as the general public ever imagines.
- The last thing in the world that a teacher will ever have is "extra" time.

I knew from the beginning that if I came up with some hot new classroom management procedure that cost the

The last thing in the world that a teacher will ever have is 'extra' time.

teacher extra time for planning or record keeping, I could forget it. If a system of classroom management is to truly help the teacher, it must *save* time. It must make your life easier.

The Naturals Make It Look Easy

How do the natural teachers manage an entire classroom while making it look easy? I decided to hang out in these classrooms until I figured it out. Little did I know that this was the beginning of a new career.

Yogi Berra once said, "You can see a lot by looking." So, I looked. I couldn't see a thing. What does Yogi know about classrooms? I was driven to desperation.

When you watch a natural at work, do not expect to see a big show. Effective management is, for the most part, invisible.

You will certainly not see most of the things we associate with classroom management in our memories of school. You will not see much rule enforcement. You will not hear nagging. You will not see students singled out.

Since effective management is hard to see, we tend to invent a mythology about the skills of these natural teachers. Maybe they are born with it – as though there are genes for classroom management. Maybe it is magic. Who knows?

Making Method Out of Magic

Over a period of two decades, I worked continuously with classroom teachers in every imaginable setting. Whatever they were most concerned with in their class-

rooms became my research agenda. A succession of natural teachers, excellent graduate students, my wife Jo Lynne, and I spent many an afternoon brainstorming following a day of classroom observation.

We would focus on a problem, and we would experiment until we solved it. Yet, whenever we solved a problem, our teachers would say, "That really helps. But, my main problem now is ..." And, off we would go on our next project.

Beyond The Naturals

We learned more from the natural teachers than we ever taught them.

Yet, over the course of decades we developed a knowledge of classroom management that far exceeds the practices of any single teacher.

We did our share of formal research and publication, but for every article there were dozens of little experiments that delineated the fine points of practice. We learned more from the natural teachers than we ever taught them. But, over the course of decades, we developed a knowledge of classroom management that far exceeded the practices of any single teacher.

Over the years, enough problems were solved to enable us to discern the outlines of the puzzle of classroom management. The puzzle is complex, but it is not overwhelming. This book contains the pieces of that puzzle.

Chapter Two

Focusing on Prevention

Preview

- This chapter is an overview of the topics described in the book.

- This book focuses on the fundamental skills of classroom management. These skills replace working hard with working smart.

- Instructional practices focus on making learning interactive while replacing helpless handraising with independent learning.

- The management of motivation focuses on helping students to internalize values of hard work and conscientiousness. Incentives for productivity combine enjoyment with accountability.

- Discipline management builds classroom structure that makes cooperation and responsible behavior a matter of routine. In addition, we will describe the subtle skills of meaning business.

Positive Classroom Management

Areas of Management

The pieces of the classroom management puzzle fall into three broad areas:

- **Instruction** – We will look at the *process* of instruction rather than *content*. How do we exploit *learning by doing* so that students learn rapidly with as little chance of error as possible? How do we exploit the visual modality of learning? How do we replace *helpless handraising* with *independent learning*?

- **Motivation** – We will look at motivation in terms of the incentives that a teacher can deliver during the teaching of a lesson. How do we give students a reason to work hard? How do we train them to be conscientious? How do we hold students accountable for achieving higher standards while increasing their enjoyment of learning?

- **Discipline** – We will look at increasing time-on-task while reducing both time wasting and fooling around. How do we prevent most of the goofing off in a typical classroom with structure that costs the teacher nothing in terms of time and energy? How do we "mean business" when setting limits on misbehavior? How do we train students to be responsible and to cooperate with each other – even the most alienated students who typically produce most of our office referrals?

A Classroom Management System

While all of these aspects of classroom management might seem to pull the teacher in many different directions at once, in fact, they do quite the opposite. Key elements of instruction, motivation, and discipline occur simultaneously so that they represent a consolidation of teacher effort. Together, they define working smart instead of working hard.

The system of classroom management described in this book has the following characteristics:

- **Specificity** – This book answers the question, "What do I *do?*" It deals in specifics rather than generalities. For example, rather than telling you that you need to *mean business*, which you already know, it describes exactly *how* to mean business. In addition, we will explain *why* procedures are used in specific situations so that, when you need to improvise, you will know what to do.

This book, however, does not contain an endless array of "handy hints" and prescriptions for solving problems. These prescriptions are not flexible enough to deal with the ever-changing realities of the classroom. And, you could never keep them all straight anyway.

Rather, we will focus on fundamentals – the basic skills and procedures of managing a classroom. The fundamentals never change. They are present in every management situation, and mastery allows you to adapt to situations as they unfold.

- **Economy** – Over the years I have thrown out more procedures that "worked" than I have kept. I threw them out because they were too expensive – too much planning, record keeping, and hassle.

The procedures that are included in this book have one thing in common. They produce dramatic results while *reducing* the teacher's workload. By sheer efficiency, they replace the stress of teaching with the enjoyment of teaching.

- **Prevention** – For classroom management to be affordable, the prevention of problems must take center stage. You cannot afford to be constantly interrupted by fooling around in the classroom. Nor, can you afford to have your time consumed during every lesson by helpless handraisers who greet you with, "I don't understand how to do this."

When you observe the classrooms of natural teachers, you simply see a room full of kids at work. It takes a few minutes for you to realize that something is missing. What is missing is the constant stream of hassles and diversions that normally consume the teacher's time and energy.

For teaching to be enjoyable, you must be able to simply relax and teach. Classroom management must be built from the ground up so that most potential problems simply do not occur.

While instruction, motivation, and discipline are intertwined in classroom management, it is possible to find a

Prevention and Enjoyment

For teaching to be enjoyable, you must be able to simply relax and teach. Classroom management must be built from the ground up so that most potential problems simply do not occur.

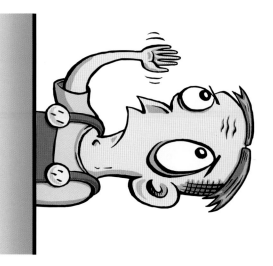

The natural enemy of working the crowd is the helpless handraiser.

starting point from which one thing logically leads to another. We will begin with instruction.

Instruction

Mobility and Proximity

The easiest way to prevent goofing off is *location*. The students who are *near* the teacher tend to be on their best behavior. It is the students on the far side of the classroom that you have to worry about.

Effective teachers make an art form out of working the crowd – otherwise known as "management by walking around." Rather than spending all of their time in the front of the classroom, they put the students to work and then walk among the students as they supervise.

As they move among the students, these teachers' proximity serves as a powerful deterrent to goofing off. While such teachers are typically more concerned with supervising the students' work than with discipline management, they nevertheless get a significant amount of discipline management for free.

Before these teachers can work the crowd, however, they must have *walkways*. To get walkways in classrooms that are already crowded, we will need to examine the arrangement of furniture.

Chapter Two: Focusing on Prevention

Learned Helplessness

Once teachers focus on mobility, they immediately confront the natural enemy of working the crowd – the *helpless handraisers*. Helpless handraising is epidemic during Guided Practice – that portion of the lesson during which students are supposed to be "working independently."

Every classroom seems to have five or six helpless handraisers who constantly demand the teacher's undivided time and attention. These students just sit with their hands raised and wait for help. When the teacher finally arrives, they say, "I don't understand what to do here."

The teacher then ends up tutoring these students through the lesson that he or she just taught the rest of the class not ten minutes before. This process of tutoring usually takes three to six minutes.

Unfortunately, the teacher pays a very high price for such tutoring. By the time ten seconds have passed, the classroom has become noisy. By the time twenty seconds have passed, students are wandering around the room. For the sake of tutoring the helpless handraisers, the teacher has lost the class.

Helpless handraising is epidemic for a reason. By playing helpless, these students get the teacher's attention for several minutes while the teacher does their assignment for them. The teacher's helping supplies the incentive for the help-seeking itself.

For this reason, learned helplessness is one of the most widespread learning disabilities in education. What other learning disability can you name that consistently occurs at a rate of five to six per classroom?

Understanding the teaching practices that foster learned helplessness in the classroom is the beginning of curing the problem. How, exactly, do you help a students who are stuck so that they do not become more helpless?

Even beyond that, how do you cure students who have been chronic helpless handraisers for as long as they have been in school?

If working the crowd is to have a chance, we must free the helpless handraisers from their dependency on the teacher and make them into *independent learners*. Accomplishing this, however, will impact almost everything else that we do in the classroom.

The Verbal Modality

As we just mentioned, a typical helping interaction during Guided Practice lasts three to six minutes. During that time, the teacher typically reteaches a major portion of the lesson. The more time the teacher spends with the helpless handraiser, the more he or she reinforces helplessness.

This dilemma raises a crucial methodological question that is typically ignored in teacher training. Exactly how do you help a student who is stuck?

To begin with, how much information can the student accurately store on the basis of one helping interaction? All learning takes place "one step at a time" for a reason – probably because that is all we can keep straight in short-term memory.

If we teach the student just one step rather than attempting to teach a major portion of the lesson, we can reduce cognitive overload while reducing the duration of the helping interaction. By teaching just one step, we can reduce the duration of the helping interaction to less than a minute.

Corrective feedback, therefore, focuses on giving a single prompt which answers the question, "What do I do next?" This pattern of giving corrective feedback is called Praise, Prompt, and Leave.

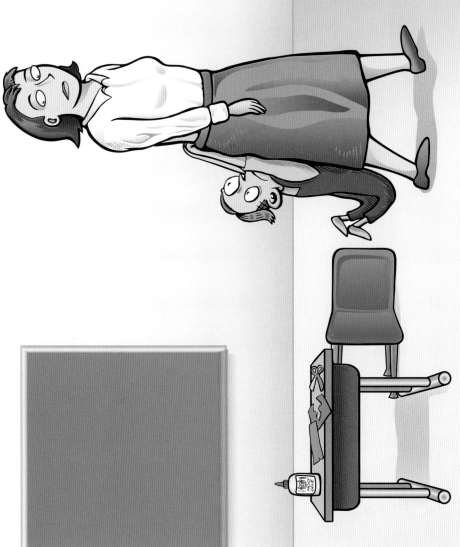

If working the crowd is to have a chance, we must free the helpless handraisers from their dependency on the teacher.

Simplifying the verbal modality of instruction in this fashion allows the teacher to do a better job of working the crowd. However, while a helping interaction of less than a minute is a great improvement, it is not good enough. The class gets noisy in 10 seconds.

The Visual Modality

The only way to reduce the duration of corrective feedback further is to *substitute pictures for words*. Good graphics provide the student with a picture for every step of performance. This *set of plans* prepackages the information normally contained in the teacher's prompts.

With good graphics, the teacher can briefly point out critical features of an operation or concept when helping a student and be gone. This can reduce the duration of a helping interaction to less than 5 seconds. Only at that point does working the crowd become the continuous pattern of movement that prevents most disruptions.

Say, See, Do Teaching

The better the lesson is taught, the less helplessness will be produced. Consequently, we will examine the process of instruction as one of the avenues to preventing learned helplessness.

We will focus on learning by doing. But, learning by doing can be undermined if the students must sit through an entire lesson presentation before they get to do anything.

One of the crucial junctures in the instructional process is the *time delay between input and output*. If output is immediate, the students have excellent recall. But, if output must wait until the end of a lengthy lesson presentation, cognitive overload and forgetting will be the norm, as will helpless handraising.

Consequently, we will pair one step at a time teaching with immediate output. The result is an input-output cycle that we call a *Say, See, Do Cycle*:

- Explain what to do next.
- Demonstrate how to do it.
- Have the students do it right away.

A lesson is a series of Say, See, Do cycles with enough repetition to create ease of performance *prior to* Guided Practice. Different lesson formats represent different ways of structuring how students learn by doing. Doing a concept in the social studies is quite different, for example, than doing a math problem.

Motivation

Why Should I?

Students who do not care about the lesson can be just as frustrating to the teacher as students who disrupt or constantly seek help. Before an unmotivated student will work hard, the teacher must answer one simple question, "Why should I?"

The answer to that question is known generically as an *incentive*. Any classroom teacher will have to know a thing or two about the design of incentive systems.

Some students have internalized incentives for working hard and being conscientious. They congratulate themselves and feel good when they do their best. We usually refer to this pattern among our better students as *a good work ethic*.

However, many, if not most, of our students have not yet internalized these values. And, they may never internalize these values unless we have a management structure that helps them do so.

On a lesson by lesson basis, these students need a *short-term goal* – a reinforcer for being diligent that occurs immediately. The rewards that we will use are called "preferred activities" – *learning* activities that the students look forward to doing. Students will be excused to do the preferred activities as soon as they complete the assignment.

Over time, good work habits can be internalized by those students who need help with motivation. The trick of incentive management is to make winners out of the weaker students so that they can consistently participate in the preferred activities. Otherwise, they are required to work without incentives until the bell rings.

Excellence and Accountability

Before a student can be excused from the assignment to do the preferred activity, the work must be completed *correctly*. If you excuse the student to do a preferred activity without first checking the work, you create a *speed incentive* in which you literally pay the student to go through the assignment as fast as possible regardless of errors.

The barrier to offering incentives for conscientiousness in the classroom is, therefore, *work check*. During Guided Practice, an entire room full of students is producing a lot of work. If the teacher falls too far behind in work check, incentives for diligence cannot be offered. The only alternative left is simply working until the bell rings.

Thus, in a program to manage motivation, incentives and accountability must always occur together. Fortunately, Say, See, Do Teaching plus our weaning program for the helpless handraisers leave the teacher relatively *unem-*

ployed during Guided Practice. Therefore, during Guided Practice, teachers have time to check work instead of tutoring helpless handraisers.

For teachers, the management of motivation actually represents *less time and effort*. The work check that used to occur in the evening can now occur *in class*. Consequently, work time after school is freed up. Teachers can now use it for planning tomorrow's instruction rather than having it consumed with paper grading.

> ## The mindset of meaning business is, 'I say what I mean, and I mean what I say.'

Discipline

Rules and Routines

While all teachers have some *general* rules for the classroom, such as *treat each other with respect*, these general rules might best be thought of as values clarification statements. The rules that generate behavior on a day-to-day basis are *specific* rules – the procedures and routines by which things get done.

Each procedure is a lesson and must be taught with the care and precision of any other lesson. Since there are many procedures and routines, teaching them is labor-intensive. Yet, while teaching classroom procedures takes a lot of time at the beginning of the semester, it more than pays for itself in time saved over the course of a semester.

The careful teaching of routines is crucial in establishing high standards for behavior in the classroom. Only by practicing routines to mastery do students learn that the teacher embodies the mindset of *meaning business*, namely, "I say what I mean, and I mean what I say," and, "We are going to keep doing this until we get it right."

Only when students realize that routines will be practiced when performance becomes sloppy do the "goof kids" put pressure on the "goof offs" to shape up. Only with the assistance of these students can the teacher's job of maintaining high standards become affordable.

Meaning Business

Effective classroom structure such as Say, See, Do Teaching, working the crowd, and well established routines can prevent most goofing off in the classroom. But,

Eighty percent of the goofing off in any classroom is "talking to neighbors."

the teacher will still have to respond to student disruptions on occasion. What do these disruptions look like?

While the school discipline code tends to focus on major infractions, those are not the problems that produce most of the stress and most of the lost learning time in the classroom. The bane of the teacher's existence is the *small disruption* that occurs at a *high rate*.

Of these small disruptions, 80 percent of them consist of students talking to their neighbors when they should be doing their work. The other 15 percent consists of students being out of their seats when they should be doing their work. These disruptions account for the high noise level in the classroom, and they squander huge amounts of learning time.

Teachers must have an effective way of dealing with these common disruptions if they are to increase time-on-task in the classroom. It is in dealing with these typical disruptions that teachers first demonstrate to the class the skills of meaning business.

But, how do you *mean business?* Meaning business is hard to see. The teachers who mean business rarely have discipline problems, rarely raise their voices, and almost never send students to the office. Since meaning business is intangible, we have developed a mythology about it which includes the notion that it is something natural teachers are born with.

Meaning business is hard to see because it is transmitted through *body language*, and body language is subtle. Yet, using body language to your advantage can be taught just like any other skill. In this book you will receive a crash course in body language.

Students instinctively understand body language. They have been reading it since before they could walk. They can read you like a book.

You have only two choices. You can learn about body language so that you can use it to create learning. Or, you can spend your life in front of a room full of students who are one step ahead of you.

Responsibility Training

How do you train a classroom full of students to be responsible? Once again, we must answer the question, "Why should I?" as in, "Why should I bring a pencil to class? Why should I sharpen my pencil during the break? Why should I be in my seat when the bell rings? Why should I hustle during a lesson transition?"

As mentioned earlier, the answer to the question, "Why should I?" is called an incentive. In discipline management, incentives are used to produce cooperation and responsible behavior. Incentives can save huge amounts of learning time by having students ready to work when the bell rings and by eliminating dawdling.

The incentive system that achieves these goals for the entire class most efficiently is called Responsibility Training. Responsibility Training is a group management program which embodies the principle, *one for all, and all for one.*

Omission Training

Unfortunately, there is usually at least one student in any class who would ruin any group incentive just to prove that he or she can. How do you succeed with the highly alienated and oppositional student?

Omission Training is a specialized incentive system for dealing with these difficult students. It can be added to Responsibility Training at very little effort to the teacher.

Omission Training provides a powerful incentive for the alienated student to work with the group rather than against the group. Once this is accomplished, the teacher's need for severe disciplinary actions decreases dramatically. As a by-product, these alienated students, who are often highly unpopular, are rapidly accepted into the peer group.

The Backup System

The Backup System has as its objective the management of severe and chronic misbehavior. The school discipline code is the part of the Backup System with which people are most familiar.

The logic of the school discipline code is simple and timeless – the punishment fits the crime. The bigger the

We must answer the question, "Why should I?" as in, "Why should I sharpen my pencil during the break?"

crime, the bigger the punishment. The result is a "hierarchy of consequences" which usually begins with a verbal warning and ends with suspension and expulsion.

Unfortunately, the school discipline code has never worked all that well. The same 5 percent of the student body produces 95 percent of the office referrals for the entire duration of their "academic careers."

Part of the Backup System, however, occurs inside of the classroom and is under the teacher's control. These small backup responses attempt to nip problems in the bud before they become so large that the student has to be sent out of the classroom. The small backup responses are described in detail so that you will know exactly what to do the first time an obnoxious behavior occurs.

Small backup responses are not so much sanctions as communications. They are given privately so as not to embarrass the student in front of his or her peers. While the specific wording will be your own, the general message is as follows:

"A word to the wise. We are entering the backup system. This would be a good time to stop what you are doing if you want to avoid getting into trouble."

If the student takes the teacher seriously and "shapes up," management is cheap for everyone concerned. But, if the student does not take the teacher seriously, the communication will have no effect. The ability of the teacher to keep small problems from becoming large problems, therefore, hinges on the student's perception of the teacher as meaning business rather than on the size of the sanction employed.

Building on Fundamentals

Once you master the fundamentals of classroom management, you can adapt successfully to the unpredictable.

But, without that mastery, you are constantly left wondering what to do next, and you are forced to invent on the spot.

You do not have much of a choice as a teacher other than to master these fundamentals. Take *meaning business* as an example. It is conveyed through body language, and the human species has only one body language. It has operated in the same predictable fashion since we lived in caves.

Say, See, Do Teaching is another example. You must teach to the brain the way it is built. If you do, learning will be relatively rapid, errors will be infrequent, and forgetting will be slow. But, if you do not, learning will be difficult and teaching will be exasperating.

Working the crowd is another example. The biggest single variable that governs the likelihood of a student goofing off in class is his or her physical distance from your body. You can either exploit mobility and proximity to create time on task, or you can pay the price.

Once you master the fundamentals, however, you will be able to manage a class without working yourself to death. Some of our most typical feedback from teachers is,

"I have energy at the end of the day. I have a life after school."

"I have recouped large amounts of time that the students used to waste. This gives me time for the enrichment activities and learning games that the students love."

"Why didn't I get this twenty years ago?"

Being truly good at classroom management will free you up for the fun part of this profession – teaching students who want to learn.

Section Two

Exploiting Proximity

Chapter Three

Working the Crowd

Physical Proximity

Where Does Goofing Off Start?

I'll bet you already know the most important single fact about the management of goofing off in the classroom. After all, you spent the whole first part of your life calculating the odds.

Look at the diagram of a classroom at the right. The "X" marks the spot where the teacher is standing. Imagine that you are the teacher and that you are helping a student who is stuck.

Now, place your finger on the spot in the classroom where goofing off is most likely to begin.

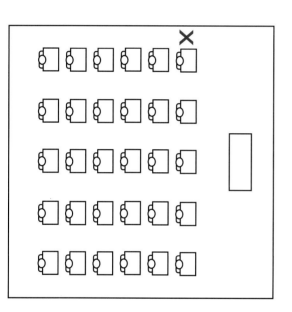

Preview

- The most basic factor that governs the likelihood of students goofing off in the classroom is their physical distance from the teacher's body.

- Effective teachers make an art form of working the crowd. They know that either you work the crowd, or the crowd works you.

- By using mobility and proximity as tools of management, teachers constantly disrupt the students' impulse to be disruptive.

- Since these teachers are typically supervising the students' work as they move about the room, they get discipline management for free.

- Working the crowd provides perfect camouflage for setting limits on disruptions when they do occur. Since the teacher can speak to the student from close range, he or she can avoid embarrassing the student in front of the peer group.

You Know How It Works

Chances are, you put your finger on the corner of the room that is farthest from the teacher. You know how it works.

When the teacher is standing near you, you cool it. If you are not working, you at least make it *look* as though you are working. But, when the teacher is on the far side of the room, well, that is a different story.

The most basic factor that governs the likelihood of students goofing off in the classroom is *physical distance from the teacher's body*. The closer the teacher is, the *less* likely they are to goof off. The farther away the teacher is, the *more* likely they are to goof off.

Proximity and Mobility

Watching Natural Teachers

When you watch natural teachers, you do not see very many things that you would label as "management techniques." Rather, you see a room full of students who are busy working.

While the students work, the teacher *walks*. The teacher meanders around the classroom supervising the students' work in a most unremarkable fashion.

If you were to ask a naive observer what the teacher was doing, the answer would probably be *nothing*. The observers might occasionally see the teacher lean over to help a student. But typically it looks as though the teacher is just "cruising" around. Only after you watch a lot of classrooms and note

the differences between the effective and ineffective teachers does the importance of this cruising become apparent.

Crowd Control

As I mentioned in the previous chapter, once a discipline problem occurs, management cannot be truly cheap. When a problem occurs, you must stop and deal with the problem or declare "open season" on yourself. If you stop and deal with the problem, it will take time and energy, and it will pull you away from instruction.

Consequently, before we get into complicated discipline management techniques, think in *simple* terms. In a classroom there are roughly 30 students. That is a *crowd*. The most basic level of discipline management is *crowd control*.

Crowd control does not create a perfect classroom. Rather, crowd control gets *most* of the students to do *most* of what they are supposed to be doing *most* of the time. If teachers can get most of the management they need cheaply through crowd control, they can then afford to give their undivided attention to the few problems that are left over.

Working the Crowd

The most basic technique of crowd control is called "working the crowd." Anyone who earns a living in front of a crowd will come to understand working the crowd. Singers, comedians, teachers and preachers – they all work the crowd. They know that, *Either you work the crowd, or the crowd works you.*

Either you work the crowd, or the crowd works you.

Entertainers will work the crowd with *movement, eye contact* and *energy*. If they feel that they are losing part of the room, they will work that area all the harder.

If, for example, people at a table are talking instead of paying attention, performers will direct everything to that table until they have eye contact. Thereafter, they will focus on that table as often as they need to in order to keep from losing it. If they were to allow that table to "leave," they would probably lose the table next to it and the table next to it until they were playing to the backs of peoples' heads over the noise of conversation.

Natural teachers instinctively work the crowd. They have an innate sense of being "in contact" with the students. They use the proximity of their bodies as an instrument of management. They *move*.

Psychological Distance

Zones of Proximity

Imagine a teacher walking among the students. Picture three *zones of proximity* surrounding the teacher's body in concentric circles. We will use the colors of a stoplight to represent these three zones: *red, yellow* and *green*.

Next, think of every student in the classroom as having a computer whirring in the back of his or her brain dedicated to answering the question, *Is the coast clear?* This computer is operating at all times, even though it may not be at a conscious level. It calculates such things as how far away the teacher is, which direction the teacher is facing, and whether he or she is preoccupied.

The *red zone* is a circular area around the teacher roughly eight feet in radius. Using the stoplight as our analogy, *red* means *stop*.

Students in the red zone cool it. Their computer says, "Goofing off now would be really stupid. You would get nailed." Very few problems occur in the red zone.

Outside of the red zone is the *yellow* zone. The yellow zone extends another six feet in every direction. *Yellow* signals *caution*.

Calculating the Odds

All students have computers in their brains dedicated to answering the question,

Is the coast clear?

In the yellow zone students act much the way students in the red zone act – as long as the teacher is facing in their direction. But if the teacher should become distracted by helping a student for a little too long, especially if the teacher's back is turned, the computer signals, *Coast clear.* Suddenly a part of the student's brain wakes up – the part that likes to goof off.

Outside of the yellow zone lies the *green zone* – *green* as in *go!* When students in the green zone look up to see that the teacher is on the far side of the room, particularly if the teacher is preoccupied, the little computer in the back of the brain gets excited and says, *Why not?*

Students in the green zone, however, do not start goofing off immediately. They have to be in the green zone for a little while before things start to happen. The brain needs a little time to notice that the coast is clear, to cook up a plan, and to cast an eye about for an accomplice.

The longer students are in the green zone, the more likely goofing off becomes. Imagine students in the back half of the classroom of a teacher who spends all of his or her time standing in the front. These students will spend the whole semester in the green zone. Oh my!

Disrupting Disruptions

As effective teachers work the crowd, they constantly cause the zones to change. Imagine students who look up to see that they are in the green zone. But just when their computers signal, *Coast clear*, the teacher looks their way and casually strolls in their direction.

Dang! says the computer. *I hate it when that happens! Oh, well, back to work.*

When a teacher is working the crowd, two or three steps will switch a student from the green zone to the yellow zone or from the yellow zone to the red zone. Thus, through mobility, the teacher is constantly disrupting the students' impulse to disrupt.

Kids feel safer goofing off in the green zone.

Of course, neither the teacher nor the students monitor these calculations at a conscious level. It is *subconscious* — on the edge of awareness.

When I asked teachers who work the crowd why they move among the students, they said, "So I can see how they are doing." They always looked at me as though it were the most obvious thing in the world.

But I asked the question because I wanted to know whether their use of proximity was conscious or instinctive. I found that it was instinctive.

So I asked the students, "What are you thinking about as the teacher strolls among you?" They responded, "Oh, nothing. Why?"

Only when you watch these students in the classroom of a teacher who does *not* work the crowd do you come to appreciate the subconscious calculations of the classroom. By the time these previously well-behaved students have been in the green zone for five minutes, they become living proof of the statement, *Either you work the crowd, or the crowd works you.*

Working the Crowd from the Front

Working the Near and Far Zones

Let's imagine that you are talking to the class from the *front* of the room. When you are in front of the class, you work the crowd just like an entertainer would work a room in Las Vegas. You continuously move, and you direct your energy and eye contact with a purpose.

Think once again of the *zones of proximity*, with the *red* zone near your body and the *green* zone on the far side of the room. To maximize contact, you would let physical proximity take care of the red zone while you directed most of your eye contact to the green zone.

It is best to make eye contact with *individual people* on the far side of the room. Don't just scan an area. Make eye contact for about a second. Then, move on to another target in the green zone and then another.

Interspersed between these moments of eye contact with people on the far side of the room are more fleeting "scans" of people in the green zone. Thus, while you do make eye contact with everyone in the room, most of your time and attention is directed to the far side.

As you talk, you walk. Your general pattern of movement is roughly an arc as pictured below.

This general pattern of movement accomplishes several goals simultaneously. *First,* you constantly change the zone in which a student is sitting, so that no one is in the green

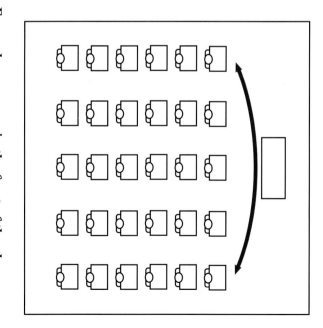

Even when you are in the front of the class, you move.

zone very long. *Secondly,* you constantly change everyone's visual field by forcing them to watch a moving target. If you stand still, you create a stationary target, a "talking head," and the brain "zones out," in a matter of seconds. *Finally,* you provide yourself with *camouflage* should you need to set limits on a student who is goofing off.

Camouflage for Setting Limits

Camouflage is an important concept when dealing with a student who is goofing off. You want to get them back on task, but you do not want to embarrass them in front of the group. Your normal pattern of movement creates the perfect camouflage needed to "work" individual students without it being blatant.

Imagine, for example, that you catch two students goofing off on the far side of the room. You can't allow that to happen! These students suddenly become the two most important people in the room.

Of course, you could stop and ask the students to get back to work and pay attention. This would be about as subtle as an entertainer stopping in the middle of a song and saying to the patrons of the lounge, "Group, I am simply going to wait until I have full attention."

Body Language and Finesse

Rather than embarrassing the student, you can use *finesse.* Without breaking your train of thought as you talk to the group, turn slowly toward the whisperers and talk directly to them. Typically they will notice you because smart students always keep an eye out for the teacher.

You now have eye contact with the disruptors. Talk directly to them as you stroll a step or two in their direction. Then, pause and half turn as you continue addressing the group, as though nothing special were happening. This is your normal pattern of moving, pausing, and scanning. By the time you have repeated this sequence a few times, you will be standing next to the disruptors. Stay there a little longer than usual.

Having "disrupted the disruption," you can now begin to move away. However, when you scan toward the disruptors, make eye contact with them for that extra half-second. Turn your body a little further toward them. This reminds the students that you are still thinking about them.

To an old pro, all of this would take place with hardly a conscious thought. But when first starting out, remember that working the crowd is *work.* Think of yourself as an Australian sheepdog that must constantly keep its charges from wandering off.

Working inside the Crowd

Mixing with the Audience

While teachers can work the crowd from the front of the room, they can work the crowd more intimately if they place themselves among the students. Even entertainers will move off stage to mingle with the audience if they want more intense contact.

I have often seen good teachers walk among the students while they explain a concept or act out a part, ges-

---

Three Rules of Movement

- **Constantly change the zones of proximity so that no one is in the green zone very long.**

- **Stimulate the brain to attend by constantly changing everyone's visual field.**

- **Use movement as camouflage for dealing with the disruptive student.**

turing dramatically as students watch wide-eyed. You can read a story as you cruise among the desks. You can facilitate a discussion as you move. If you need to write periodically on the chalkboard or overhead, you can do so and then work the crowd as you explain your point.

During Guided Practice

The most frequent occasion for a teacher to move among the students is during Guided Practice. Working the crowd enables the teacher to supervise students as they work on an assignment.

Teachers who work the crowd in this fashion cannot imagine *not* doing it. They say, "How else would you know what the students are doing? You have to check their work, especially when they are beginning the assignment, or they could do it all wrong, and you would never know it."

As teachers supervise work, they get discipline management for free as a by-product. You might wonder why any teacher would *not* work the crowd. Yet, most do not.

Obstacles to Working the Crowd

When something that is as sensible and beneficial as working the crowd fails to happen, there has to be a reason. Something must be blocking common sense.

One thing that blocks working the crowd is your years of being in the classrooms of teachers who stand in the front. Years of such modeling will strongly predispose you to do the same thing unless you understand the importance of working the crowd.

Another common factor that blocks working the crowd is the use of the *overhead projector*. Rarely do teachers who are using an overhead get more than three steps away from it. It is as though they were tethered to the machine. They take a step or two while making a remark to the class, and then they head back to the projector.

One simple way of using an overhead projector while working the crowd is to quit doing all of the work yourself. Let one of your students write on the transparency. Make it a privilege. Assign a different person to do it every week.

Yet, while the overhead projector can present a formidable barrier to working the crowd, it is not the main barrier. The main barrier to movement is the furniture. We will spend the entire *next chapter* dealing with that topic.

Body Language Is Subtle

As we describe working the crowd, we are beginning to learn about body language. Body language gets much more complex as the teacher attempts to remediate disruptions that are already in progress. In subsequent chapters on meaning business, for example, we will learn how to deal with disruptions that escalate into back talk and beyond.

Yet, the simple interactions described in this chapter reveal a key characteristic of body language in discipline management. Body language allows the teacher to use *finesse* to *protect* the students from embarrassment while dealing effectively with their imperfections. It can be subtle.

Consequently, body language allows the teacher to deal in a nonadversarial fashion with the common, everyday disruptions of the classroom. Without such a powerful yet gentle method of management, a classroom can be a very stressful place for everyone.

Chapter Four

Arranging the Room

Barriers to Mobility

Tripping over the Furniture

Once the importance of mobility and proximity become clear, the next logical step is to make working the crowd as easy for the teacher as possible. Are there any obstacles that the teacher must overcome?

Look around a typical class, and you will see a whole room full of obstacles. The biggest impediment to working the crowd in a typical classroom is the *furniture*.

The Custodial Room Arrangement

The most common room arrangement in education is pictured in the diagram on the following page. Now, ask yourself, *Who arranged the furniture in this classroom?*

During training, teachers respond in unison, "The custodian!"

Now, ask yourself, *What is the custodian's vested interest in the arrangement of furniture?*

Teachers respond, "Cleaning."

Students' feet are almost always under the chair in front of them. With students at their desks, the custodian's room arrangement produces *five impermeable barriers* between the left side of the room and the right side of the room.

A Lot of Work for Nothing

Imagine that you are standing at the "X" in the diagram on the following page. You know where the disruptions will begin. We

Preview

- The biggest obstacle to working the crowd in a typical classroom is the furniture.

- The custodial room arrangement makes cleaning easy, but it creates barriers to movement.

- The best room arrangement allows the teacher to get from any student to any other student in the fewest possible steps.

- Teachers gain proximity by removing their desks from the front of the room and moving the students' desks forward.

- Teachers need walkways. These are not little, narrow walkways, but rather, boulevards.

- The most efficient pattern of movement takes the form of an interior loop. This general pattern is adaptable to a wide variety of teaching situations.

29

talked about that in the previous chapter. Imagine, further, that you are helping a student who is stuck. You look up to see two students *talking to neighbors* in the far corner. What are you going to do about it?

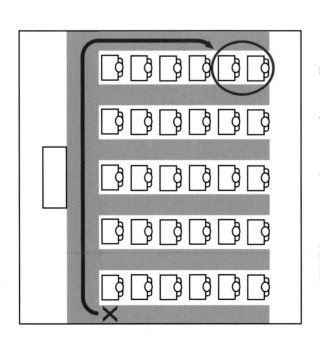

Walking across the room is usually an expensive response to a small problem.

If you ignore the talking, you signal to the class that you have no intention of dealing with this kind of misbehavior. Other students will take note and say to themselves, *Oh great! I wanted to talk too.* In previous chapters, the nickname given to this error of management was *declaring open season on yourself.*

You need to do something. But, what?

You could stop what you are doing, walk all the way over to the disruptive students, and have one of the truly silly conversations so typical of classroom management.

"I am tired of looking up and seeing nothing but talking over here."

"Okay."

"I want you to turn around in your seats and get some work done."

"Okay."

"And, when I look over here, I want to see you working instead of all of this fooling around."

"Okay."

Unfortunately, the students' repentance tends to be short-lived in this situation. Any trace of it has disappeared by time you get back across the room to the student who is stuck.

Having gone to all of this effort, how long do you think it will take for those kids in the corner to start goofing off again? How many trips across the classroom can you make before the futility of this exercise becomes apparent? We need a new strategy.

Economy Measures

The day may come when you decide to save yourself the useless trip across the classroom and, in the interest of economy, say:

"Roger! Philip! I am sick and tired of looking up to see nothing but talking over there. Would you please turn around in your seats and get some work done for a change? Blah, blah, blah."

When it becomes too expensive to use the body in classroom management, we use the mouth. You might think of nagging in this situation as a labor-saving device. If you are

The biggest impediment to working the crowd in a typical classroom is the furniture.

Arranging the Room for Teaching

The custodian's room arrangement that is designed for cleaning is the *worst* possible room arrangement for instruction. Attempting to work the crowd with the custodian's room arrangement will be so frustrating that you may give up the whole idea.

You will have to rearrange the furniture to make working the crowd as easy as possible. In so doing, you will carefully analyze space, distance, and movement.

The Teacher's Desk

Get Rid of It

The first step in room arrangement is to get the teacher's desk away from its traditional location in the front of the classroom. Where should the desk go?

Most teachers just shove it into the corner so they can conveniently lay things on it. Other teachers place it in the back of the room.

Why get rid of the teacher's desk? Because, it costs you almost *eight feet of proximity* with every student in the classroom!

I used to carry a tape measure with me when I visited classrooms. With the teacher's desk in the front, the distance from the chalkboard to the students in the front row was roughly thirteen feet.

Now, stand in front of a colleague who is seated, and imagine that you are conversing with him or her. Make it a comfortable conversational distance. Look down to see how far your kneecap is from your colleague's kneecap. It is usually about three feet.

Next, imagine that you are addressing the class. Take the comfortable conversational distance described above and add another two feet. This extra space gives the students to the side a decent viewing angle when you are writing

Because you are not going to fail anyway, you may as well fail at the lowest price.

ing on the board. You are now approximately five feet from the students in the front row. This would place you eight feet closer to every student in the class than when the desk was in the front.

The Cost of Eight Feet

Is eight feet important? In terms of the zones of proximity described in the previous chapter, it is the difference between the *red* zone and the *green* zone.

To feel the difference, stand about thirteen feet from a group of your colleagues who assume the role of typical students. Have them imagine that they would like to begin talking in class. Now, ask them, "Would you start if I were standing here?"

Next, walk toward them until you are standing five feet away. Once again, have them imagine that they are the same students who are thinking of goofing off. Again, ask them, "Would you? Could you?"

You will find that when you are thirteen feet away, the students feel free to goof off. But, when you are five feet away, they wouldn't dare.

This experiment will give you a feeling for the relationship between proximity and goofing off. In your classroom, *eight feet* is the difference between *prevention* and *remediation* for every student all day long.

Leaving Your Comfort Zone

I must warn you that, when you first bring the students forward, you may feel a bit claustrophobic. Just do it, and get used to it. It takes a few hours in the classroom for your comfort zone to readjust. You will soon come to enjoy the intimacy and control that proximity gives you.

The Students' Desks

Analyzing the Use of Space

I will show you some sample room arrangements. Do not jump to the conclusion that they are "correct." They are generic examples that demonstrate key features of room arrangement as they relate to working the crowd.

These room arrangements make mobility easy. Once you become familiar with them, you will be able to rearrange your own classroom in a way that is best for you.

As we look at space, think of teachers in one of two different places. One is standing in front of the classroom as they address the group or facilitate a discussion. The second is walking among the students supervising work during Guided Practice. A good room arrangement must serve you well in both of these situations.

Make Room Arrangements Compact

Let's start with the fairly traditional room arrangement pictured on the following page. In this diagram the teacher is in the front of the room, and the students are separated and facing forward.

For starters, you only need *two aisles* running from the front of the classroom to the back, rather than the six

The objective of room arrangement is to create walkways.

aisles that the custodian typically provides. As a result, you can make the room arrangement more compact by placing desks where four of the custodian's aisles used to be.

Think of the rows of desks as running *from side to side* rather than from front to back, as in the custodian's room arrangement. There are now eight students in the front row rather than the five or six that the custodian would place there.

In addition, these students are much closer to you than they were before we moved your desk to the corner. We are following two strategies to make the room arrangement more compact. We are *moving the students forward* and *packing them sideways*.

Making Walkways

Now, imagine yourself positioning the *second* row of desks. *First*, sit in a chair in the second row and relax your legs (bent, not straight out in front of you). *Second*, with a tape measure, measure eighteen inches from your toe to the back leg of the chair in front of you. That distance will provide you with an adequate walkway for working the crowd.

When you first look at the distance separating the first row from the second row, it seems huge. How can you afford that kind of space in a crowded classroom? The extra space that we need for wide walkways will come from the space we *saved* by moving the students forward and by packing them sideways.

The Key to Room Arrangement

The most important feature of room arrangement is *not* where the furniture goes, but, rather, where the furniture *does not go*. The objective of room arrangement is to create *walkways*. I do not mean little, narrow walkways. I mean *boulevards*.

I want you to be able to stroll down the boulevards with-

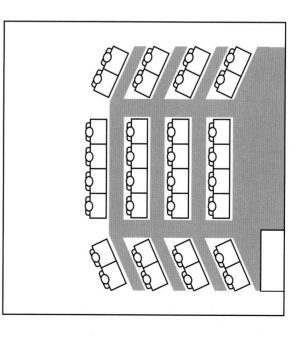

The space for walkways is created by bringing the students forward and packing them sideways.

out kicking students' feet, tripping over backpacks, or being blocked because a student is tall. In addition, I do not want you to pull students off task because they are worried about being stepped on.

The diagram pictured above has four rows running from side to side with eight students per row for a class of thirty-two students. We can now work the crowd with easy access to every student.

Patterns of Mobility

Proximity and Supervision

Imagine yourself working the crowd during Guided Practice as you supervise students' work. To supervise work, you must be able to *read* it. How far can you be from a student's work and still read it?

With normal eyesight, you can read the work of the student sitting on the aisle as well as the student sitting next to them. However, you cannot read the work of the third student over because the writing appears too small.

Normal eyesight limits you to supervising *two students to your right and two students to your left* as you work the crowd. This fact will play a major role in determining the placement of furniture as you attempt to work the crowd.

Shortest Distance, Fewest Steps

What is the shortest distance you can walk that will allow you to read the work of every student in the class? It is pic-

tured in the diagram below on the left. We will call this pattern of movement an *interior loop.*

It is no accident that, as you work the crowd along this interior loop, every student in the class is within two seats of an aisle. In addition, because distances are so short, you are only a few steps from any student in the class. Consequently, as you work the crowd, no student will be in the green zone for very long.

Effective teachers instinctively *avoid the periphery of the room.* Imagine standing at the edge of this room arrangement. Look at the distance and the physical barriers separating you from the far corner. You would pay for being in this location for any length of time.

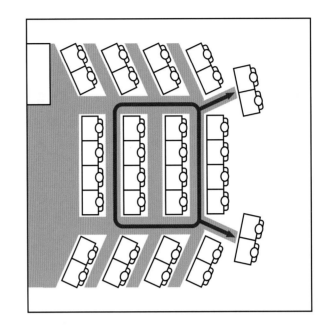

*An interior loop allows you
to work the crowd with the fewest steps.*

*With overcrowding, you may need
to use an interior loop with ears.*

Mobility with Overcrowding

What if you have more than thirty-two students? Where will you place the overflow?

Don't make a fifth row! The middle section of it would be in the green zone for too long. Place the extra students at the *ends* of the two walkways that run from front to back instead. These locations are the most accessible to you as you work the interior loop.

Of course, you will need to take a step or two out of the loop to see how these students are doing. This produces the elaborated pattern of movement shown on the previous page which I will refer to as *an interior loop with ears*.

The placement of ears will depend on the idiosyncrasies of your classroom. You will find that one of these ears is no trouble and two is doable. If you have three of them, however, the whole idea collapses because you are in the ears more than you are in the interior loop.

Cooperative Learning

You may wish to have students work together in small groups as in cooperative learning or committee work. The diagram to the right shows a room arrangement in which students are working in groups of four. They may be seated at large tables, or they may have shoved their desks together.

As you can see, this room arrangement looks very different from the preceding two diagrams. However, when you start working the crowd, you will discover that it is not so different after all. You will find your *interior loop with ears* soon enough.

Count Your Steps

When first rearranging their classrooms, many teachers create aisles but fail to count the steps. For example, it is not uncommon for a teacher to show me a picture like the one at the upper left on the following page and say,

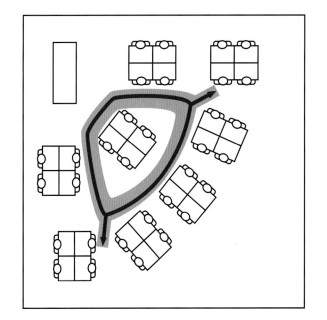

An interior loop with ears fits a wide variety of furniture configurations.

"I think my room arrangement is close to what you are describing. I have a central aisle that allows me to get around the room fairly easily."

While the first room arrangement on the next page might allow teachers to move easily as they address the group, its weakness becomes apparent when you picture yourself supervising work during Guided Practice. In order to read the students' work, you must work the crowd using a loop that is 60 percent longer than an interior loop. Half of this loop is on the periphery.

Sometimes, however, due to the crowding typical of portable classrooms, the teacher simply cannot have the

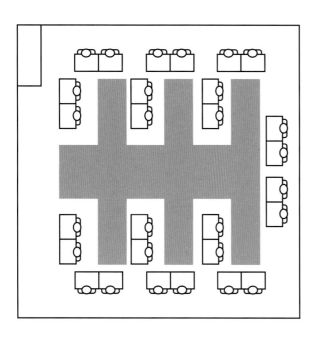

The "Double E" works well with two-person desks.

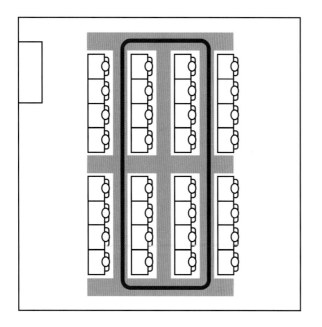

Count your steps. A central aisle increases the size of the loop by 60 percent.

aisles necessary for an interior loop. Having a central aisle with a lateral aisle halfway back to cut the class into quarters permits a reasonable amount of proximity.

Variations on Room Arrangement

There are patterns of room arrangement other than those shown previously that can work beautifully. The common element is that the teacher can get from any student to any other student with very few steps.

"Double E"

The arrangement pictured above and to the right works well with two-person desks. It is called a "double E" because it resembles two capital E's facing each other.

The teacher can easily stroll the middle area between the two E's while addressing the group. It is popular in social studies since students are facing each other during group discussions rather than facing forward.

Computer Labs

Another variation that many teachers like to use is the "horseshoe" or "U." It is very practical in small classes such as resource rooms and special education classes with fewer than fifteen students.

With normal size classes, the "U" is so large that the teacher tends to be too far from students on the opposite side. However, this arrangement may be the pattern of choice when students are at workstations. The diagram at

A "U" shaped arrangement works for computer labs.

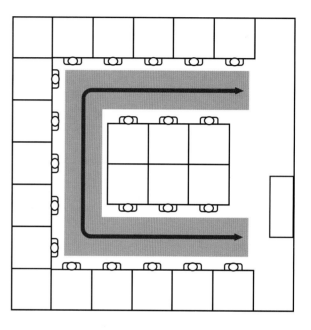

the top left of this page shows a computer lab with workstations placed in the interior part of the "U." Using this arrangement, the teacher can look over students' shoulders with a minimum of walking.

Instrumental and Choral Music

Instrumental and choral music teachers often ask for ideas that might help them during rehearsals. They feel cut off from the students in the back where most of the fooling around occurs.

These teachers typically arrange the students for rehearsal exactly as they would for a concert. Breaking this tradition opens the door to looking at the use of space in new ways.

A *variation on the "U" facilitates supervision during rehearsal for instrumental and choral music.*

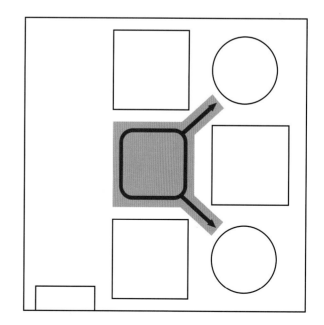

One practical solution is to arrange the subunits of the ensemble around three sides of an open square as shown above. Teachers can easily work the crowd by moving around the central area. Vocal music teachers often report that they can hear the altos and sopranos clearly for the first time. The spaces between these subunits provide walkways for the band director to reach the percussion and rhythm instruments represented by circles in the diagram.

Mobility with Small Groups

At Arm's Length

Teachers who work with small groups of students seated around them at arms length often ask during training what they should do about room arrangement. The answer is usually: *nothing*.

It is helpful to remember that both room arrangement and mobility are simply means to an end. The objective of room arrangement is *proximity*. If you already have proximity without moving, you needn't go any further.

For example, primary teachers might have all of the proximity they need while sitting on the carpet and reading to students at their feet. Management of minor disruptions might be accomplished by stopping, turning toward the disruptor, looking at them and simply waiting until the student becomes quiet before proceeding.

Reading Groups

Teachers in reading groups often find working the crowd to be crucial for instruction even though it may play a minor role in discipline management.

Traditionally, the teacher sits with the students in a circle and has each student read aloud. This time honored format has two disadvantages:

Low time-on-task – If there are eight students in the reading group, only one of them is reading while seven out of eight are relatively passive. How can we increase the ratio of students who are actively engaged in reading without sacrificing teacher supervision?

One way might be to have the students work in partners in which one student reads while the other lis-

tens. Another way might be to have all of the students "whisper read" by themselves.

With both of these arrangements, the teacher can supervise by moving around the *periphery* of the group while leaning down to listen to students read. The teacher will hear one student at a time just as before.

Once up and about, the teacher can then cruise among the students not in the reading circle from time to time. The teacher's mobility will pay a sizeable dividend by reducing goofing off in those students who are supposed to be working independently.

Performance Anxiety – Some students get nervous when they have to read out loud. They block due to anxiety which causes other students to giggle. This causes the student who is reading to block all the more. Partner reading and whisper reading eliminate most of this problem.

People Issues

Teacher Inertia

Over the years I have repeatedly seen resistance on the part of experienced teachers to changing their room arrangements. I suppose this inertia is not surprising. We all resist changing what is familiar and comfortable.

This resistance is so great that, as part of training, you will probably want to break into groups, go to the participating teachers' classrooms and say, "Where do you want the furniture?" The teachers will often give you a funny look as though they are surprised that they really have to

The most important feature of room arrangement is not where the furniture goes, but, rather, where it does not go.

go through with it. But then, they usually give in and say, "Well, let's start with my desk."

Without your furniture moving committee, over a third of trainees never rearrange their furniture. This then impairs the effectiveness of working the crowd and most of the other management skills described in this book.

The Custodian's Cooperation

Teachers who rearrange their furniture without having a talk with the custodian are asking for resistance. I have known teachers who rearranged their furniture on Monday only to find it back in rows on Tuesday.

For one thing, the room arrangements pictured in this chapter *do* make cleaning more difficult than room arrangements with traditional rows. But, perhaps more importantly, nobody likes to have their world changed without being consulted.

If you want the custodians to go to the extra effort to give you an optimal room arrangement, treat them like colleagues. Have a joint planning meeting to explain the rationale for the changes and to discuss implementation. They are an important part of the staff.

Section Three

Creating
Independent Learners

Chapter Five

Weaning the Helpless Handraisers

Preview

- Most lessons go smoothly until Guided Practice when the teacher is met with hands waving in the air. They are the same students every day.

- Students will not become independent learners if we constantly reinforce their helplessness with our time and attention.

- In addition, while the teacher tutors the helpless handraiser, the noise level in the class increases so that the teacher must reprimand.

- No discipline management program can succeed if the teacher loses control of the class as the price of helping students.

- How can we help a student who is stuck without reinforcing helplessness? Only by answering this question can we replace helpless handraising with independent learning during Guided Practice.

Typical Lesson, Typical Day

Bop 'til You Drop

I have spent many years observing teachers in all subject areas at all grade levels, looking for what works and what doesn't. In almost every classroom from kindergarten through twelfth grade, one pattern emerges day after day that makes teachers want to scream.

At the beginning of the lesson when the teacher is presenting material, the students attend fairly well. They seem to enjoy watching the teacher work out. Call this portion of the lesson "Bop 'til You Drop."

While teachers often find five matinees a day exhausting, it is easy compared to what comes next. The hard part of the lesson begins with Guided Practice. That is when the teacher attempts to put the *students* to work.

Guided Practice

Imagine a math lesson. Can you remember these timeless words as the teacher transitions from input to Guided Practice?

"Class, if there are no more questions, would you please open your books to page sixty-seven? As you can see, the problems at the top of the page are like the ones we have been working on. We have 20 minutes until the bell rings, and that is enough time to get started on the assignment.

44

"If you are having difficulty with any of the problems, look at my example on the board. Try to do it on your own. If, however, you are still having difficulty, you are having difficulty with the first problem, go to the next problem.

These words hardly leave the teacher's mouth before hands start waving in the air. I ask teachers, "Are they the same students every day?" They just roll their eyes.

The teacher then goes to the first hand-waver and asks, "Where do you need help?"

The student says, "I don't know what to do here."

The teacher says, "What part don't you understand?"

The student responds, "All of it."

I'll bet you recognize this student. I'll bet you have more than one in your class.

At this point, the teacher typically begins a process of *reteaching*, walking the student through the lesson step by step. As the teacher reteaches, the noise level in the room rises. At *five* seconds there is whispering; At *ten* seconds there is talking all over the room. At *fifteen* seconds students are out of their seats. As the noise level rises, the teacher turns to the class and says,

"Class! There is altogether too much talking. You

all have work to do, and the assignment is up on the board.

"I cannot be everywhere at once. If you are having difficulty with the first problem, go to the next problem."

The teacher resumes tutoring. The noise level creeps back up. The teacher stops again and says,

"All right class, this is the second time I've had to talk to you. When I look up, I expect to see people working. Robert, would you please take your seat?"

When the teacher has finished working with the first student, he or she moves to the second hand-waver and begins again.

"I'm sorry you had to wait. Show me where you are having difficulty."

The student says, not surprisingly, "I don't know what to do here."

The teacher says, "What part don't you understand?"

By the time the teacher has finished tutoring the second student, the handraisers on the far side of the classroom have been waiting for five to ten minutes. What do you think they have been doing all of this time?

"All right class, it is still too noisy in here!"

"I'll be around to help you as soon as I can."

When it is all over, the teacher will be tired and exasperated from having retaught the lesson a half-dozen times.

We Have a Pattern

Tutoring the same students during Guided Practice day after day is the most predictable pattern of behavior in the typical classroom. Ask yourself:

Are They the Same Students Every Day?

Any teacher could give you their names.

How Many Are in a Typical Class?

The national average is five or six.

How Long Does Helping Take?

The vast majority of tutoring interactions take three to six minutes (Mean: 4.23 minutes. Standard Deviation: 1.27 minutes). It is very difficult for a teacher to tutor in less than three minutes since half of the time is spent in checking for understanding as the student works.

The Kindergarten Laboratory

We will use kindergarten as our laboratory for understanding the dynamics of the classroom that foster chronic dependency and help-seeking. Using kindergarten as our laboratory allows us to see patterns easily because the kids have not gotten "slick" yet. Hang in there if you teach high school because *nothing changes*.

You Can Spot Them a Mile Away

Kindergarten teachers have repeatedly demonstrated the ability to predict which students will "bomb" in math and reading when they get to first grade. Most will tell you that they spotted these students on the first day of school.

How did they know? One test is to see who is clinging to your leg and crying.

Teachers label these students "immature." However, the term used in the teachers' lounge is "babies." How can a kindergarten teacher spot babies in the classroom?

- They do not follow verbal instructions.
- They do not do what they are supposed to do unless you are standing right over them and helping them.

The reason that kindergarten teachers can spot the babies a mile away is because their behavior is anything but subtle. These students exhibit the immaturity and clinginess typical of three-year-old toddlers. Their social-emotional development is lagging behind their physical development by almost *half of their life span*.

If the babies only work when "mommy" or "daddy" is helping them, they will fall further and further behind their peers the longer they are in school. They are a learning disability waiting to happen.

Toddler Behavior

In order to picture this immaturity, visualize a toddler at home with a parent. What room of the house is the toddler in?

Parents instinctively respond, "Wherever I am." The child is still in a *symbiotic* stage of social-emotional development. They are mommy and daddy's little helper. They follow you around and get upset if they are left alone.

Being clingy is age-appropriate for three-year-olds. So are some other primitive behaviors. Ask yourself:

- Do they share? *Yeah, right!*
- Do they take turns? *In your dreams!*
- What if they do not get their way? *They cry, hit, bite, tantrum,* or *whack their little playmate over the head with a Tonka truck.*

That is to say, they are not *civilized* yet. Their parents will work very hard to civilize them to the point where, by five

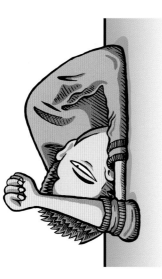

years of age, they will be ready for kindergarten. *Most children* have outgrown toddler behavior by the time we ship them off to school. But, not *all* of them.

The Squeaky Wheel Gets the Grease

Picture yourself as the kindergarten teacher, and imagine the *clinginess* typical of toddlers.

- Do they share your *body?*
- Do they take turns for your *body?*
- What do they do if they cannot get your *body?*

The answer to the last question is, *Whatever it takes.* Their objective is to get your undivided attention, and they will be ruthless because they are not yet civilized.

The Sociology of the Classroom

The following sociological realities drive the help-seeking behavior in *any* classroom. Let's continue to imagine kindergarten.

Everybody Wants Your Body

Your loving and caring time and attention are the most powerful reinforcers in the classroom.

There Is Never Enough Teacher to Go Around

While everybody wants your body, some want it more than others – especially the babies. There are more of them than you can service at any given time.

The Classroom Is an Ecosystem

A sociological ecosystem is analogous to a biological ecosystem. There are niches in which creatures specialize to compete for limited resources. Within these niches, it is survival of the fittest.

There Is a Pecking Order

Because there is never enough teacher to go around, there is *competition* for your body. This creates a "pecking

order." Among the students who want your body, only the most ruthless competitors will actually get your body.

The Same Cast of Characters Every Year

First year teachers are usually amazed at the strange characters that populate their classrooms. But more experienced teachers realize that you will get the same cast of characters year after year. One reason is that the niches in the classroom ecosystem never change.

While the teacher helps the first student, the helpless handraisers wait.

Many of these niches are for students who want the teacher's body. See if you recognize any of these characters:

- **The Clinger** – What is the most direct way to monopolize the teacher's body? Grab it, of course!
- **The Student Who Does Not Listen Carefully to Instructions** – Will you have to spend some extra time with this student before he or she gets started?
- **The Student Who Falls Out of His or Her Chair** – Ask the secondary teachers. They are still doing it in junior high and high school!

Avoiding Ridicule

As these "clingers" get older, they eventually realize that they are paying a high price for their babyishness. The other students ostracize them and call them names. Baby is the nicest one I can think of.

Consequently, during first and second grade, the clingers begin to clean up their act. They learn to look less babyish in order to avoid ridicule.

How can immature students avoid looking like babies in the upper grades while monopolizing as much of the teacher's body as possible? They will have to alter their game plan.

Handraisers may have to wait for ten or fifteen minutes.

Helpless Handraising

Fortunately for these students, there is a perfect way of monopolizing the teacher's body that avoids looking like a baby. It is, of course, *helpless handraising*.

In addition to avoiding peer disapproval, helpless handraising also gets a sympathetic response from the teacher. It is the perfect ruse. These students appear to be hungering and thirsting after knowledge while doing absolutely nothing.

Keep in mind, however, that some helpless handraisers will be on the opposite side of the classroom from where the teacher begins tutoring during Guided Practice. These students might have to wait ten or fifteen minutes before the teacher even gets to them. This creates a severe dilemma for these helpless handraisers.

How can these students hold their arms up for *ten or fifteen minutes*? They are faced with a problem of sheer endurance.

The Four Basic Positions

As handraisers tire, their handraising typically deteriorates through the following four positions:

1. **The Beginning Position:** Helpless handraisers begin with their arms held straight up. We will call this the beginning position. The problem with the beginning position is that the blood drains from the arm. The student experiences mild numbness followed by a pin-prickling sensation all over the hand.

2. **Half-Mast:** One day while waiting, the helpless handraiser looks up to see a classmate modeling a perfect solution to the dilemma. The discomfort can be remedied by lowering the arm and providing a bit of support. This produces hand raising position number two, half-mast.

3. **The Broken Wing:** While an improvement, half-mast still requires the student to hold up his or her arm for an extended period. Less work is required if you rotate the arm a quarter turn and relax. This produces position number three, the *broken wing*.

4. **Out Cold:** While some students can maintain the broken wing indefinitely, others lose their "train of thought." When the teacher finally arrives, the student is *out cold*.

"I Don't Know What to Do Here."

When beginning to work with a helpless handraiser, the teacher typically asks, "Where do you need help?"

The student responds, "I don't know what to do here."

The teacher says, "What part don't you understand?"

The student responds, "All of it."

Being clueless is a very shrewd strategy. If the student were to respond, "I don't understand what to do on step

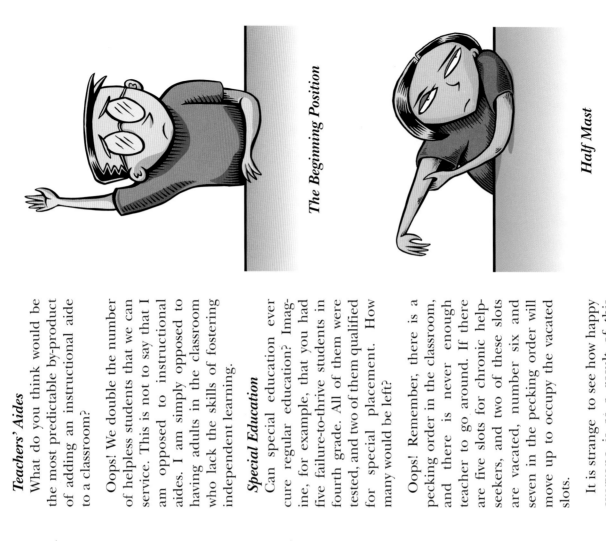

The Beginning Position

Half Mast

"five," the teacher would only explain step five and be gone in 30 seconds.

To be so specific would be a tactical error on the part of helpless handraisers. The more they know, the quicker the teacher leaves. To monopolize the teacher's body, it is best to be clueless.

Why should helpless handraisers even pay attention during the lesson presentation? If they did, they would have to *fake* being clueless. If they "zone out," they can get the same result at no effort.

Learned Helplessness

The way in which we give corrective feedback during Guided Practice creates an incentive for seeking help. In so doing, we inadvertently create the most widespread learning disability in American education – *learned helplessness*. No other disability occurs consistently at a rate of five to six per classroom nationwide.

Helping the Help-Seekers

Students will never grow up if we reinforce them daily for remaining infantile. Almost everything we have done in the past 40 years to deal with the problem of chronic neediness in the classroom has inadvertently made the problem worse. These "cures" include:

Hustle

The classic response of a truly dedicated teacher is to go the extra mile, work harder, hustle! What if, for example, you were to *speed up* so that you could consistently get to *eight* students during Guided Practice instead of the normal five. In addition to exhausting yourself, how many chronic help-seekers would you have?

Oops! You will have exactly the number of chronically helpless students that you can help chronically.

Teachers' Aides

What do you think would be the most predictable by-product of adding an instructional aide to a classroom?

Oops! We double the number of helpless students that we can service. This is not to say that I am opposed to instructional aides. I am simply opposed to having adults in the classroom who lack the skills of fostering independent learning.

Special Education

Can special education ever cure regular education? Imagine, for example, that you had five failure-to-thrive students in fourth grade. All of them were tested, and two of them qualified for special placement. How many would be left?

Oops! Remember, there is a pecking order in the classroom, and there is never enough teacher to go around. If there are five slots for chronic help-seekers, and two of these slots are vacated, number six and seven in the pecking order will move up to occupy the vacated slots.

It is strange to see how happy everyone is as a result of this process. The students being

The Broken Wing

Out Cold

referred out are thrilled to be in the resource room with a two-to-one student-teacher ratio. Ironically, teachers seem equally happy. They say,

"I am so glad that I finally have time for some of these other students who need the individual attention."

Creating Independence

Helping Is Tricky

How do you help students without making them increasingly helpless? It's tricky.

You can look in vain for this topic in the methodology of teacher training. Yet a careful systems analysis of the classroom reveals that giving corrective feedback to helpless handraisers is the source of most of the teacher's chronic headaches.

- **Discipline:** When teachers give corrective feedback, they relinquish working the crowd, and the noise level rises. Thus, by giving help in the traditional fashion, teachers generate discipline problems faster than they can be remediated.

- **Instruction:** Why should students pay attention and then fake not understanding when

they can zone out and achieve the same result? Children will never work if we pay them for being helpless. Rather, they will fall further and further behind each day.

- **Motivation:** How long can students play this game before they fall so far behind that there is no real point in attending anymore? After all, what is the point of paying attention to a lesson on the multiplication of fractions when you are not sure of your addition facts?

Ceasing to pay attention in class pertains to students dropping out of school. When do you think students actually drop out? How about *fourth grade?* When do teachers start seeing it blatantly? How about *fifth grade?* High school "at risk" programs are sometimes a bit late.

A Full Scale Weaning Program

The babies in kindergarten stick out like a sore thumb. By the time they reach fifth grade, they will have patterns of *chronic* learned helplessness that are over a half-decade old.

You will not be able to reverse such chronic patterns with only a few minor adjustments. These students *like* being taken care of. They are not about to give it up without a *fight.*

To *wean* the chronic help-seekers, you will have to redesign the process of instruction from the ground up to build independence. Furthermore, your weaning program must be *airtight.* If there are six ways to beat your weaning program and you fix five of them, all of the babies will remain helpless in the way left open to them.

In the following chapter we will begin to build our weaning program. We will start with the pivotal question: *How do you help a student who is stuck?*

Chapter Six

Simplifying the Verbal Modality

Common Sense

How do you help a student who is stuck? The whole human race seems to do it the same way. It is so widespread that we might call it "common sense."

Imagine a student doing an assignment in the classroom with his or her hand raised. This is not a helpless handraiser necessarily – just a student who is having difficulty in the middle of a task. Imagine a math problem since it is easy to visualize helping a student with the next step of a calculation.

Typically the teacher would spend three to six minutes with the student, showing him or her what to do and checking for understanding. When the teacher was satisfied that the student could proceed, the teacher would leave and go to the next student needing help. This common sense approach to corrective feedback could be summarized as: *Show the student how to do it.*

It is not too surprising that corrective feedback has never become a topic of research. Can you imagine trying to get tenure at a university by investigating something so obvious?

Limits of Long-Term Memory

While common sense gives us a strategy for giving corrective feedback, it does not describe how the brain works. To put corrective feedback into a proper perspective,

Preview

- How do you help students who are stuck? Common sense says we show them how to do it and check for understanding before we leave.

- This process usually takes three to five minutes. In addition to reinforcing helplessness, this much input produces cognitive overload.

- To fit the limitations of auditory memory, corrective feedback must be brief. It must simply answer the question, "What do I do next?"

- Since our eye immediately finds things in the visual field that do not "belong," we have a natural tendency to focus on error.

- Focusing on error is typically irrelevant to instruction since it is useless in teaching a student how to do something right.

- We will organize corrective feedback into three steps: Praise, Prompt, and Leave.

we need to focus on *long-term memory*, and, in particular, long-term memory in the *auditory modality*.

To make a long story short, I would not trust your long-term auditory memory very far. Without getting mired in the research, just ask yourself these questions:

- Have you ever forgotten the name of a person you just met while standing there talking to him or her?
- Have you ever forgotten a set of directions to get somewhere by the time you have gotten into your car?
- Have you ever forgotten a phone number by the time you have found a scrap of paper to write it down?

These are universal experiences that convince most of us that we have some kind of memory problem. In fact, we do, but we share it with the rest of the species. While long-term visual memory may be great and long-term kinesthetic memory may be good, long-term *auditory* memory will get you lost on the way to my house.

Cognitive Overload

Learning One Step at a Time

How much long-term memory can you count on as you instruct a student during corrective feedback? The research varies depending on the material being learned, but I would not gamble on much more than a few sentences.

This can explain, at most, the *next step* of the task. That is why learning takes place "one step at a time."

Let's return to the helping interaction between the math teacher and student. Imagine that the math problem has *eleven* steps. The student is stuck on step number *seven*.

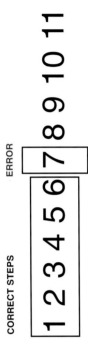

The teacher helps the student by showing him or her what to do on step number seven. If the student understands, the teacher typically proceeds to step number eight.

If the student continues to understand the input, the teacher will often walk the student through the remainder of the problem before leaving. After all, the student seems to be "getting it." In social studies, the teacher might spend a similar amount of time explaining a concept.

Returning to our math problem, let's examine the demands made upon long-term memory by the teacher walking the student through the remainder of the calculation. The teacher will spend three to six minutes asking the student to *encode, store, decode, and perform five steps of new learning.*

What are the odds that a student could keep all of this straight? Not much considering that we learn one step at a time.

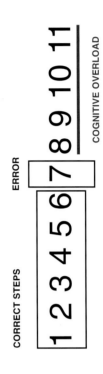

a time. To teach all the way to the end of the task (steps 8-11 in this case) would represent cognitive overload to a factor of roughly *500 percent*.

Short-Term versus Long-Term Memory

How could such a gross overestimate in the student's ability to assimilate input go unrecognized in classroom after classroom, day after day? My best explanation is that we are *faked out*. We are faked out by the difference between *short-term* and *long-term* memory.

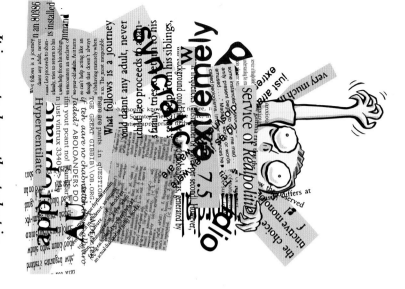

Short-term memory is nearly total recall, and it requires no work. It is simply a by-product of perception. The only problem is that it does not last very long.

Long-term memory, on the other hand, requires a great deal of work, particularly with the subjects we study at school. Remember all of the studying we did for those tests in college? Remember studying the same material for the midterm? Remember cramming it again for the final? If we had been forced to take the final again a month later without studying, we would have flunked it cold.

Short-term memory and long-term memory follow different rules. But they

both *feel* the same. You either remember or you don't. The student cannot tell which one is operating.

Returning to our math problem, let's imagine that the teacher shows the student how to do step number eight, and the student understands. When the teacher and the student receive confirmation that learning has occurred.

So, why *not* keep going? Several steps later, the student seems to understand how to do the whole problem, and the teacher feels confident enough to leave. Everyone has "closure," but all of this learning is in *short-term memory*.

After the teacher leaves, the student copies the next problem and begins to solve it by doing steps one through six. By the time the student gets to step seven – the new learning – *two minutes have passed*. Now, the student must rely on *long-term memory*. The student finds that the specifics of solving the math problem have faded.

How can the math student explain this confusion? Other students in class seem to be able to do this stuff, and they didn't have extra time with the teacher. The most obvious explanation is that, *I must be S,T,U,P,I,D.*

Simplifying Corrective Feedback

One Step at a Time

We are going to do radical surgery on the traditional method of giving corrective feedback. We are going to have to cut it down to size. We must align it with what the brain can actually do, which is captured in that ancient truism: *All learning takes place one step at a time.*

All learning takes place one step at a time for one simple reason. That is about all you can store accurately long enough to get to the second ancient truism of learning: *You learn by doing.*

It is easy to drown the student in cognitive overload with our explanations.

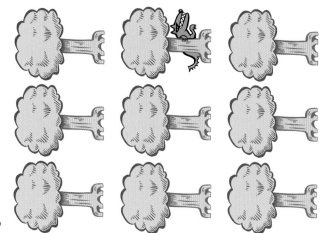

A Simple Prompt

Do not approach corrective feedback with a fancy model of instruction. And, do not engage in complex dialogue. Keep it short and simple.

When stripped of its excess baggage, corrective feedback can be reduced to a simple answer to a simple question: *What do I do next?*

In learning theory the answer to this question is called a *prompt*. The heart of corrective feedback is a good prompt. Keep the prompt brief and get to the point.

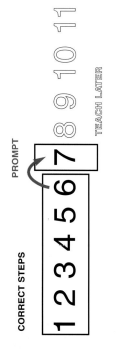

CORRECT STEPS   PROMPT

1 2 3 4 5 6 7 8 9 10 11

TEACH LATER

When giving corrective feedback, therefore, the less said the better. Simplify, simplify, simplify! Remember:

- *Simplicity is clarity is brevity is memory.*

- Teaching need never be more difficult than taking students from where they are to wherever you want them to be – *one step at a time.*

- In order to progress, all the student needs to know is *what to do next.*

- Be *clear.* Be *brief.* Be *gone.*

Common Sense and Negative Transfer

Common Sense Is Biology

When people all seem to do the same thing in the same way, we tend to call it common sense. The way in which

people give each other corrective feedback is a prime example.

Since there is no training program to produce such uniformity among people, we are most likely dealing with a behavior that has a strong biological component. To help in pinpointing the biological component in the giving of corrective feedback, ask yourself the following question:

When you look at a piece of work that is part right and part wrong, which part catches your eye – the part that is right or the part that is wrong?

Everyone answers, somewhat sheepishly, "the part that is wrong." Let me assure you that this behavior has nothing to do with personality traits such as negativism or fault-finding. This piece of behavior is built-in.

The Eye Finds the Error

This universal tendency to focus first upon the error has to do with the structure of the visual cortex. Finding the "thing that does not belong" in the visual field has to do with survival – with finding the danger in the environment as rapidly as possible.

We filter out the familiar and focus on the unexpected. The thing that does not belong in the visual field is the thing that could "eat you up." This operation takes place instantaneously.

When giving corrective feedback on a piece of schoolwork like our math problem, therefore, we scan past the part that is right – the part that matches our example on the board – and *stop at the error.* Having found what the student is having difficulty with, we are now ready to give corrective feedback.

Our Emotional Response

When we see something that is surprising or upsetting, we have an emotional response. It is a reflex that we studied in our first high school biology class – the *fight-flight reflex*.

In the classroom the intensity of this response is mild compared to a life-threatening situation, but it contains the same physiological components. These include a tensing of muscles and a shot of adrenaline. The *mild* version of the fight-flight reflex is usually referred to as *exasperation*.

> **Simplicity is clarity, is brevity, is memory.**

Typical Openers

What you see is what you *say*. If we are looking at the error and begin to speak, we will be talking about the error.

What pops out at such times are patterns of speech that we have been hearing all of our lives. They are so common that we do not even stop to analyze them. I will refer to these remarks as "typical openers."

I will list five of the most common openers. But they will not sound like much – just the background noise of life.

To hear them with fresh ears, I want you to imagine that you are *failing* my class. Your self-esteem is *nil*. You are *vulnerable*. These are the kids who really hear the openers.

The strong students don't seem to mind them as much. To further help you hear the real message implied by these openers, I will paraphrase.

- **Ask Them** – Ask the student where he or she is having difficulty.

"Okay, Billy, show me where you are having difficulty."

This hardly sounds like a hurtful message. It even sounds helpful. See how invisible these openers are? Now, let's paraphrase:

"Okay, Billy, how did you mess it up this time?"

By focusing upon the error when we begin helping, we trigger one of the most frightening facets of Billy's already shaky self-concept – the thought that he might be S,T,U,P,I,D. And, upon this experience we will attempt to build learning. Lots of luck!

- **Tell Them** – Sometimes it is not worth asking the students where they are having difficulty because they seem lost. In such cases, we usually just jump in.

"Okay, Billy, let's look here at this first problem. Yesterday, you'll remember, we were adding fractions with *like* denominators. Today the denominators are *different*. We will have to begin by finding a common denominator. Do you remember how we do that? Let's look at our example on the board."

Let's paraphrase to see how it sounds to Billy.

"Okay, Billy, let's look at the very first thing you were supposed to do today - finding the common denominator. Do you remember how to do that? Apparently not. So, let's look at my example which is right in front of you on the board as plain as day."

- **"Yes, But" Compliment** – Wouldn't it be better if we used *praise*? Unfortunately, when you begin with the error, praise won't save you. All you get is a sugar-coated failure message known in the therapy trade as a *yes, but compliment.* Yes, but compliments always follow the same form; *first* the good news, *then* the bad news.

"You are off to a good start, Billy. You have found your lowest common denominator. You have checked it and inserted it into the equation. Great! Now, let's look at the numerator. Do you remember what we said about "adjusting the numerator?" Let's look here at step number five."

Do you want to hear it from Billy's point of view?

"Okay, Billy, you have done the first part right. We spent all day yesterday on that. Now, I want you to look at 'adjusting the numerator.' That is what you were supposed to do on today's problems. Do you remember anything about it?"

It is almost impossible for a person's remarks to be interpreted as anything but negative when they are focusing upon the error. For example, has a supervisor ever given you feedback on your performance after visiting your classroom? It usually begins with the "good news."

"Today, when I was in your class, I saw some real strengths that I want to mention...blah, blah, blah."

You know what part is coming next, don't you? Shall we call it "needs improvement" or "areas of potential growth?" Why don't we just call it, "Things I did not especially like."

• **S & M** – "S & M" does not stand for sado-masochism. This is a classroom, after all. "S & M" stands for "Sighs and Moans" – the sighs and moans of martyrdom.

When we have a fight-flight reflex, even the mild one we call exasperation, muscles tense. One of these muscles is the diaphragm. We breathe in. Then, after we fill our lungs, we speak.

To hear the sigh, breathe in deeply, and then relax and gently exhale as you say,

(Sigh) "Okay, let's see here..."

or,

"Hmmmmm..."

The teacher may as well look to the heavens and say, "Why me, Lord?"

• **Zaps and Zingers** – Sometimes, as a result of repeated exasperation – particularly with the same students day after day – the thin veneer of civilization finally cracks. Frustration boils to the surface, and we "let fly."

Zaps and zingers refer to *sarcasm.* All sarcasm can be paraphrased as, *I don't understand how you could be so stupid!*

Let's look at some common examples in the order of increasing exasperation and imagine how they might make Billy feel.

Okay, Billy, let's go over this *one more time.*

Billy, we just went over this at the board!

Billy, I don't understand why you are still having difficulty with this.

Billy, I want you to pay attention this time. Where were you ten minutes ago?

Billy, I am sick and tired of coming back here day after day only to find that you have not been listening to a word I have said.

Corrective Feedback Makes People Defensive

Frankly, it does not matter which typical opener you use. They all begin the process of corrective feedback by rubbing the student's face in his or her inadequacy. Would you be surprised if the student's attitude toward learning was less than enthusiastic?

Let me ask you another question about corrective feedback. Have you ever tried to give corrective feedback to your spouse or child or loved one? Have you ever noticed how easily people get *defensive* when you try to help them? No matter how you phrase it?

"Dear, you know this is for your own good..."

"Honey, I wouldn't tell you this if I didn't love you..."

These words hardly leave your mouth before the hairs on back of the other person's neck begin to rise. Corrective feedback is indeed a tricky business.

Vulnerable Students Get the Most Failure Messages

Who do you think receives corrective feedback most often, the top third of the class or the bottom third of the class? Who do you think has the lowest self-esteem, the top third of the class or the bottom third of the class?

The bottom third of the class, the students with the least self-confidence about learning, receive ten times as much corrective feedback as the top third of the class. In addition, they tend to be *sensitive* to failure messages, whereas, the stronger students often take them in stride.

Students begin public education with many beliefs about themselves which they bring from home. But, there is one important facet of self-concept that must be learned at school. Either I am *smart* with school work, or I am *stupid*. Giving corrective feedback in the natural, common-sense fashion will polarize this perception among students.

A New Perspective on Error

Consider the following when your eyes find their way to the shortcomings in someone's performance: *There are a million ways to mess up anything; Each is as useless to remember as the next.*

Why spend precious instructional time going over something with students that you never want them to repeat? Not only does it make them feel defensive, but it also fills up limited memory with throw-away information.

Corrective Feedback in Detail

Your Physical Response

When you look at a piece of work that is part right and part wrong, you will see the part that is *wrong* first whether you want to or not. You will also have a fight-flight reflex that may range in intensity from the imperceptible to real exasperation. The question is, *What do you do about it?*

First, take a *relaxing breath*. During this relaxing breath you will *not* be mildly exasperated and focused on the error. Rather, you will be ready to formulate a plan of action. This relaxing breath will calm you and allow time for the fight-flight reflex to come and go.

Second, take *another* relaxing breath. During the second relaxing breath, take a fresh look at the task. Scan the stu-

> The degree of error is irrelevant. If the student is on square one, teach square one.

dent's work with fresh eyes, and ask yourself, *What has the student done right, so far?*

Third, starting from this point in their work, ask yourself, *What do I want the student to do next?*

Your Verbal Response

The heart of corrective feedback is the prompt which answers the question, *What do I do next?* However, there are some additional elements that you may wish to consider along with the prompt.

- **Praise** – The label "Praise" simply serves as a reminder to focus upon what the student has done *right so far* rather than upon what he or she has done *wrong.* Rather than being gratuitous "nice, nice talk," praise describes one or two aspects of the student's performance in simple, declarative sentences. Most commonly, you would:

  - *focus* the student's attention on that portion of performance that is relevant to the upcoming prompt.

  - *review* what the student has done right so far as a bridge into the prompt.

Let's look again at our graphic of the math problem containing an error. Which step would be the most useful to review as the bridge to teaching step seven? During training, teachers respond in unison, *Step six.*

CORRECT STEPS   ERROR

1 2 3 4 5 6 7 8 9 10 11

*You might review step 6
as a bridge to teaching step 7.*

Knowing what we know about verbal memory, would it be useful to review steps one through six? Trainees respond, *No!*

Don't use the *praise* step if you do not need it. While the praise step may be useful in some situations, it is competing for short-term memory with the *prompt.*

It is most often useful the *first time* you help a student. You have no idea what he or she might be thinking about when you first walk up to them, and the praise step prepares them for your prompt. However, the *second time* you help the student, praise is usually superfluous if he or she has been working on task since you left. In that case, *dump* the praise and go straight to the prompt. The less said, the better.

- **Prompt** – Good prompts are brief and clear. All modalities of learning can be utilized in the service of clarity. Prompting with the visual and physical modalities will be the subject of subsequent chapters.

For now, let's focus upon what we *say.* A good verbal prompt provides a clear guide to performance while avoiding cognitive overload. Follow these guidelines:

- One step at a time
- Short and simple
- Specific

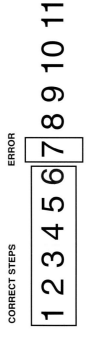

Teaching is never more difficult than taking the student forward one step at a time.

Our eternal enemy is *verbosity*. We explain and explain, and, if the student looks confused, we *paraphrase*. Remember, simplicity is clarity is brevity is memory.

Another impediment to a good prompt is, of course, the *typical opener*. Beware of the following three transitions as you begin the prompt:

- But
- However
- Instead of

Your instinct may tell you to check for understanding; but, with helpless handraisers, that is usually a bad idea. Leave, because, if you stay, you:

- signal that you think they may need more help
- offer your body as the reinforcer if they seek help

Make a helpless handraiser an offer like this, and you won't have to guess about the outcome. Leave because you really have no choice.

Deal with your worry about this student's success by giving a *more effective prompt*, not by staying to check for understanding. The following chapters on the visual and physical modalities of instruction deal with more effective prompting.

Beware as you transition to the prompt.

You can watch the student's face drop as you utter these words. Your attempt to help has just become a *yes, but compliment*. Now the student is waiting for the other shoe to drop.

Begin the prompt with the following phrase, and you will pass through the transition safely:

"The next thing to do is…"

- **Leave** – When you give a student a prompt, it would be logical to check for understanding before you leave. If your instincts tell you that this would be a wise thing to do, then, by all means, do it.

But, I am preoccupied with the *helpless handraisers*. They constantly exploit corrective feedback for *attention* rather than for learning. With our babies, you have to play the game differently.

After you give the prompt, turn on your heel and leave. Leave *before* you see the student carry out the prompt.

Leave because you really have no choice.

Prompting Variations

Praise, Prompt, and Leave is the simple, generic pattern for giving corrective feedback. It is better to stay with this simple version at the beginning, lest you slide back into verbosity. As you become more comfortable, however, you may find the following elaborations useful.

Question Asking

Should you ever ask the students questions? Giving a simple prompt does not leave much room for dialogue.

Beginning corrective feedback with a question is, in fact, one of the most common patterns that teachers utilize. However, there are some problems to consider when beginning the interaction with a question:

- **It takes time** – Dialogue usually takes a minute or two. During that time you are not working the crowd. The predictable outcome will be time off task and noise.

- **It produces verbosity** – The best way to guarantee that you talk for three minutes is to talk for one minute. In addition, verbosity produces cognitive overload.

- **It sets the student up for failure** – While there are many sophisticated questioning strategies in the literature, I rarely see them used in the classroom. Rather, I usually observe a series of leading questions.

Teachers often refer to this as the "Socratic method." However, most of the time leading questions are questions leading nowhere. The teacher is simply fishing. When the student fails to grasp the teacher's drift, he or she feels even more stupid.

- **It plays into the helpless handraisers** – While some dialogue with curious students may yield rich dividends, to helpless handraisers it is a golden opportunity to hang onto your body. They will play it like a violin.

An alternative use of questioning is to check for understanding *after* the prompt. The student can answer the question readily because you have just supplied the information.

Discussion Facilitation

The skills of facilitating a group discussion are an extension of Praise, Prompt, and Leave. They enable the teacher to guide the discussion while creating a degree of safety that encourages the quiet students to talk.

Imagine that a given student's comment is mediocre – somewhat off the point or partially incorrect. Our normal focus would tend to be on the error. If, however, we direct attention to the error, we will not get any more participation from that student in the future.

As an alternative, use this sequence:

1. **Selective reinforcement** – Take the best and leave the rest.

2. **Key issue** – Where does the student's comment lead? You get to choose. By highlighting a particular key issue, you can guide the discussion without taking it over.

3. **Open-ended prompt** – Direct the key issue to the class in the form of an open-ended question. You can direct the prompt to the student who gave the mediocre response if you wish to engage him or her in idea building.

   "Sarah, what do you think about..."

4. **Wait time** – Give time for the wheels to turn after a prompt. When you speak, you shut down student participation.

Discrimination Training

Can the teacher ever point out the student's error? Well, sometimes.

Prelude to a Prompt
The next thing to do is…

In this case, the error is already in memory, and the student thinks it is correct. Discrimination training focuses upon discriminating correct from incorrect as a prelude to replacing old learning with new learning.

To produce a discrimination, the teacher must place both ideas into the student's awareness and then contrast critical features. This is a fairly complex process and usually requires more extensive instruction than we would attempt during corrective feedback.

When we are first starting out with Praise, Prompt, and Leave, it is better to play it safe. Get to the prompt, and get out of there.

Painless Prompts

Initiating and Terminating Requests
As a means of getting closure on corrective feedback, consider that a prompt is simply a request for behavior. There are two basic kinds of requests: *initiating* requests and *terminating* requests.

Initiating Requests
An initiating request asks a person:

- **to do** something
- to do something **more**

An initiating request is emotionally *safe* because it carries **no implied judgement**. You can ask anybody to do anything, to turn cartwheels or quack like a duck, and it car-

Pointing out the error usually does more harm than good. But the situation changes when you are attempting to correct a *misconception* or break a *bad habit.*

ries no implication that what he or she was doing previously was wrong.

Terminating Requests
A terminating request asks a person:

- **not to do** something
- to do something **less**

A terminating request is emotionally *dangerous* because it always carries an **implied judgement.**

"Don't swing at a pitch when it's over your head!"

"How many times do I have to ask you not to leave your clothes on the floor?"

"Don't drive so fast!"

*Terminating requests are *natural*. We see a problem, and we respond instinctively. Unfortunately, terminating requests make people defensive. And, they make poor prompts because they do not tell the person exactly what to do.

*Initiating requests are *not* natural. They represent a learned pattern that takes a lot of *practice*. Since this pattern is learned, it is subject to forgetting. For as long as we live, it will be easy for us to slip back into giving corrective feedback with terminating requests, especially when we are tired or upset.

Shaping
Shaping is the name given by learning theory to the basic process of instruction. Shaping is *the prompting and reinforcing of successive approximations of task completion.*

A given instance of corrective feedback is simply one step in the shaping process. Instruction always comes down to the same basic question: *What do I do next?*

Chapter Seven

Teaching to the Visual Modality

Limitations of Verbal Prompts

The problem with which we began this section was the *helpless handraisers*, and, in particular, their interruption of teachers' attempts to *work the crowd* during Guided Practice. As a first step in our weaning program, we focused on the verbal modality since extensive tutoring caused helping interactions to last from three to six minutes.

However, training teachers to use brief, yet effective verbal prompts produced mixed results. Immediately after training, teachers were able to prompt efficiently and work the crowd. But three months later, the majority had slipped back into old habits of verbosity.

Why was backsliding so common? Old habits are hard to break, we all know that. But there were also other factors at work.

Strong Habits Win

Habit strength is a simple and useful concept in learning theory that helps to explain the difficulty of breaking old habits. In a nutshell, a behavior that you have repeated 10,000 times has more habit strength than a behavior you have repeated 100 times. It coincides perfectly with the characterization of an old habit as having a "deep groove."

During training, we were asking teachers to change life-long patterns of speech. These patterns have *very* deep grooves.

Preview

- An efficient verbal prompt takes the teacher about 30 seconds.

- Unfortunately, it only takes the class 10 seconds to get noisy.

- We must reduce the duration of corrective feedback to less than 10 seconds, and we must reduce the verbosity that creates cognitive overload.

- If words are getting us into trouble, eliminate the words. After all, a picture is worth a thousand words.

- In order to wean the helpless handraiser, we must go beyond effective verbal prompts to supply the student with effective visual prompts.

- A Visual Instructional Plan (VIP) is a lesson plan in visual form. It is a string of visual prompts that provides a clear set of plans for correct performance.

Our training was attempting to replace habits that were three or four decades old with habits that were three or four hours old. On the basis of habit strength, which patterns of speech do you think would win out over the next three months?

Wallowing Weaners

In addition to habit strength, the second reason that trainees tended to backslide was the fact that helpless handraisers resist being weaned from their chronic help-seeking. They *like* being waited on hand and foot.

Do not imagine for one minute that helpless handraisers are going to be weaned easily. They will not give up their pampered lifestyle to become independent learners without a *fight*.

When weaners fight back, their primary tactic is *wallowing*. The refrain of the wallowing weaner is, "Yeah, but."

- Yeah, but I don't understand what to do on this next part.
- Yeah, but that's not what you said at the board.
- Yeah, but you didn't explain that.
- Yeah, but I still didn't understand.
- Yeah, but I'm going to play helpless as long as I can to keep you here forever.

Worried Teachers Hover

The third reason that trainees tended to backslide was the fact that caring teachers naturally worry about those students who chronically struggle. A simple verbal prompt, so cut-and-dried, seems too brief to a teacher who is accustomed to tutoring the chronically needy.

Watch these teachers attempt to leave a wallowing weaner, and you will often be treated to a bit of visual comedy. They give the prompt, and then they look at the student hesitantly. They straighten up, and then they look at the student again before slowly moving away. They seem to be thinking, *Does the student really know what to do? How can I be sure? I worry that they can't continue on their own. After all, I didn't really spend much time with them.*

This hovering is an open invitation to wallowing. No weaner worth his or her salt will miss such a blatant cue. And once they murmur, "Yeah, but," it seems so cold-hearted to such a caring teacher to continue walking away. But, then, co-dependency is a two-way street.

The refrain of the wallowing weaner is, 'Yeah, but ...'

Beyond the Verbal Modality

Wean to What?

After watching my trainees backslide, I concluded that I was blocked – at least temporarily. Then one day, as I watched a teacher tutoring a helpless handraiser on a math assignment, I saw the teacher point to her *example on the board* as she spoke. When I looked at the board, I saw the solution to my problem.

In order to cure problems of verbosity, we will have to deal with the *entire context of the teacher's verbosity*, not just the talking itself. We will have to deal with a topic that I had never worried about before – *lesson plans.*

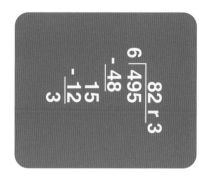

A summary graphic hides the individual steps of a lesson.

A Picture Is Worth a Thousand Words

If words get us into trouble, one way of getting out of trouble is to eliminate words. A prompt does not need to be a *verbal* prompt.

In fact, verbal prompts are rather inefficient. It takes a lot of talking to explain something. Since a picture is worth a thousand words, wouldn't a picture be more efficient? This simple observation brings us to our next topic – the pictures that teachers typically use.

Lesson Plans

Summary Graphics

Imagine a teacher explaining to the class how to divide 495 by 6. We will stick with math, as usual, because it is easy to visualize. The humanities will come later.

The teacher would typically explain and demonstrate the calculation to the class one step at a time. As the teacher walked the students through the problem, he or she would construct an *example on the board* as illustrated to the left. It is so unremarkable that I would never have given it a second look were it not for the wallowing weaners.

Shift perspective for a moment, and imagine that you are a student struggling with the first problem of the practice set as you begin Guided Practice. You are stuck on step four. You look at the teacher's *example on the board* for help with step four. Look at the illustration to the left. Where is step four?

I will call this a *summary graphic* because it summarizes the steps of the calculation. A summary graphic does not *reproduce* the steps of the calculation. The individual steps are nowhere to be seen.

Our normal and traditional pattern of writing when we put an example on the board is to lay *one step over another* until we finish the task. While this pattern effectively walks the students through performance, it leaves behind a poor visual record. The students are only left with a picture of how the problem should look when it is *completed*. There is no path for them to follow in order to get there.

Opening the Door to Wallowing

Imagine that you are a helpless handraiser looking for a good excuse to wallow. Looking at the summary graphic for long division, you would have a very good case for saying, "I don't understand what to do here."

As I watch teachers constructing their summary graphics on the board, I am reminded of a scene from old-time western movies in which the outlaws are being pursued across the rocky badlands by the posse. One of the outlaws dismounts and breaks off a piece of sagebrush in order to wipe out the tracks of their horses. With the trail obliterated, the posse cannot follow.

With our summary graphics, we also *obliterate the trail* so that no student can follow. Once the *visual* modality is gone, all the teacher has left is the *verbal* modality. It is on the verbal modality that the helpless handraiser will hang the teacher with wallowing.

"But, I don't understand what to do here."

A New Perspective on Graphics

To get a new perspective on the visual modality of instruction, let's step out of the classroom for a moment. Imagine that you are shopping for a birthday present for a ten-year-old. As you pass a hobby shop, you notice model airplanes in the window. You decide to buy one.

On the box of the model airplane is a picture of the model built perfectly by a professional. There are no flaws – no glue drops or bent decals. It is beautiful. Your *example on the board* is this perfect model built by you, the professional.

When you get home, curiosity gets the best of you, and you take the cellophane off the box to look inside. On top of all the parts lie the instructions. Spread them out on the table. What format do they follow?

• One step at a time
• A picture for every step
• Minimal reliance on words

The model airplane company learned some important lessons about *lesson plans* long before I was born. They understood, for example, that they would not know the kid who was building the model airplane – age, IQ, reading ability, or mother tongue. And they also knew that if this model did not go together right the first time *without a teacher*, the kid would never buy another one.

Consequently, they were forced to answer the question, "What do I do next?" clearly and without language. They had no choice but to draw up a good *set of plans* based upon *pictures*. This format is as clear as a bell, and it has worked beautifully for generations.

Think of lesson plans from the perspective of the model airplane company. A lesson plan is for the person who has to "put this thing together." While it may also be of use to the teacher's supervisor or to a substitute, these are secondary functions. First and foremost, it is for the student.

A lesson plan is nothing more than a *set of plans* for building something – a calculation, a sentence, a paragraph.

If the steps are not clear, the door is open for wallowing.

graph, an essay, a wooden bench in shop class, or a play on the football field. If the student cannot infer correct performance from the set of plans, then, by default, he or she is thrown back on the only other resource in the classroom. That resource is *you*. Once you begin to explain, the door is open for wallowing.

Visual Instructional Plans (VIPs)

I will refer to a lesson plan with good graphics as a Visual Instructional Plan or "VIP." A VIP is nothing more than a string of visual prompts. It is simple, clear, and permanent. The student can refer to it at any time in order to answer the question, "What do I do next?"

Do not jump to the conclusion, however, that "visual" only refers to pictures. Steps of thinking can also be represented graphically.

Sticking with our long division example for the time being, imagine that, in contrast to covering up our tracks, we were to provide a separate picture for each step. The VIP might look like the illustration below.

However, the old habit of laying one step over another to produce a summary graphic is very hard to break. As an

aid to providing a separate picture for each step, try telling yourself to *step to the right*. Each time you take a step, you will be faced with a blank section of chalkboard. This will prompt you to draw a new picture.

VIPs Accelerate Learning

VIPs dramatically accelerate learning. This VIP of long division was developed during a workshop in twenty minutes by a fifth grade teacher. When I talked to him the following year, he said,

"Last year I spent the entire first semester on long division, and by December, I still had a half-dozen kids who couldn't do it. This year, with good graphics, we all mastered single-digit division in one week and double-digit the following week."

VIPs Aid Weaning

Apart from accelerating learning, VIPs are an indispensible part of the weaning process. As an aid to creating independent learning, VIPs serve three functions.

Reducing the Duration of a Prompt

When teachers give efficient verbal prompts, they reduce the duration of a helping interaction from 3-6 minutes to an average of 30-35 *seconds*. While this is certainly a step in the right direction, it is not yet good enough.

When the teacher is giving corrective feedback, the class typically becomes noisy within 10-15 seconds. In 20 seconds, students are out of their seats. A 30-second prompt will still produce too many discipline problems.

Compare	÷	X	−	Compare	Bring Down

A Visual Instructional Plan (VIP) shows each step of the lesson.

Only when prompts average less than 10 seconds can the teacher work the crowd effectively. A teacher can consistently produce 5-10 second prompts only when a picture is substituted for the words.

With an adequate graphic, the explanation is *prepackaged*. The teacher can point out a critical feature and be gone. It is not uncommon for a prompt to sound like this:

"Look at Step Four up on the board. That is what you do right here."

Reducing Cognitive Overload

In the verbal modality, we hit cognitive overload within a few sentences. That is hardly enough explanation to produce clarity with a complex concept or operation.

How can you present information without constantly being hamstrung by the limitations of verbal recall? The answer, of course, is to *go visual*.

Creating a Halfway House for Weaning

You cannot wean a helpless handraiser by simply removing the help. If you try to go "cold turkey" with chronic help-seekers, they will increase the intensity of their help seeking.

Rather, you must wean the student from your body to a *body substitute*. This body substitute must be able to answer the question, "What do I do next?" in your absence.

By providing a permanent display that can be referred to at will, the VIP guides performance just as you would if you were tutoring. Through repeated reference to the *string of visual prompts* provided by the VIP, students eventually *wean themselves*.

Types of VIPs

As I mentioned earlier, VIPs do not have to be pictures as in our long division example. Some lessons lend them-

selves to pictures, and some do not. But, every type of VIP must answer the question, "What do I do next?" in a permanent, visual form.

There are *three* basic types of VIPs appropriate to different types of assignments. They are:

Performance Illustration

A performance illustration is primarily a series of pictures as in our long division example. Pictures are most useful for tasks which involve computation or physical performance. I saw a good one recently at a public swimming pool – three pictures for mouth-to-mouth resuscitation that left little doubt as to what to do.

A common question asked by primary teachers is, "What do you do if the students cannot read?" The answer is, "Omit words." Pictured below is a lesson plan for a classroom procedure – carrying a chair properly.

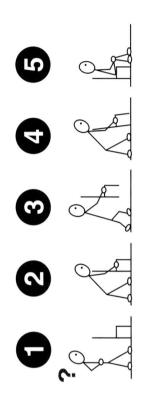

For students who cannot read, omit words.

To appreciate the use of this lesson plan, imagine a student dragging his or her chair across the room a week after this lesson was taught. Imagine, also, that this simple graphic has been posted in the room where it can easily be seen. The teacher might simply stop the child, point to the graphic and wait. Usually, nothing would need to be said.

Performance Outlines

An outline is one of the most common and familiar ways of organizing ideas. However, outlines are most useful for guiding students' work if they retain a focus on performance — what we want the student to *do*.

As a reminder to focus on doing, we will call a lesson plan in outline form a "performance outline." Performance outlines are typically used with tasks that involve writing, research, and discussion. They are the norm in the social studies.

The most common error in the humanities regarding the structuring of performance is not so much *covering up our tracks*, but rather, *providing no tracks at all*. For example, social studies teachers will often explain a topic to the class with no visual representation of the material whatsoever. Where will the details be when it is time to discuss or write? It is equally common to observe a group discussion in which no one is recording what is being said.

Research papers are one of the most common examples of an assignment without adequate structure for performance. Few students are actually taught how to do research much less how to write it up. Students from elementary school through graduate school are sent to the library with little more than a topic. Then, teachers wonder out loud at the quality of the work.

I had this experience as a teacher myself. I would receive some papers that covered only part of the topic

A lesson plan is nothing more than a string of visual prompts.

while others never quite grasped the topic at all. But it was difficult to attribute the poor outcomes to laziness or stupidity since I was dealing with doctoral students at one of the top universities in the country.

Stripped of easy rationalizations, I had to examine *my* contribution in order to explain the high degree of variability in quality. One day I experienced a blinding flash of the obvious. We were playing a game — *a game of hide-and-seek*.

Rather than teaching the students exactly how to produce an excellent paper, I was conducting a *contest*. I knew the subject, the key issues and the relevant literature. They did not. While I had discussed the topic in class, I had stopped short of preparing the students for the *performance* I wanted.

On the next paper, I gave the students a handout which describes exactly what I wanted from them. I outlined not only the major issues, but also the subordinate issues and how they related to the major issues. In addition, I provided a bibliography for each topic.

This time I received a batch of consistently excellent papers. They showed plenty of individual style and creativity, but they were focused and thorough.

Give the students a road map, and they will probably reach their objective. But as the old saying goes, *If you don't know where you are going, you are not too likely to get there.*

Teachers often report a gut feeling that giving the students this much direction is somehow *wrong*. They feel as though they are *giving them the answers*, or *doing their work for them*. Teachers have said to me, "You mean we can actually show them *exactly* what we want?"

If you want to teach, provide adequate structure for performance. If you want to have a contest, provide a mini-

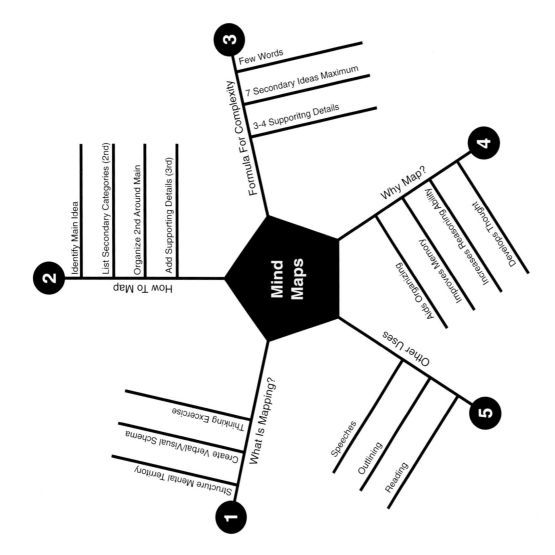

Mind Maps

central graphic with branches:

Mind Maps

2 How To Map
- Identify Main Idea
- List Secondary Categories (2nd)
- Organize 2nd Around Main
- Add Supporting Details (3rd)

3 Formula For Complexity
- Few Words
- 7 Secondary Ideas Maximum
- 3-4 Supporitng Details

4 Why Map?
- Aids Organizing
- Improves Memory
- Increases Reasoning Ability
- Develops Thought

5 Other Uses
- Speeches
- Outlining
- Reading

1 What Is Mapping?
- Structure Mental Territory
- Create Verbal/Visual Schema
- Thinking Excercise

A mind map shows someone how to organize an idea, solve a problem, or perform a series of operations.

mum of structure, and see who can succeed without any outside help.

Mind Maps

Mind maps combine the information of an outline with the clarity of a picture in an easy-to-read diagram. A mind map is literally any graphic that shows someone how to organize an idea, solve a problem, or perform a series of operations. The graphic to the right is a mind map of mind mapping.

Most descriptions of mind mapping focus on clarifying the relationship between main ideas and secondary ideas. But in mind mapping, necessity is the mother of invention. Sometimes mind maps illustrate a linear sequence with no secondary ideas at all, something that could just as easily have been presented in the form of a list.

The illustrations on the left side of the following page show a variety of schema for mind maps. You are probably familiar with all of them. You probably made some of your own that were far more complex when you were studying for finals in college. Balloons with arrows are a perennial favorite.

VIPs versus Simple Visual Aids

It is important to discriminate VIPs from other common types of visual aids. Over the years teachers have developed many devices for representing performance in graphic form. Many of them are far too cryptic to serve as VIPs.

Long division, for example, has traditionally been summarized in the four steps pictured at the top right of the next page. It would be more accurate to think of this graphic as a *vestige* of a VIP rather than the VIP itself. It might be useful as a

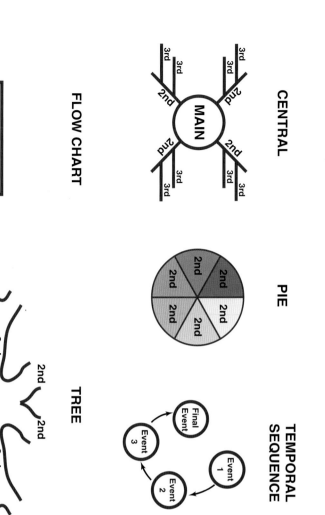

CENTRAL

PIE

TEMPORAL SEQUENCE

FLOW CHART

TREE

In mind mapping, necessity is the mother of invention.

memory aid for test review. But, it would omit far too much information to be of much help to a student who was struggling with initial acquisition.

A memory aid is useful for test review, but it omits the information needed for acquisition.

Task Analysis and Performance

Task analysis is the term commonly used in education for dividing a task into the steps of performance. I have learned that logic alone is not a reliable guide to task analysis. You can logically divide any task into any number of steps. I have seen a protocol for long division with over twenty steps!

To be useful, dividing the task into steps must bear a close relationship to what you want the students to *do*. The steps must correspond to *meaningful acts*.

Merely *thinking* the process through makes it easy to assume too much or to leave out minor steps, especially if you are highly familiar with the task. A helpless handraiser can spot a missing step a mile away.

In order to see the task with the fresh eyes of new learning, actually manipulate the equipment, do the calculation, or walk through performance while developing your task analysis. From the student's vantage point, keep asking yourself, "What do I do next?"

Chapter Eight

Integrating with the Physical Modality

Continuing the Weaning Process

Effective verbal and visual prompts take us halfway to our goal of replacing learned helplessness with independent learning. To take the next step in weaning the helpless handraisers, we will need to focus on the *physical* modality of learning.

Up to this point, our objective in weaning has been to replace tutoring during Guided Practice with brief, yet rich helping interactions. The focus of this chapter will be to reduce the need for corrective feedback during Guided Practice to an absolute minimum.

The most effective way to minimize the need for corrective feedback after a lesson has been taught is to teach it right in the first place. How do you teach a lesson so that mastery is the natural outcome of instruction?

Teaching for Mastery

Goals of Instruction

The twin goals of instruction are *comprehension* and *long-term memory*. We want the students to get it and to keep it.

Comprehension and long-term memory are two sides of the same coin. They occur simultaneously and for the same reason – the integration of learning modalities.

In most classroom work we teach to three modalities: auditory, visual, and physical.

Preview

- With effective verbal and visual prompts, we are halfway to our goal of weaning the helpless handraisers.

- By teaching the lesson right the first time so that mastery is the natural outcome, we can prevent most of the helplessness.

- Both comprehension and long-term memory are maximized when we integrate the verbal, visual, and physical modalities of learning.

- Integration occurs when all modalities are used simultaneously. Teaching one step at a time with all three modalities produces a series of Say, See, Do Cycles.

- Structured Practice slowly walks the students through these cycles often enough so that they approach automaticity before Guided Practice.

In this book I use the term verbal modality rather than auditory modality to reflect my focus on the perspective of the classroom teacher who must constantly rely upon language to convey ideas. It might best be thought of as the *verbal modality of teaching*.

Comprehension

The strength of the *verbal* modality is in the area of comprehension. While weak in terms of memory, it is unique in its ability to convey meaning. The efficiency of the verbal modality in this regard seduces us into relying on it too heavily during instruction.

When we teach by talking, we rapidly load information onto the verbal modality in which storage is poor. This is a prescription for exasperation for teacher and student alike. As the saying goes, *In one ear and out the other.*

The *visual* modality, in contrast, seems capable of producing immediate comprehension almost effortlessly. Hence, the saying, *a picture is worth a thousand words.*

The *physical* modality produces a unique depth of understanding. Hence, the saying, *We learn by doing.*

This understanding of learning is not new. A Chinese proverb states it most succinctly:

I hear, and I forget.

I see, and I remember.

I do, and I understand.

Long-Term Memory

The verbal, visual, and physical modalities, as we know from experience, have quite different capacities for storage. While the *verbal* modality is limited, the *visual* modality is nothing short of phenomenal.

When we sleep, we dream so realistically that we sometimes wake thinking that we were actually there. We can conjure up sights decades old in holographic color at the equivalent of thirty frames a second – a movie from the past.

The physical modality is somewhere between the verbal and visual modalities in terms of memory. As with auditory memory, significant practice is required to get results. Nevertheless, once skills are acquired, the "feel" stays with us. As the saying goes, *Once you learn to ride a bicycle, you never forget how.*

Combining Modalities

We have three learning systems, each with its own strengths and weaknesses. We can maximize both comprehension and long-term memory by integrating the three systems so that the student can profit from the strengths of each. How can this integration best be accomplished in the classroom?

Surprisingly, it is not as difficult as you might think. The brain simply constructs and decodes *patterns*. If all three modalities can be "welded together" into a *single pattern*, the strong modalities can carry the weak.

Either you teach to the brain exactly as it is built, or you fail.

How do you weld all three modalities together? Simple – *use them simultaneously*. Whatever neurons are firing at a given instant become integrated into a single pattern or "memory trace."

The diagram to the left represents this welding together or linking of modalities. For simplicity's sake, let's refer to these three modalities as *say, see, and do.*

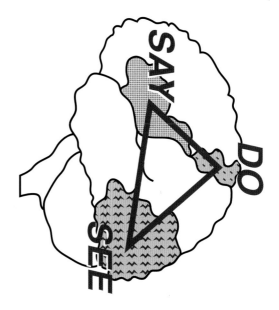

We weld the three modalities into a single pattern by using them simultaneously.

A Model for Learning

We already know that we learn by doing and that we *learn one step at a time.* Put these two notions together and you get a simple, yet powerful model for the teaching process.

This model is comprised of the repetition of a simple unit which we will call a "Say, See, Do Cycle." A Say, See, Do Cycle integrates one "chunk" of input as follows:

- Let me explain what to do next.
- Watch as I show you.
- Now, you do it.

The cycle is repeated as often as necessary in order to complete a lesson. We will call this pattern "Say, See, Do Teaching." The presentation of the lesson would be interactive by its nature, with the students *learning by doing one step at a time* through a series of Say, See, Do Cycles as represented in the figure above and to the right.

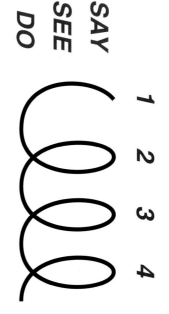

SAY
SEE
DO

1 2 3 4

We teach one step at a time with a series of Say, See, Do Cycles.

Learning and Forgetting

Memory and Time

While the integration of modalities builds comprehension and long-term memory, maximizing this integration in the classroom depends upon *the packaging of our presentation.* The eternal enemy of memory is time. Memory, particularly auditory memory, slips away second by second.

The picture on the following page shows a generic learning curve. The ascending "S" curve is familiar to us from the opening chapters of learning textbooks.

Sadly, however, there is only one predictable outcome of learning, and that is *forgetting.* Pictured beside the learning curve is a forgetting curve – a learning curve turned upside down.

As you can see, retention drops as a function of time. It drops like a stone in the auditory modality. Seconds after you explain something to another person, the memory pattern begins to deteriorate.

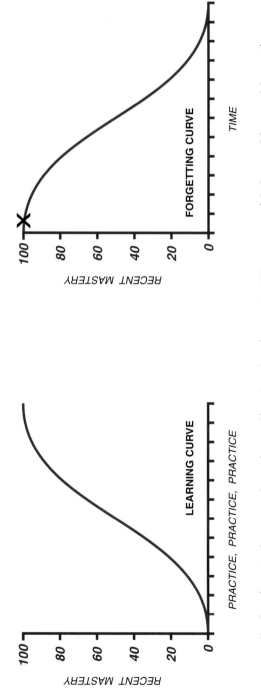

LEARNING CURVE

RECENT MASTERY

100 · 80 · 60 · 40 · 20 · 0

PRACTICE, PRACTICE, PRACTICE

FORGETTING CURVE

RECENT MASTERY

100 · 80 · 60 · 40 · 20 · 0

TIME

By having students perform immediately after input (at X), you avoid the problems of forgetting.

Perform Immediately

While long-term memory deteriorates rapidly, short-term memory has nearly total recall. You are at the top of the forgetting curve *two or three seconds after input.* If you ask the students to perform immediately after input, you exploit the recall of short-term memory while avoiding the problems of forgetting inherent in long-term memory.

Compare this simple model with the packaging of input and output in the typical classroom, especially at the secondary level. Routinely the teacher's presentation will last twenty minutes or more. During this time, the students are relatively passive. They are supposed to be "taking it in" when, in fact, they are experiencing both cognitive overload and forgetting.

Even if the students were to do something with the material before the end of the period, the loss of the input would be great. This would maximize help-seeking.

We have referred to this general model of teaching previously as *Bop 'til You Drop.* It could more accurately be characterized as:

> *Input, Input, Input, Input – **Output***

Imagine, in contrast, packaging the students' efforts so that *doing* consistently occurred *immediately after* input when retention was at its maximum. This model of teaching would be characterized as:

> *Input, **Output**, Input, **Output**, Input, **Output***

Of course, the second model is far better aligned with Say, See, Do Teaching, but they are not the same. If you were to say too much and wait too long before doing, you could undermine both comprehension and long-term memory. As with the execution of so many skills, success is in the *timing.* Say, See, Do Teaching delivers its full potential when *input is brief and output is immediate.*

Packaging a Lesson

It is helpful to have a simple model in mind for packaging the presentation of a lesson. It allows you to do a quick check during lesson planning to see if anything has been left out.

Lessons, regardless of the subject area, tend to have three sections. Like a play, they have a beginning, a middle, and an end. The *beginning* sets the stage. The *middle* is the "meat and potatoes" of the lesson – the new stuff. The *end* is "practice, practice, practice" with "variations on a theme" being optional.

Setting the Stage

Setting the stage represents the preliminary business of the lesson: a series of decisions by the teacher as to what the students need to have in mind before they encounter the new material. The items listed below are typical. Any combination of these may be presented in any given lesson, and you may wish to add a few items of your own:

- **Raising the Level of Concern:** Why is this lesson important?

- **Review and Background:** What skills from yesterday need to be rehearsed? What information is needed to create a context for today's lesson?

- **Goals and Objectives:** Where will this lesson take us? What specifically will we learn? Sometimes the teacher can present a "preview of the coming attraction" called an "advance organizer."

To create

long-term memory,

you must integrate

Say, See, and Do.

Acquisition

Acquisition is the label we will give to the middle part of the lesson – the meat and potatoes. This is the main event. During acquisition we put the new stuff into the students' heads one way or another.

During acquisition we will pointedly teach to all three modalities, and we will maximize their integration. The following items are alternative labels for the elements of the Say, See, Do Cycle.

- **Explanation (Say):** What do we do next? As in all shaping, it is just one step, and the less said the better.

- **Modeling (See):** What does this step look or sound like? Modeling is a broad term in learning theory that is synonymous with "demonstration." It applies to anything from a computation to an athletic skill to a passage of music.

- **Structured Practice (Do):** What does correct performance feel like? The purpose of Structured Practice is to build correct performance without building bad habits. It is practice that is so highly structured that the likelihood of error approaches zero.

Consolidation

Consolidation in most cases is synonymous with practice, practice, practice. There is, of course, no end in the quest for mastery. How many times must a professional musician practice a passage or a professional basketball player practice a shot before it is mastered to their satisfaction?

Yet, even at the level of normal classroom learning, performance must be taken to the point of being second nature, or it will soon be lost.

- **Guided Practice:** Guided Practice is practice at a level of Acquisition that requires coaching to perfect performance and to maintain it. Error readily invades performance and it often goes undetected by the learner. Without the supervision of a teacher or coach, bad habits can creep into performance where they are inadvertently practiced to mastery.

- **Independent Practice:** With Independent Practice you are *your own coach*. You must be able to discriminate error as soon as it occurs. And then, you must be able to reinstruct yourself in order to correct the error.

- **Generalization and Discrimination:** Generalization and discrimination constitute, in effect, the "fine tuning" of the lesson. Generalization refers to teaching variations on a theme. In mathematics, there might be variations of a procedure. In the humanities, there might be different interpretations of a historic event from different perspectives. In football, there might be different ways to crack a particular defense.

  Discrimination refers to delineating correct from incorrect performance. If the error does not exist in the student's repertoire, you are better off not bringing up the issue. But, if the error is already there, you need to train the student to consciously discriminate correct performance from error.

The diagram to the right shows the three-phase lesson design in its entirety. Acquisition, of course, is the main event with Say, See, Do at center stage. Note also the repetitions of the skill (R1, R2, etc.) during Structured Practice to make performance nearly automatic *prior to*

Guided Practice. Consequently, there should be a greatly reduced need for corrective feedback *during* Guided Practice.

Structured Practice

One of the most noticeable characteristics of lesson presentation when you watch an effective teacher, regardless of the subject area, is that Structured Practice comprises the bulk of the lesson. Only during Structured Practice do we have enough control over performance to produce perfect practice. If we "pay our dues" during Structured Practice, the students should need help only occasionally during Guided Practice.

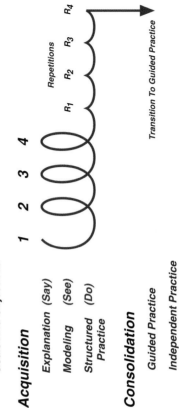

Setting The Stage

    Raising The Level Of Concern

    Review And Background

    Goals And Objectives

Acquisition

    Explanation (Say)

    Modeling (See)

    Structured (Do)
    Practice

Consolidation

    Guided Practice

    Independent Practice

    Generalization And Discrimination

If we build performance carefully during Acquisition, students will need very little help during Guided Practice.

Walk through Slowly

The traditional method of "getting it right the first time" is to slow down and walk students through performance one step at a time. Typically students gain fluency and speed with additional repetitions until they approach what Benjamin Bloome refers to as *automaticity*.

With a musical instrument, for example, the teacher would have the students play the passage slowly at the beginning in order to play it "cleanly." Once it was played cleanly, the students could slowly increase speed as long as they maintained a clean and fluid performance. If they were to go too fast, errors would immediately creep in, and the passage would become "ragged."

Students, of course, always want to go for speed too soon. They want to play "hot licks" like their heroes. Coaching a sport is no different. The kids want to scrimmage before they learn the fundamentals. The eternal struggle of the teacher is to slow students down until they can increase speed without increasing error.

The role of Structured Practice in building correct performance while avoiding bad habits was most succinctly stated by Vince Lombardi, the legendary coach of the Green Bay Packers. He said, *Practice does not make perfect.*
Only perfect practice makes perfect.

Structured Practice in the Humanities

In the humanities, the central question of Say, See, Do Teaching is, "How do you do a concept?" There are a limited number of answers to that question. You can:

- **Talk** – anything from quickly paraphrasing a concept with a partner to an English-style debate.

- **Write** – anything from a quick in-class essay to a dissertation.

- **Perform** – anything from some role playing to an internship.

My own prejudice, however, gained from writing this and previous books, is that thinking is not rigorous until the thoughts are clearly written. Rewriting is the crucible in which the fragments of ideas that pass for understanding in our consciousness are forged into clarity. Clear writing is clear thinking.

Practice does not make perfect.
Only perfect practice makes perfect.

Regardless of your subject area, if students cannot write a clear essay on a given topic, they probably do not understand it very well. We are, then, all teachers of English composition. When writing becomes a process rather than an assignment, it fits very nicely into the say, see, do framework.

During Structured Practice, for example, students might discuss chunks of a concept with partners after you present each step of the lesson. They might then write a ten-minute essay followed by practice of the concept as they read each others' papers. The teacher might then read some of the best papers in order to create an outline of a well-written essay. Guided Practice would be the writing of the second draft.

Mastery, Helplessness, and Weaning

You Get What You Pay For

The three-phase lesson design gives us a simple language for describing the teaching process. If this process is carried out thoroughly, *mastery* should be the natural outcome. But insofar as the process is abbreviated, *failure* will be the outcome. The students' casualty rate on a lesson is a good index of the degree to which the teaching process has been abrogated.

Missing Lesson Parts

The part of the lesson that is most commonly omitted is Structured Practice. Taking mathematics as our model once again, it is not uncommon to see a teacher walk the

class through only one or two examples before going to Guided Practice. It is equally common to see the teacher model all of the steps of the computation on the board, pausing only for questions before going straight to Guided Practice. Sometimes there is no practice whatsoever, and new material is assigned for homework.

Whether this is because the teacher is naive or simply in a hurry, this failure to produce automaticity or anything even approaching it will soon cost the teacher and the students dearly. As we say during training, "All the chickens come home to roost in Guided Practice."

Cognitive overload is the first cousin of learned helplessness.

Weaners Think Like Lawyers

Cognitive overload is the first cousin of learned helplessness. For any student who is near cognitive overload or simply dependent by nature, the door has just been thrown open for help-seeking. The helpless handraisers will be waving their arms in the air as soon as the teacher says, "Let's get to work."

Weaners would like you to spend as much time with them as possible, of course. But, they want your *nurturance*, not your scorn for having done nothing. They want to enroll your helping instincts.

To do this, they must think like lawyers. They must *have a case.*

Skillful weaners, therefore, are sophisticated consumers of teaching. They can tell a faulty product when they see one. They know when a step of the task analysis has been provides the *preventative* component of our *weaning program for the helpless handraiser.*

Teaching the lesson thoroughly ruins the weaner's case for help-seeking. How can the weaner convincingly say, "I don't understand how to do this," after you have just walked him or her through several correct performances?

Weaners may, of course, give help-seeking a try out of pure habit. But, having laid the groundwork for weaning with both thorough teaching and a good VIP, you can now begin a successful *extinction program.* You might simply refer to some critical feature of the VIP and be gone. Sometimes just pointing is enough to get that slightly embarrassed, "Oh" from the student.

With thorough teaching, therefore, you work yourself *out of a job* during Guided Practice. With incomplete teaching, you work yourself *into a job* during Guided Practice.

Like lawyers, weaners must have a case.

left out. They know when a step is too big. They know when the teacher has assumed too much. They know when they have a good case for seeking help.

When weaners have a good case, they will pursue it with zeal. With their hands waving helplessly in the blue, they will nail you for five minutes of individualized attention.

Preempting Helplessness

The dividends of teaching a lesson thoroughly go beyond the acquisition of learning. Teaching thoroughly

Section Four

Raising Expectations

Chapter Nine

Creating Motivation

Preview

- The management of productivity in the classroom focuses on building *diligence* (working hard) and *excellence* (working conscientiously).

- In order to get more and better work, we must answer the basic question of motivation, "Why should I?" The answer to this question is called an *incentive*.

- A simple incentive is the juxtaposition of two events: a task and a preferred activity. The best preferred activities in the classroom combine fun with learning.

- Since preferred activities can only be given after the task has been completed correctly, work must be checked as it is being done.

- Say, See, Do Teaching plus the weaning of helpless handraisers frees the teacher to check work in the classroom during Guided Practice rather than at home.

Beyond Weaning

A successful weaning program must build *independent learning* so that the teacher's time is no longer consumed during Guided Practice with tutoring the helpless handraisers. Once the teacher's time is liberated, possibilities open up for the management of *motivation* and *accountability* that were not previously available.

This chapter will focus on *motivation* – the building of *diligence* in the classroom. The following chapter will focus on *accountability* – the building of *excellence* in the classroom.

What tools can the teacher bring into play in the classroom to give students a reason to be diligent – to work hard? For many students, working hard on school assignments is a novel idea. How can the teacher build a good work ethic in these students – one that is often lacking?

Focus on Motivation

During training, teachers express frustration not only with students who disrupt, but also with students who won't do *anything*.

"Do we have to do this?"

"This is boring."

"We did this last year."

"This stuff is dumb."

How do you motivate the student who simply *does not care?* Motivation is a very complex topic since there are many reasons for the failure of students to apply themselves in the classroom. A few of them we can control, but most of them we cannot.

Things We Do Not Control

A student's attitude toward learning is largely a function of *enrichment in the home environment.* One of the largest single correlates of success in reading during first grade is the amount the child has been read to *before* first grade. Contrast a home in which snuggling with children and reading is a daily nurturing ritual to a home in which books are not present and neglect is the norm. However, you have no control over the student's home life.

Abusive child rearing practices can also seriously handicap a child in school. A child raised by the "yell and hit" method of parenting is likely to harbor a deep resentment toward adult authority. That resentment will be transferred to the teacher once the child comes to school. There are few handicaps to learning greater than a habitual passive-aggressive response to the teacher's instruction. However, you cannot quickly alter the child's personality.

A student's attitude toward learning is also a function of the *ills of society.* Drugs, violence, and constant danger stunt a child's imagination and dreams. However, we cannot wait until the ills of society have been cured before we begin to teach.

A student who has been allowed to substitute *television and video games* for reading may show a short attention span and little interest in classroom tasks. However, you will not have influence over the child's access to video.

We do have some control over the curriculum, but this is not a book about the content of the curriculum. This is

a book about the *process* of instruction. What elements of the instructional process do we control that might increase the students' motivation to learn?

Things We Do Control

We do control the students' experience of learning in the classroom. We can affect the students' willingness to work if we create a learning experience that has crucial elements of motivation built in. Our management of academic productivity will focus on two things:

- *Quantity* of work or diligence
- *Quality* of work or excellence

Ideally, we would like the students to *work hard* (diligence), and we would like them to *work conscientiously* (excellence). If we can gain some leverage over these two aspects of performance, we can go a long way toward overcoming disadvantages that children bring from outside of the classroom.

A Dynamic Tension

When students work on a task, quantity and quality are constantly in dynamic tension. If they work too fast, quality suffers. But, if they obsess and dawdle, quantity suffers.

Ideally, we would like students to work as fast as they can *short* of becoming sloppy – to push hard without pushing too hard. This balance point between diligence and excellence is different for each student depending on his or her abilities.

Productivity

The management of productivity in the classroom focuses on:

- **Quantity – diligence or "working hard"**
- **Quality – excellence or "working carefully"**

Discovering Our Own Limits

We have all gone through a process of discovery in learning our own limits with various types of tasks. We have gone too rapidly and made mistakes. And, we have gone too slowly and failed to finish. We try to function somewhere between *haste makes waste* and *get on the ball and hustle!*

By pushing ourselves, we learn that we can accomplish much more than we might have thought possible. It is always sobering to see how much we can produce in a short span of time when we work under a deadline. When we are highly motivated, we focus our attention and mobilize our resources. When we want to do something badly enough, we usually can.

But, we must *want to*. To learn our limits we must *push* ourselves. Those limits will vary depending on the nature of the task. Finding out what we can accomplish in different areas of endeavor is part of discovering who we really are.

Incentives

Why Should I?

Before we will push ourselves to define our own capabilities, we must have a reason to do so. We must have a good answer to the question underlying any discussion of motivation: *Why should I?*

Why should I go to work right now? Why should I concentrate so hard? Why should I stay up late studying? Why should I keep working instead of taking another break?

Without a good reason, we will effortlessly slip into our comfort zone. Our minds will wander and our hands will slow down as we unconsciously reduce stress.

Any answer to the question, "Why should I?" is called an *incentive*. The term "incentive" is interchangeable with the term "reinforcer."

Incentives or reinforcers produce work. While you may offer a person a reward for doing something, until at least some work has been completed, you cannot say that the reward functioned as a reinforcer.

Incentives Are Everywhere

Life is full of incentives. Showing interest in what a person says can serve as an incentive for that person's continuing to talk to you. A parent's love and approval can serve as an incentive for a child's cooperation.

The opposite of an incentive is a *disincentive*. While incentives give you a reason to do something, disincentives give you a reason to stop. For example, a child might be sent to a piano teacher only to discover that, because of a lack of any natural ability, progress is agonizingly slow and the price of that progress is agonizingly high. The toil might provide a disincentive for continuing with the piano.

A second child, being gifted, might find that progress is rapid and adulation from proud parents comes at a very reasonable price. This child might find practicing the piano reinforcing. Thus, an activity that is a disincentive for one child may serve as an incentive for another child.

Incentives answer the question, 'Why should I?'

Incentives are, therefore, a matter of "cost" and "benefit." An experience in which the benefit outweighs the cost tends to be repeated.

When an incentive functions within some planful structure, we refer to the incentive and the structure for delivering it as an *incentive system.* When teachers plan ways of getting students to do things, they are designing incentive systems.

Incentive Systems

Informal Incentive Systems

Most incentive systems in life are *informal.* The universal incentive in child rearing and family life is *love.* Love is both a bond and a motivator. Children who love their parents will often do things to please their parents.

One of the most important jobs of parents is to spend a lot of time giving affection to their children – to cuddle and play, to rough-house and horsey ride, to snuggle and read stories. These "good times" serve many purposes – bonding, brain development, and emotional growth to name a few. One purpose, however, is to establish the parents as powerful reinforcers in their children's lives. Most of the cooperation that parents eventually get from their children will be

based upon all of the emotional "money in the bank" that has been stored up over the years.

As soon as you are ready for bed, it will be story time.

For example, if you ask your twelve-year-old to carry the groceries in from the car, and he or she says, "Okay," realize that your child has just given you a gift. But this gift is not given based upon nothing. You have paid for it with all of the love and good times that you and your child have shared over the years. You have just received a small dividend check from your account.

Formal Incentive Systems

Some incentive systems in life are *formal*. They represent an agreed upon exchange of goods and services. Your paycheck is such an incentive. But around the house, most of the formal incentive systems that we use as parents are simply routines to get the kids to do things. These routines are well understood in advance.

The one I remember most clearly from my childhood is "the bedtime routine." My mother would say:

"All right kids, it is 8:30 – time to get ready for bed. Time to wash your face, brush your teeth, and get your pajamas on. As soon as you are in bed, it will be story time. But, lights out at 9:00."

As you can see, the terms of the arrangement were no mystery. The faster we moved, the more time we had for snuggles and stories.

Formal incentives and informal incentives work together. No matter what the formal incentive, we always try harder for someone we love and respect.

Bribery

Due to the overuse of formal incentives in classrooms during the past several decades, educators have become understandably concerned about "bribery." We have become wary of the overuse of points, tokens, treats, and meaningless "awards." Many teachers have overgeneralized, however, to the point where they consider *all* incentives to be bribes.

In order to avoid throwing the baby out with the bath water, we need to examine the appropriate and inappropriate use of formal incentives. Within this context, it is helpful to categorize formal incentives as either *proactive* or *reactive*.

A **proactive** incentive system is an exchange that is established *in advance*. These exchanges are typically innocuous, every-day events.

Imagine, for example, that you wish to buy a box of cornflakes at the grocery store, and the price is $2.99. At the check-out stand you pay the $2.99 which gives the checker a good reason (i.e. incentive) to allow you to leave with the cornflakes. You have provided the checker with an answer to the question, "Why should I?"

A **reactive** incentive system, on the other hand, is an exchange that is established *in the heat of the moment*. Imagine a situation in which another person will not cooperate with you. From his or her perspective, there is not enough reason to do so.

In frustration, you *react* to this dilemma by offering the other person a reward if he or she will do as you want. This *reactive* incentive is a *bribe*.

Take, for example, the following argument:

Mother: "Billy, I want you to clean your room."
Billy: "I don't want to."
Mother: "Now, I want that room cleaned. It is a mess!"
Billy: "I want to go outside and play!"
Mother: "Not until you get this room cleaned!"
Billy: "I'm not doing it!"
Mother: "Oh, yes you are!"
Billy: "You can't make me!"

Mother: "Listen, I'll give you fifty cents when this room is clean, and then you can go outside and play."

Unfortunately, when you use incentives incorrectly, they usually blow up in your face and give you the *opposite* of what you want. In this example, the mother has just reinforced Billy for *noncooperation* rather than cooperation.

By digging in his heels and saying "No," Billy has just been rewarded with fifty cents. If he had simply cleaned his room without an argument, he would not have gotten a penny. What do you suppose will be going through Billy's mind the next time his mother asks him to do some chore around the house?

To put it simply, bribery is the definition of *malpractice* in incentive management. Nobody who is well trained in the technology of incentive management would even consider offering an incentive in this fashion.

Informal and Formal Classroom Incentives

In the classroom teachers will need both informal and formal incentives to motivate students. Students will naturally work harder for teachers they like. But, formal incentives will play a more prominent role in the classroom than they do in family life. For one thing, the students don't know you, much less love you, on the first day of school. And, for another thing, some students resent you just because they resent any adult authority figure.

For these reasons, any teacher will need to develop technical proficiency in the design and implementation of formal incentive systems. The trick is to motivate the students without working yourself to death.

Simple and Complex Incentive Systems

Incentive systems can be simple or complex. A simple incentive system provides a reinforcer in exchange for a specified behavior. However, incentive systems can be

extremely complex depending upon the number of bonus clauses, penalty clauses, and fail-safe mechanisms that are built in.

Incentive systems for *discipline* management in the classroom tend to be relatively complex in order to get *everyone* to cooperate with the teacher – even the most disruptive students. Incentive systems for *academic productivity*, the subject of this chapter, are relatively simple.

Simple Classroom Incentive Systems

Grandma's Rule

Simple classroom incentive systems are straightforward applications of Grandma's Rule which says:

You have to finish your dinner before you get your dessert.

Effective parents and teachers have always been instinctive incentive managers. They have a knack for pairing treats with chores in order to get the work done.

Traditional Incentives

When I was a kid in grade school, I had teachers who instinctively used incentives. They would come by my desk, look at my work, and say:

"I think you know how to do this, Fred. When you complete that example, you may put your paper on my desk and work on your science project for the remainder of the period."

I was thrilled! I loved working on my science project!

Bribery is the definition of malpractice in incentive management.

You have to finish your dinner before you get your dessert.

Most of my teachers were really into "projects." We did science projects, art projects, current events projects. My teachers did not stop what they were doing in order to get us started on our projects, either. The projects were already organized so that teachers could simply excuse us and continue working with the rest of the class.

For example, all of my elementary classrooms had an easel in the back with three jars of tempera paint in the primary colors and a few well worn brushes. Every few weeks we painted a new mural on the chalkboard depicting the theme of our social studies unit or the coming holiday. I can remember working on the horses' heads, or the

wagon trains going west, the sails of the Nina, Pinta, and Santa Maria, as well as the ghosts in the Halloween scene and the turkeys in the Thanksgiving scene.

My sixth grade teacher, Miss Bakey, had a different system. She had us all bring a shoe box from home to serve as our "project box." We put our names on the boxes and filled them with the materials needed for an art or science project. All of the project boxes were lined up on a shelf where we could easily get them if we finished our assignments early.

The Problem with Traditional Incentives

The problem with these traditional incentive systems was that the same seven or eight kids always got to paint the murals and work on their projects. They were the "smarties" who always finished early. Everyone else worked until the bell rang.

While I loved doing these projects, as far as incentive management is concerned, the whole system was backwards. The kids who already had a good work ethic got all of the incentives. Those who needed a reason to try harder almost never received an incentive.

My teachers probably weren't thinking about incentives, anyway. They were probably just trying to keep us busy. Rather than providing incentives for those in need of some motivation, our projects served more as "sponge activities" – learning activities which soak up time that would otherwise be wasted. To make the transition from a sponge activity to a cost-effective classroom incentive system, we will need to learn a lot more about the technology of incentive management.

Incentive System Design

Beyond "Grandma's Rule"

The basic structural element of a simple incentive system is, of course, Grandma's Rule. A simple incentive system is the juxtaposition of two activities:

- The thing I *have* to do
- The thing I *want* to do

The first activity is the *task*. The second activity is the *preferred activity* – otherwise known as the reinforcer or the preferred activity. The heart of an incentive system is the preferred activity. It answers the question, "Why should I?" It gives the student something to look forward to in the not-too-distant future. It should be fun. Hence, the truism of incentive management: *No joy, no work.*

Criterion of Mastery

While the heart of an incentive system is the *preferred activity*, there is an additional, equally important element; the *criterion of mastery*. Every lesson in the classroom is a learning experiment. Any learning experiment needs a working definition of when mastery has taken place.

A criterion of mastery is typically stated in terms of *consecutive correct performances.* How many *in a row* do the students have to do *correctly* before you can relax and say, "They've got it!" It is a judgement call, of course. Too few feels "thin," and too many feels like we're beating it to death.

Criteria of mastery for complex human learning typically range between five out of five and ten out of ten. This is a sensible criterion that you can use in the classroom. Notice, however, that criteria of mastery are *not* stated in the form of a percentage, such as:

> "When you pass your post-test with a score of 80% or above, you may proceed to the next unit."

While this example represents common practice in education, I would not recommend it. I would doubt if anyone reading this book would equate a 20% error rate with the normal meaning of the word "excellence." Would you buy a car built to that criterion, or would you call it a piece of junk?

Speed Incentives

Mastery implies that the work be completed *correctly.* Otherwise, you get a lot of junk. Employing a criterion of mastery, therefore, requires that you have enough time to check the work *as it is being done.*

If you were to excuse students to work on their preferred activities *without* first checking their work, you would create a *speed incentive.* Students would go slapdash through the assignment, not caring about errors, so that they could hand in their papers as quickly as possible and be off to the preferred activities.

Criterion of Mastery and Guided Practice

In the classroom, the criterion of mastery is typically employed during Guided Practice. Students must meet the criterion of mastery before they can be excused to do their preferred activities.

The transition to Guided Practice for a math assignment might sound like this:

Incentives for Diligence Have It All

- *A task:* the thing you have to do
- *A preferred activity:* the thing you want to do
- *A criterion of mastery*

The task must be done correctly and checked before the preferred activity can be given. You cannot have diligence without excellence.

Speed Incentives Omit Work Check

If you omit work check, you create a speed incentive in which the students go as fast as possible regardless of error.

Dawdling Incentives Omit Preferred Activities

If you omit the preferred activity and have the students work until the bell rings, you train them to dawdle.

"Class, I would like you to open your books to page 127 and look at the practice set on the top of the page. As you can see, the problems are very familiar. We have done the first four of them together during Structured Practice. Would you please help me check your papers by marking the first four problems 'correct'?

"We have twenty minutes until the bell rings. I will be coming around to check your work and to answer any questions. As soon as you get five in a row correct, you may hand in your papers and work on your projects for the remainder of the period."

Dynamic Tension Revisited

A criterion of mastery is stated in terms of *consecutive correct performances*. In the previous example, if a student were to do three problems correctly and then make an error on the fourth, that student would have to start over. They must do *five in a row* correctly.

Thus, the more problems a student completes correctly, the more they have to lose should they become sloppy. As the student's total of correct problems grows, they gain a greater and greater vested interest in doing the *next one carefully*.

As a result, students learn to work fast while at the same time retaining their focus on correctness. In this way a teacher can create the dynamic tension between speed and accuracy that encourages students to explore the limits of their abilities.

Criterion of Mastery and Work Check

The teacher must be able to check the work *as it is being produced*. This is fairly easy to do during Structured Practice because the teacher is slowly walking the students through the task. During Guided Practice, however, the rate of production by the students increases rapidly.

Herein lies the difficulty of using a criterion of mastery in the classroom in order to build excellence. If the teacher falls too far behind in work check during Guided Practice, he or she cannot excuse *anyone* to do a preferred activity without creating a speed incentive. If the teacher cannot keep up with work check, the whole notion of using incentives for diligence collapses.

Dawdling Incentives

When overloaded in this fashion, the teacher has few options. They can always excuse the "smarties" to do preferred activities, of course. But the rest of the class will have to work until the bell rings.

Unfortunately, this creates a *dawdling incentive*. Why work yourself to death if it doesn't get you anywhere? Students who must work until the bell rings will eventually learn to slow the rate of work in order to fill the time.

Incentive Options

As you can see, everything you do in the classroom creates an incentive system of some kind. You really only have three choices:

- An incentive for **diligence** which implies excellence.
- An incentive for **speed**.
- An incentive for **dawdling**.

Accountability, therefore, emerges as the most vexing logistical hurdle that a teacher must overcome in classroom management in order to build diligence and, with it, excellence. Work check must be so quick and cheap that it can be done *while the students are working on the assignment during Guided Practice*. The entire next chapter will be devoted to this topic.

Sponge Preferred Activities

Keep It Cheap

In addition to being desirable, preferred activities must be cheap. They must be readily available, easy to use and represent a reasonable amount of prep time for the teacher.

Preferred activities are usually organized and ready to go *before* the lesson starts. The teacher will not have time to stop what he or she is doing during Guided Practice in order to get each student started on a separate preferred activity.

The project boxes that my sixth grade teacher used were very efficient. We spent twenty minutes early in the grading period organizing our project boxes. For that investment, the teacher was free to teach without having to continually stop during Guided Practice to answer the question, "Now, what do I do?"

Types of Sponge Preferred Activities

The range of preferred activities available to a teacher in the classroom is quite broad and varied. Literally anything that the students eagerly look forward to doing can serve as a preferred activity. Many would come under the heading of "enrichment activities." The following suggestions only scratch the surface.

Art Projects: In addition to the tempera paint murals on the chalkboards of my childhood classrooms, I can remember innumerable art projects accompanying social studies and science units.

We sketched and painted everything from wild animals to cell structure, from maps with rivers and mountains to villages of thatched huts. We drew igloos and log cabins.

We would decorate the room. Every upcoming holiday or back-to-school night provided the teacher with preferred activities. We would decorate walls and bulletin boards. To this day I cannot understand why a teacher would spend valuable lesson planning time putting up bulletin boards when the net result is to preempt a wonderful preferred activity.

My high school French teacher was particularly clever. She assigned each of her five huge casement windows to a different class period. Each class had the job of transforming its blank window into a beautiful stained-glass window.

Our teacher surrounded us with examples from the cathedrals of France, and she taught us how the artisans built the windows. Our materials were colored cellophane and electrician's tape. We went through all of the stages of construction from drawing the life-size cartoons to "leading" the "glass." We rushed to complete our daily assignments so that we could get to work on our windows.

Music Projects: When the teacher does whole-group instruction, the class can have a whole-group preferred activity. Our foreign language classes were particularly well suited for doing this since so many drills and dictations were group activities.

Preferred activities should be cheap, readily available, and easy to use.

When we completed our stained-glass windows in French class, we moved right along to French folk songs. I can still sing some of them. We had to practice so that we could serenade the school before the spring break.

Listening centers make great preferred activities. Some teachers use listening centers to teach music appreciation. Other teachers put on background music to make whole-group preferred activities even more enjoyable. Sometimes small groups of students rush to complete their assignments in order to work up a routine for a student talent show.

Learning Projects: One question that I was never asked in school was, "What do you want to know?" Children are curious by their very nature. This truism even applies to students who may not be very curious about the subjects contained in our normal curriculum.

Having students describe their special interests will help you identify relevant learning projects. It may be dwarf stars or race cars, but whatever the topic, it can become a research project.

Preferred activities, therefore, provide the teacher with an avenue for teaching research skills on a topic that the student is motivated to explore. The student could also prepare a presentation to the class as part of the project, complete with visual aids.

Interest Centers and Computer Centers: Interest centers are ready-made preferred activities. In addition, access to computers or special equipment of any kind can be a powerful motivator.

Learning Games: Almost anything in the curriculum can be taught in the form of a game. Books of games have been published for learning everything from history to the multiplication of fractions. Books of learning puzzles and mind benders can also be found. Because such books have a short shelf-life, instead of listing them here, we update our web site regularly with publishers of available books on games and activities. There are also lists of web sites containing directions for specific projects.

Reading and Writing for Pleasure: Having students read their library books is a time-honored preferred activity. Journal writing is another traditional favorite. Some teachers have the class work on a class newspaper. Others have contests for writing poetry or song lyrics.

Helping the Teacher: Students who finish their work early are natural candidates for peer tutoring. Training the class to use Praise, Prompt, and Leave while helping each other gives students a valuable teaching skill in the process.

Some students like to help the teacher with work check, writing test questions, developing materials for interest centers, or even helping the teacher search for good preferred activity games and puzzles. You can often find a bright student with artistic ability who will make beautiful VIPs for you before you teach the next lesson.

Extra Work: Using preferred activity time to build up extra credit is particularly appealing to some students. Memorizing poetry, doing more advanced assignments, or preparing a special class presentation are examples.

Some students want to do their homework during preferred activity time. These are often the high achievers whose after school hours are taken up with extra-curricular activities.

Scheduling Preferred Activities

Lesson-by-Lesson

The simplest and most common way to schedule preferred activities is on a lesson-by-lesson basis. Grandma's Rule implies the juxtaposition of two activities, one that you have to do (the task) and one that you would rather do (the preferred activity). These two activities are typically scheduled back-to-back. When you finish the first activity (correctly, of course), you can work on the second activity until the period is over.

Sometimes, however, this arrangement leaves the teacher and the students feeling as though the day is too chopped up, with never enough time to really get into the preferred activity. In such situations, the teacher may want to consider a work contract.

Work Contract

A work contract is simply a preferred activity that follows the completion of a *series* of tasks. Teachers in self-contained classrooms might leave the end of the day open for preferred activity time once all of the day's assignments have been completed. Teachers in a departmentalized setting might have preferred activity time on Friday.

One clever way of organizing a work contract is called "Freaky Friday." Friday, of course, is the day on which all

No joy, no work.

of the week's assignments must be completed. Explain the rules of Freaky Friday to the class as follows:

"Class, tomorrow we are going to have Freaky Friday. Let me remind you how it works. Before you can start Freaky Friday, all of your assignments for the week must be completed and turned in. Only then can you participate.

"For Freaky Friday, I will put seven assignments on the board. You may choose any four of them and omit any three. When you have completed your four assignments to my satisfaction and handed them in, you may work on your project for the *rest of the day*."

It is hard for adults to appreciate how sweet it is for young people to have control over their own destiny. One teacher who had implemented Freaky Friday had a parent storm into her classroom after school and say,

"I understand from my son that students get to do whatever they want all day Friday. Is that true? The children only work during four days of the week?"

The parent was slightly misinformed, of course. The child simply said that, "We get to do whatever we want on Fridays." In the excitement over getting to exercise freedom of choice, the student failed to clarify that "anything we want" included a full day's worth of academic work. But, how sweet it is to choose.

A Sense of Fun

You cannot have preferred activity time without having fun. Some teachers just have a sense of fun. They bring it with them into the classroom and find ways of making it happen.

But, implementing preferred activity time must also be affordable for the teacher. Work check must be cheap, organization must be simple, and a repertoire of preferred activities must be readily at hand. Using preferred activities becomes much easier when the faculty members work together to gather preferred activity ideas and materials in a central "PAT Bank." Discovering more and more ways of making learning fun is a hallmark of our professional growth as teachers.

By understanding incentive systems, we can have our fun with learning and get motivation for free. Having fun with learning is, therefore, one of the main avenues to raising standards in education. Remember the maxim of incentive management: *No joy, no work*.

Chapter Ten

Providing Accountability

Building Excellence

Accountability and Excellence

To students, incentive systems are about preferred activities. Certainly, from the perspective of the unmotivated student, the preferred activity provides the short-term goal that drives behavior.

But, as we know, there is another key element in the equation – the criterion of mastery. The criterion of mastery requires that the work be done *correctly* before the preferred activity is given.

A criterion of mastery, therefore, requires *strict accountability*. You cannot build diligence unless you simultaneously build excellence.

The Management of Excellence

The primary work environment of a child is school. We will spend our careers trying to replace laziness with hard work and sloppiness with conscientiousness. If unmotivated students do not learn good work habits in our classrooms, they will probably go through life as we found them.

In education we talk endlessly about building excellence and raising standards. Our ability to talk about excellence would seem to be inversely proportional to our ability to produce it.

Improvement in education ultimately comes down to the classroom. If excellence is ever to be produced, it must be produced

Preview

- Incentive systems require continuous work check to ensure that students work carefully rather than just quickly.

- Quality control requires designing the work process so that excellence is the natural outcome.

- Say, See, Do Teaching and the creation of independent learning provide the new "production process" upon which the pursuit of excellence can be built.

- Quality control requires that the product be built right the first time. This occurs during a lesson in the form of thorough Structured Practice and continuous work check during Guided Practice.

- When work becomes too complex to scan and check rapidly, it is time for the teacher to get help. Training students to check their own work conscientiously solves the problem.

by us during the lessons that we teach. If we are to be builders of excellence rather than just talkers of excellence, we must understand how excellence is produced.

Excellence will be produced in our classrooms in exactly the same way that it is produced at Rolls Royce or Hewlett-Packard or Intel. The building of excellence is called *quality control*. It would be worth our while to spend some time learning about the technology of quality control.

Excellent Work from Ordinary People

The Typical Work Force

It is a rare student who wakes up in the morning and says wistfully, *Maybe today they will finally teach me how a bill becomes a law.* In fact, many students, even the good ones, haven't a clue as to the ultimate use of many of the lessons we teach.

Some will go along with us and try their best. Others, however, will take a more utilitarian approach to learning. They will habitually ask the motivational question, *Why should I?* Until they get a satisfactory answer, they will act unmotivated.

The random assortment of personalities that walks into the classroom every day is known outside of educational circles as "the typical work force." Some are "gung ho," and some are habitual heel draggers, but we must get good work from all of them.

Where Does Excellence Come From?

Part of the reason that some students do their best resides in our *lesson.* Obviously, relevant lessons are better

than irrelevant ones, and interesting lessons are better than boring ones.

But if you think that the primary source of motivation is in the ability of your lesson to grab the students' souls, keep in mind that the typical work force produces widgets day after day without having a deep love of widgets. In some places they produce excellent widgets, and in other places they produce defective widgets.

Part of the reason that some students might do their best resides in the *student.* Some students learn at an early age that, "If something is worth doing, it is worth doing *right.*"

But if you think that the primary source of motivation is the work ethic of your students, keep in mind that the craftsman driven to perfection is the exception rather than the rule. In the classroom, as in the automobile factory, you will have to produce excellence with the typical work force, or you will not produce excellence.

Organizing the Work Force

Both the captains of industry and classroom teachers will have to work with the same raw material, the human race. The question that will confront all of us is, "How do you organize a typical work force to produce excellent work?"

It is natural for us to want higher standards from our students than the students want for themselves. The goal of quality control is to train students to come up to our standards rather than for us to lower our standards to match their work ethic.

The Goal of Quality Control

The goal of quality control is to train students to come up to our standards rather than for us to lower our standards to match their work ethic.

The Locus of Quality Control

Quality control can take place at any work site in either of two places during the production process:

- *In-production quality control* – during production
- *Post-production quality control* – at the end of production

In-Production Quality Control

Imagine that a worker at an automobile factory, call him Joe, has the job of connecting some electric wires that go from the radio to the rear speakers. To do so, Joe must connect three wires: the *blue* wire on *top*, the *yellow* wire in the *middle*, and the *red* wire on the *bottom*.

However, Joe is new on the job. Instead of doing the job correctly, he puts the red wire on the top and the blue wire on the bottom.

On the production line, a quality control supervisor, call her Carol, walks from station to station checking the work. As she carefully watches the new worker, she notices the error in wiring.

What would follow, ideally, would be a short, painless, and efficient teaching interaction that would correct the error. Carol might say,

"On these speaker wires, the blue one goes on top and the red goes on the bottom. I'll sketch a quick diagram on this 3-by-5 card so you can double check."

In this example, corrective feedback has taken the form

Types of Quality Control

In-Production Quality Control

- *Quick (Praise, Prompt, and Leave)*
- *Continuous*
- *Preventative*
- *Cheap*

Post-Production Quality Control

- *Slow (Tear down and rebuild)*
- *Delayed*
- *Remedial*
- *Expensive*

---

of Praise, Prompt, and Leave with a VIP for quick reference. Teaching has been quick and efficient with little reason for defensiveness. And, the job will probably be done right for the rest of the day.

Just as importantly, Carol has done very little work. She has insured that the person responsible for the wiring does the work and does it *right*. She is free to continue walking the production line to check the work of other employees.

Post-Production Quality Control

Imagine that the error in wiring was *not* fixed during production. At the *end* of the production line, the *post-production quality control* staff takes over.

In the automobile factory these specialists are the quick diagnosis and quick-fix artists. They have a long checklist, and they go through the car piece by piece to make sure that it works.

Imagine that the inspector, Raymond, is going through his checklist. He tests the ignition, the headlights, and the radio in rapid succession. He turns the fader knob to the rear speakers, and everything goes dead.

"This is the third one of these we've had this morning!" he explodes. He turns off the ignition and begins his diagnostic procedure. Finding the problem, he reverses the wires that were installed backwards and hops back into the car to recheck the rear speakers.

The Cost of Quality Control

As you can see, the post-production quality control specialist has a far more complex and time consuming job than the in-production supervisor. Rather than investing only a few seconds in corrective feedback, the post-production specialist must *diagnose the problem, take the unit apart, and rebuild it.*

Consequently, post-production quality control is labor-intensive, time-consuming, and exasperating. It also has no effect on the production process. Rather than preventing problems, it only remediates them. New errors are being made as the old ones are being fixed.

This comparison of cost and benefit between in-production and post-production quality control leads to one of the cardinal rules of quality control:

It is always cheaper to build it right the first time.

As the saying goes:

If you don't have time to build it right the first time, when will you have time to fix it?

You may wish to consider these truths the next time you take a stack of papers home for grading.

Zero-Defects Production

Zero-defects production is a term from quality management in industry. It refers to designing the entire production process from the ground

up so that *excellence is the primary product.* Assessment is built into *each step* of the production process. Workers are trained not only to do the job, but also to check the job and certify it before passing it along. In-production quality control supervisors simply *augment* the check routines of the workers in a joint effort to build it right the first time.

Errors are, therefore, detected and corrected immediately. An often cited example is the fact that any worker

Post-production quality control is labor-intensive and exasperating.

on the Toyota production line can pull an overhead cable and stop the entire production process any time he or she sees something done incorrectly. Workers are part of a *culture of excellence.*

In contrast, naive attempts by top management to improve quality usually focus upon upgrading supervision of the *existing production process*. But, the workers are not trained and integrated into the quality control effort. As a result, there is still a large reliance upon post-production quality control, and the quest for excellence "hits the wall" long before the error rate reaches the target that defines excellence.

Zero-Defects Production in the Classroom

Quality Control During the Lesson
You might think of this book up to now as a text on zero-defects production in the classroom. To see how all of the pieces of the quality control puzzle fit together, let's return to our hypothetical math assignment.

- **Say, See, Do Teaching:** We have walked the students through the computation one step at a time, checking their work after every step.

- **Structured Practice:** We have walked the students through three or four additional examples of the computation. While the pace slowly quickens, we are still able to check their work after every step. We are creating *perfect practice*, and the students are approaching *automaticity*.

It is always cheaper to build it right the first time.

- **Visual Instructional Plan:** A VIP for the lesson is clearly visible. During Guided Practice, the students will be able to review prior instruction at any time by simply glancing at the VIP.

- **Guided Practice:** During Guided Practice, the pace of production quickens as students start working "on their own." We work the crowd in order to supervise "production," but very few students need help, and weaners have a very weak case for seeking it.

- **Praise, Prompt, and Leave:** If a student does need help, we can use Praise, Prompt, and Leave in conjunction with our VIP and be gone in seconds. If a helpless handraiser tries to play helpless, we can operate an extinction program.

- **In-Production Quality Control:** During Guided Practice we should be relatively *unemployed*. Being freed from the burden of reteaching during Guided Practice, we can now do in-production quality control by checking the students' work as it is being done.

Consequently, relatively little work check should remain to be done after the students go home. Of course, the final drafts of essays must be read, and words of praise written in the margins. And, some paper grading may be left over due to the interruptions and distractions typical of life in the classroom.

Nevertheless, insofar as work check can be done during Guided Practice, to that extent our time will be freed up later in the day. If we plan to work after

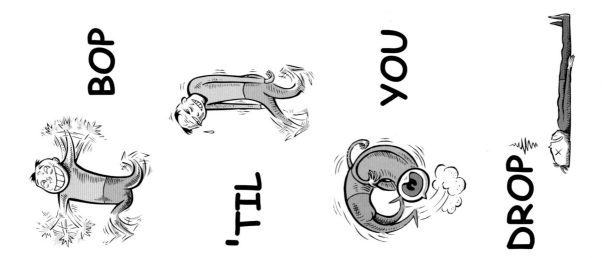

school or in the evening, better that we invest our work where it will pay a dividend – in planning tomorrow's instruction rather than in doing yesterday's clerical work.

The Paper Grading Trap

American education has a folklore concerning the production of excellence that, unfortunately, has little to do with either motivation or excellence. Teachers take papers home to grade in the hope that this added effort will somehow translate into better learning. Students throw most of these papers into the wastebasket.

The students are trying to teach us a lesson about quality control. When we accept a student's work, we clearly signal that the production process is over. In the students' minds, they are *done* with the assignment. Rekindling their enthusiasm for the task tomorrow will be like raising Lazarus from the dead.

In addition, by accepting faulty work, the teacher has taught the students that mediocre work is acceptable. After all, you accepted it. This common error in quality control is expressed in the following rule:

The standard of excellence on any job site is defined by the sloppiest piece of work that you will accept.

Going over Work in Class

Many teachers, in an attempt to keep last night's paper-grading from going to waste, go over the same assignment again the following day in class item by item. This is both *very* boring and *very* inefficient – a process guaranteed to render most of the class comatose.

"Would anyone like me to go over problem number *one* from yesterday?"

Imagine that half-a-dozen students really cared. This means that twenty four students out of thirty don't care –

a maximum of 5 for the class or one-fifth. A rowdy classroom will be the teacher's reward.

The Cost of Accountability

In-Production *versus* Post-Production

If you want to make accountability in the classroom *cheap*, build it right the first time and do a good job of in-production quality control *during Guided Practice*. If you want to make accountability *expensive*, do it *after the lesson is finished*. You will be grading papers instead of spending time with your family.

From the practical perspective of teacher overwork, we are simply taking the time and effort you would normally spend grading papers in the evening and inserting it during Guided Practice. In that way, we reduce your work load by freeing up your evening!

Say, See, Do versus Bop 'til You Drop

Contrast the quality control procedures that are built into Say, See, Do Teaching with those of Bop 'til You Drop Teaching. With Bop 'til You Drop, you work hard in presenting the lesson, and then you work even harder during Guided Practice as you tutor the helpless handraisers. You are too busy during the lesson to implement any system of quality control.

The chronic overwork that accompanies Bop 'til You Drop Teaching in contrast to the generous amount of time available for work check during Say, See, Do Teaching creates the following irony of quality control:

The harder you work, the less excellence you can produce.

The less you work, the more excellence you can produce.

The Natural Teachers in Action

The classrooms of natural teachers look very different from those of their colleagues. Effective teachers do not work as hard. They put the *students* to work. During Structured Practice the students learn by doing, and during Guided Practice the students continue working as the teacher supervises.

In order to dramatize the difference between Say, See, Do Teaching and Bop 'til You Drop Teaching, I have trainees recite the following saying together. It may sound tongue-in-cheek when you first read it, but it is an accurate depiction of your proper role during Structured Practice and Guided Practice.

It is not your job to work yourself to death while the students watch.

It is your job to work the students to death while you watch.

If you don't have time to build it right the first time, when will you have time to fix it?

Work Check

Cruising and Checking

Typically, quality control during Guided Practice amounts to "cruising and checking" on the part of the teacher. As students reach the criterion of mastery, they are excused from the assignment.

Trainees typically report an entirely different feel during Guided Practice. Being freed from the helpless handraisers, teachers can now spend more time with students who want to learn. In addition to checking work, they have time to discuss the lesson and brainstorm ideas with students. It is a much more enjoyable and satisfying experience for the teacher.

Scanning Complex Work

Teachers' ability to check work as they move among the students is largely a function of the *complexity* of the work. If teachers can quickly scan and check the work, they can keep cruising. But, if the work becomes sufficiently complex, teachers may no longer be able to rapidly scan and check.

If work check falls too far behind production, the teacher cannot utilize a criterion of mastery. Consequently, incentives for diligence and excellence remain out of reach.

When you feel defeated by either the volume or complexity of the work check, it is time to *switch strategies*. If you cannot keep up, it is time to *get help*.

Getting Help

Where is the handiest source of free labor in a classroom? The *students*, of course! Work check that might take one person thirty minutes will take thirty people one minute. Teachers have always exploited this logic by having the students exchange papers for grading.

But, you must train the students to check work *carefully* and *honestly*. How do you organize the class so that the students are efficient and honest checkers? After all, we wouldn't want students helping out their buddies, would we?

Building Work Groups

Dealing with the practical problems of work check will eventually drive us toward organizing the class into *work groups*. This is the same logic that drives quality control managers in industry to build quality control circles. We may not be able to check all of the work ourselves, but we *can* supervise the functioning of a handful of work groups that check the work.

First we will need to divide the class into groups. Then, we will need to train the groups to check work properly. With a little ingenuity, we might even be able to make the whole thing fun.

Often the groups are already organized in the form of cooperative learning groups, lab partners, or squads as in physical education. Consequently, having the students help with work check may simply represent an extension of group responsibilities.

Classroom Examples

Foreign Language Class

A high school foreign language teacher complained to me of her "lost weekends." She described filling her car with students' language notebooks three times a semester,

and getting nothing done all weekend except grading six weeks worth of language assignments.

In order to reduce her workload while making work check more relevant, we reorganized the class to facilitate student work check. She divided the room into groups of four with a student in each group who could serve as a leader. She then had the leaders drill their group members for the upcoming test. Test scores jumped.

She then developed a *competition* between the groups. Review prior to the test became far more task-oriented and intense. Again, test scores jumped.

Next, she developed a VIP for each type of language exercise contained in the notebooks. She drew the VIPs on butcher paper and posted them so that the students had a good visual guide as they checked work.

The last step in problem solving was to devise a means of training the students to check work conscientiously and honestly. We had the groups *exchange papers* for grading. She said, "The students would never cheat for another group because the grading is tied into our contest." Then, she had students double check their own work when they got it back. Students got *double points* if they could *find an error in the work check.*

It worked like a charm. The teacher said, "Last week we checked the notebooks in twelve minutes flat! No more 'lost weekends'!"

The standard of excellence on any job site is defined by the sloppiest piece of work that you will accept.

Mathematics Class

Having teams check each other's work as part of a contest with double points for catching the other person's checking errors gave us a simple structure for keeping students honest that could be used in almost any subject. In mathematics we went so far as to have the assignment itself be a contest.

The class was divided into two teams with members of opposing teams paired up. The class was given a fixed amount of time for completing each problem. When the time was up, the teacher said:

• Exchange your papers.
• The answer is...
• Grade them and return them.
• How many got it right on team one? (students raise their hands)
• How many on team two?

In the check routine, everybody kept everybody else honest. Nobody would give his or her opponent any extra time to work. Nobody would cheat for another team. Nobody would allow themselves to be cheated. And nobody would allow an opponent to hold up his or her hand if they had not gotten it right. The students had fun, and the teacher had no papers to take home.

New Perspectives

In general, the more the teaching format resembles a series of Say, See, Do Cycles, the more work check and corrective feedback can be integrated into the learning process to be performed by the students. In contrast, the more the teacher monopolizes the learning process, the more work check and corrective feedback are separated from learning to be done by the teacher as a separate job.

In addition, the more adept you become at utilizing zero-defects production, the more you teach the students to be independent of you as they learn. Rather than doing all of the work yourself, they do both the work *and the work check* while you supervise. Eventually, you may feel more like an activities director than a traditional Bop 'til You Drop teacher.

A New Perspective on Motivation

The big step in thinking about motivation is to realize that it is something you build, not something you are given.

Section Five

Building
Classroom Structure

Chapter Eleven

Succeeding from Day One

A Quick Start

Scoping You Out

Let's imagine that it is the first day of your teaching career. You are as green as grass.

Imagine a departmentalized setting. You will start the day a half-dozen times before the final bell. You are teaching World History in Room 101 at the local high school.

Classroom management gets off to a quick start. If first period begins at eight o'clock in the morning, the students will know how good you are at classroom management by eight o'clock. They are very astute.

However, the students will give you a 48-hour honeymoon. They gamble conservatively until they have had time to "scope you out." After the honeymoon, you will find out what the real rules in the classroom are.

Reality Is the Law

You may, of course, have rules of your own. Teachers love to tell students about their rules.

In a few classrooms the teacher's desires actually become implemented, but in most classrooms they are not. Students know that words are cheap and actions are expensive. The real rules in any classroom are defined by *reality* — by what the teacher actually permits. So, the students watch.

Preview

- Students are astute at assessing the absence of effective structure. They can tell whether their teachers are proactive or reactive, whether they are "old pros" or rookies.

- The rules in any classroom are defined by reality - "whatever any student can get away with."

- Much of the management in a typical classroom is by default. Students fool around because the teacher has not structured anything better for them to do.

- Structure begins as the students enter the classroom.

- Well-developed routines including Bell Work, signal from the beginning that the classroom is both a work environment and a friendly, personal environment.

Section Five: Building Classroom Structure

If, for example, you ask the class to pay attention while you are speaking, but you fail to deal effectively with side conversations, students know that paying attention is optional. If you ask the class to take turns as they speak, but you occasionally attend to someone who interrupts because they have a good idea, students know that they are free to cut each other off during the discussions.

Classroom rules are ultimately defined by whatever any student can get away with. So, the students just watch. Everything you do is a lesson. You will have taught a half-dozen lessons by the time first period begins.

First Lessons

Entering the Class

Imagine that you have *thirteen* minutes before the bell rings for first period. The first student enters your classroom. You have just taught the *first* lesson of the school year: *You may enter my class however you wish.*

How does the student know this? Because, he or she just did it! Remember, your rules are defined by reality.

There was no greeting, no communication of expectations, nothing specific to do. Since you have abdicated structuring this situation, structure is left to the student.

Do not be surprised if, after the honeymoon is over, the students come rolling into your classroom joking, laughing, and pushing each other. You asked for it.

Much of the management in a typical classroom is by default. Students fool around because the teacher has not structured anything better for them to do.

A Second Student Enters

You have *twelve* minutes before the bell rings. A second student enters the classroom. You now have two students in your classroom. What do you think they will do?

"Hey, Jackson, where have you been?"

"Hangin' out. I heard you were out of town."

"Naw. Just for a week. Say, I hear you're goin' out with Sharon again..."

Big surprise! They are socializing. You have just taught the *second* lesson of the school year: *After you enter my classroom, you may socialize.*

The kids have important events to catch-up on. Do *you* have anything important for them to do?

Now it is *ten* minutes before the bell rings. Eight kids are in the classroom standing around, talking, and laughing.

Now it is *five* minutes before the bell rings. Twenty kids are in the classroom standing around, talking, and laughing.

It is *one* minute before the bell rings. *Everybody* is standing around, talking, and laughing. Now that you have allowed this gab-fest to start, how will you stop it?

The Bell Rings

The eight o'clock bell rings. You just taught the *third* lesson of the school year: *Do not even think about being in your seat when the bell rings.*

Why should they worry about it? You don't. There is no routine to get the students seated and ready to work *before* the bell rings, is there? Do not expect the students to take classroom structure more seriously than *you* do.

Students fool around because the teacher has not structured anything better for them to do.

Getting Them into Their Seats

Since the students are not in their seats when the bell rings, how will you get them there?

"Class, the bell has rung. Let's all take our seats. We have a lot to cover today, so let's get started. Everybody, let's take our seats!"

The students have just observed your first *overt act of* classroom management. But, what classroom management "technique" did they see? It was the most widespread management technique in the world: *Nag, nag, nag.* You have just taught the *fourth* lesson of the school year: *In order to get you to do things, I nag.*

While nagging may be the most widespread management technique in the world, it is also one of the least effective. Your students learned to tune it out before they went to kindergarten.

A Lesson about Killing Time

The students will now give you a lesson about killing time. For the record, students like *brief lessons with great big breaks in between.*

Consequently, no matter how much time you give the students for a lesson transition, it will never be long enough. If you give the students three minutes, they will need five. If you give them five minutes, they will need seven. Students know how to stretch a break by *dawdling.*

So, when you tell the class to take their seats, three students interpret this to mean, "Now is a good time to sharpen pencils." Where does this leave you?

"Those of you over at the pencil sharpener, please take your seats. You had plenty of time to sharpen your pencils before school. Everyone, just find a seat so we can get started."

You have just taught the *fifth* lesson of the school year: *If nagging does not work, I will nag some more.*

Giving Away the Furniture

"Everyone, just find a seat." Are you kidding? You just *gave away the furniture!* The *sixth* lesson of the school year is: *You may sit wherever you want.*

Do you remember Larry – the student who will cause you to age significantly this year? Imagine that Larry is in your class – every class has at least one.

If you say, "Everyone, just find a seat," where do you think Larry will end up sitting? He will end up sitting in the *back of the class,* of course, along with his buddies. That is where all of the goof-offs will sit if you give them the chance.

This is not looking good. The students are rubbing their hands together thinking, "All right! In first period we get to *kick back.*"

The students are rating you on your skills of classroom management, and, so far, they have not seen much *style.* They are rating you along the most basic dimension of leadership ability – *proactive* versus *reactive.*

Proactive versus Reactive

Getting Organized

Proactive means "active ahead of time." Proactive people are the natural teachers, the natural parents, the born leaders. They know how to get organized, and they get organized well *in advance.*

Being Proactive

Proactive people know how to get organized, and they get organized well in advance.

For example, let's imagine that you have a four-year-old and a seven-year-old, and you are planning to visit grandmother next week. She lives three hours away.

What will you do to get ready for this trip? I remember my wife, Jo Lynne, doing it. She had an entire routine.

A week before the trip she bought some coloring books and new crayons. At the grocery store that week she stocked up on apples and oranges and the makings of a picnic.

On the morning of the trip, the coloring book and crayons along with pencils and tablets went into one paper bag while pieces of apple and orange with some crackers went into another paper bag. In addition she collected some story books and games plus the Etch-a-Sketch for good measure.

The kids were occupied with their new crayons and coloring books as we backed the car out of the driveway. The snacks were given out as we rode along accompanied by praise for "behaving so nicely." In addition to the snacks, we stopped for a picnic halfway to grandmother's at our favorite roadside park that had a swing set.

Jo Lynne was in charge, and she was actively planning and organizing the trip to grandmother's a week in advance. She

knew what the trip to grandmother's would be like without some *organization.*

But some people don't think this way. They just put the kids in the back seat and take off down the road.

Before they have gone a half-mile, the big kid takes something from the little kid, the little kid lets out a shriek and grabs it back, the big kid shoves the little kid, the little kid hits the big kid (a bad idea) and the big kid whacks the little kid who starts crying.

Reactive management always sounds the same: Nag, nag, nag.

One of the parents turns around and snaps:

"I want you to stop this fighting *right now!* You sit on *your* side, and you sit on *your* side, and I want both of you to keep your *hands to yourselves!* I do not want to listen to that fussing all the way to grandmother's!"

The parents might not want to listen to "that fussing," but they will. Having no plan to prevent it, they must now live with it.

The Sound of Reactive Management

There is a pattern of speech that is endemic to reactive management. That pattern of speech is: *Nag, nag, nag.*

When you nag, you label the procedure that you have failed to train the other person to perform. For example:

"I am *sick and tired* of coming into your room and seeing your clothes *all over the floor!* Let me tell you something! I was not put on this earth to spend my life *picking up after you.*"

Have you ever heard this speech? What procedure has this parent failed to train the child to perform? How about: *Pick up after yourself. It either goes in the closet or in the hamper.*

Focus on Procedure

What sets *proactive* people apart is not their goals and objectives, but, rather, their *procedures.* Proactive people know how to organize an activity in order to get things done. Reactive people either *do not know* how to organize an activity or *are too lazy* to go to the trouble. Consequently, they must *react* to the disaster that has been created by a lack of structure.

Classroom Structure

Getting a room full of young people to do things quickly and smoothly will place the structuring of behavior on

a plane far above your normal, everyday experience. In detail and precision, it will exceed what you remember from your parents. Your parents, after all, were not trying to manage thirty children. And they were not trying to manage one complex activity after another all day long.

Getting accustomed to the level of structure required in the classroom is a big step for a new teacher. Chances are you have never acted or sounded like this before. You have never given yourself permission to be this "controlling."

Let's give our green teacher another crack at starting the school year. In so doing, let's take a close look at proactive management by examining a few of the routines that might be most helpful.

Starting Over Again

The Day Before

When the students show up, it is too late to be proactive. The day before school begins, stand at the front of your classroom, and just look around. How big is this room? Space can be your friend by giving you elbow room, or it can be your enemy by running your legs off. The first factor in a classroom that we must take full responsibility for managing is *space.*

Room Arrangement

Where will you place the furniture? Can you get around easily? The first crucial element of classroom structure is room arrangement. This topic has been dealt with thoroughly in chapter 3, "Working the Crowd" and chapter 4 "Arranging the Room." By way of review, the biggest single variable that governs the likelihood of students goofing off in your class is their physical distance from you. Proximity is the name of the game.

Teachers who make classroom discipline look easy *move.* They produce proximity through mobility. They *work the* crowd because they know that *either you work the crowd, or the crowd works you.*

The biggest obstacle to mobility is the *furniture.* You need *walkways* – nice, broad walkways so that you can move among the students easily. Room arrangement is the art of producing walkways within the normally crowded conditions of the classroom. The optimal room arrangement allows you to get from any student to any other student in the fewest steps.

One of your first jobs in structuring the classroom is to take responsibility for where the furniture goes. This may require a conference with the principal and the custodian to gain their understanding and cooperation.

Desk Creep

What do you think will happen to your lovely room arrangement when thirty students occupy those desks? Students are full of energy, and they move. They twist and turn and squirm and scoot, and their desks will move with them.

The next obstacle that we must overcome in working the crowd is *desk creep.* A desk can block a walkway by creeping less than a foot.

To contain desk creep, you will need *visual markers* to show the students where the furniture goes. Furniture must be "straightened up" during each lesson transition, or the walkways will disappear. With clear visual markers, you can say during a lesson transition:

"...and after you have handed in your papers and sharpened your pencils, put your desks back on their marks before you take your seats."

One of the cheapest visual markers is a "tape dot." A tape dot is simply a small piece of masking tape that you tear off the end of the roll and stick on the floor. It is no

bigger than the end of your finger. Two dots where the front legs of a desk touch the floor locates the desk.

On the day before the students show up, you may be placing tape dots all over the floor after you have arranged the furniture. But rest assured that this is the *last* time *you* will ever do it. When tape dots have to be replaced due to normal wear and tear, you will have the *students* do it. It will be one of their weekly classroom chores.

Sometimes administrators and custodians get apoplectic when they see tape dots suddenly appear on their newly polished or carpeted floors. This is another reason for having a preliminary conference with the interested parties. If you do not do a little team building proactively, you will get the hassles that go with reactive management.

Incidentally, there are alternatives to tape dots. By fifth grade, if the teacher is using horizontal rows (see chapter 4), students can line up their desks with marks on the wall. I have also seen teachers use different colored dots for different room arrangements within the same classroom. The stationery store carries packages of different colored dots for pricing items at yard sales. Whatever the specific method, you will need *visual prompts* for locating the furniture.

Greet Them and Put Them to Work

Where do you stand at the beginning of the class period? Let me make a strong suggestion that you stand *in the doorway.*

In the hall, students laugh and joke and flirt as they pass from class to class. This is normal behavior for the hallway. The classroom, in contrast, is a work environment.

Students would love to bring their social environment from the hall into the classroom. They would love to spend the first part of the class period finishing their con-

101

Define the entrance to your classroom as a doorway between two different worlds.

versations. And, they will, unless you clearly structure a change in behavior.

Do everything you can to define the entrance into your classroom as a doorway between *two different worlds.* Clearly separate the social world from the world of schoolwork.

You can only define a work environment through *work.* Stand in the doorway, greet the students warmly, and, above all else, *give them a job.*

But what job will you give them? This brings us to the topic of *Bell Work.*

Bell Work

Bell Work, as the name implies, is the schoolwork that students are doing *when the bell rings.* It is always the first task of the class period.

When you describe Bell Work to your students on the first day of school, instruct them never to ask you whether there is Bell Work today. There is Bell Work *every* day. It will always be posted on the board in the same place. Tell the students,

"As soon as you reach your seat, look at the board for today's Bell Work, and get started."

Bell Work, as you might imagine, is a bit of a misnomer because many students enter the class minutes before the bell rings. Say to the students,

"If you want to talk and socialize, stay out in the hall. That is what halls are for. When you are ready to work, come in."

Bell Work consumes the first five minutes of the class period. Consequently, students who arrive early might have eight or ten minutes of Bell Work. Structuring work at the beginning of the class period eliminates the problem of "settling in."

Bell Work and "Settling In"

A typical class period is not on task until five to eight minutes *after* the bell rings. Teachers take roll, and students talk, sharpen pencils, and listen to announcements over the P.A. as they amble toward their seats. This daily ritual is called "settling in."

Settling in is so ingrained in the daily life of the classroom that few teachers regard it as a problem. It is just the normal way of starting a class period. I regard it as a problem – a *big* problem.

If, for example, a class period lasts fifty minutes, and you take five minutes for settling in each day, you consume *one-tenth of your total instructional time with this class period for the entire year.* That is a high price to pay for the privilege of settling in.

But, what if you try to start on time *without a plan?* When are you going to take roll? At the elementary level you don't just take roll – you collect lunch money, milk money, book club money, and money for the field trip on Friday. The district should issue you a cash register. In addition, there are the announcements over the P.A. that interrupt you just as you are getting started. And then a student comes in late with a note from the nurse.

The school district is not organized to start when the bell rings. That's why nobody does it. Try starting on time, and see how far you get. How many days in a row can you juggle all of the distractions listed above before you say, "Oh, forget it! Let's just settle in."

The fact of the matter is that you *do* need to take roll and collect lunch money, milk money, and so on. The question is, how can we do this without wasting the first five minutes of instruction? What you need is a meaningful learning experience that *does not require your active teaching.* You need Bell Work.

What Do You Do for Bell Work?

First, keep it simple. *Second,* make sure that it serves a purpose in getting the day's instruction started. Use it as a warm-up activity. It probably incorporates the review that you would have done anyway *after* settling in.

If you are a science teacher, how about four questions from yesterday? If you are a math teacher, how about four problems from yesterday? Make them doable. This is not the midterm exam. If the students were here yesterday and were not comatose, they can start answering those questions or doing those problems.

But review is just one of many possibilities for Bell Work. Some teachers use journal writing or silent reading. Others put word games or mind benders on the board. I remember one teacher who had a student read to the class from a library book while he took roll. The sky is the limit as long as it makes sense in terms of your classroom.

Do *not* saddle yourself with an extra stack of papers to grade. Some teachers flip through Bell Work quickly and put an "X" in a column of the grade book for those students who gave it a decent try. Other teachers farm this job out to students who are on the "clerical work committee" this week. Some teachers collect the papers with due seriousness, glance over them, and then drop them into the circular file after school. After all, the purpose is to start kids thinking, not to assess performance.

> ## Bell Work
>
> Bell Work begins as soon as a student enters your class and continues until five minutes after the bell rings. It provides a useful learning activity while you look after the organizational chores.

Until the students know that you care, they don't care what you know.

Bell Work on Day One

What will you do for Bell Work on the first day of school? You will need something.

You may already have a routine that works for you. I have seen, for example, social studies teachers get off to a quick start with a political opinion survey or questionnaire. I know primary teachers who have the children draw pictures of their families, sort blocks by color, shape, and size, or assemble a puzzle.

You might also consider handing out 3-by-5 cards as you greet the students at the door. On the blank side of the card is a seat number. All of the desks have numbers taped to them. Greet the student and say:

"This is your seat number. Find your seat, then turn the card over and fill it out according to the instructions on the board."

On the board is a picture showing students how to fill out the card – name, birthday, home address, home phone, parents work phone, and so on. It may sound basic, but at least you put the kids to work. And they get a message that can only be conveyed behaviorally: *When you enter the room, expect to get right to work.*

Introduce Yourself

On the first day of school, the *first* question in the students' minds is, "Who are *you?*" You will introduce yourself, of course, but you might also talk about yourself a little bit.

Deal with obvious questions like, "Why are you here?" Sometimes students show surprise when you confide to them that you get great pleasure from seeing young people learn. Eyes may widen when you tell them that school should be fun. Don't beat it to death. But, a few words from the heart are in order.

Icebreakers

On the first day of school, the *second* question in the students' minds is, "Who are *they?*" If you think that the students all know each other, think again.

I used to have teachers hand out a blank seating chart in mid-November and ask the students to fill in the first and last names of everyone in the class. Rarely did the number of correct papers exceed 25 percent. Teachers were typically shocked, but most had to admit that they had invested little time in making it otherwise.

Students do better in class both academically and socially when they are comfortable, relaxed, and "at home." They do not do so well in an impersonal environment.

The question facing the teacher is, *Do you care? Is it worth your time in order to make the students feel at home?* I would strongly suggest that you devote the lion's share of the first class period of the year to creating comfort. Spend at least a half-hour doing an "icebreaking" activity.

Many teachers feel that it is all-important to "set the tone" of the class by getting right into a meaty assignment during the first class period. While well intentioned, this objective is not aligned with the students' needs.

Think of yourself suddenly thrown together with a group of your peers, some you know and some you don't, plus a few good friends that you haven't seen in months. Some social "settling in" is needed.

If you invest time and energy in producing comfort, you signal to the students that you care about them as people. If you do not invest, you signal that they are nothing but warm bodies occupying a chair in your class. Do not expect a lot of warmth and consideration coming back to you from students who are treated in this fashion.

Since the objective of breaking the ice is social, have some fun with it. Anything that gets the students to interact with each other and laugh is golden.

Sample Icebreakers

Here are some sample icebreakers that you can use on the first day of school. Customize them to fit your needs. Your colleagues can give you even more.

Games

- **Scavenger Hunt:** Hand out a sheet of paper with ten questions about things the students are likely to have in common (the last movie you saw, your favorite sport, your favorite flavor of ice cream, how you got to school, etc.). To the right of the questions are four columns. Students write the answer to each question in column one. They must then find three students who have the same answer for each question. These students sign the sheet in one of the three remaining columns. Give the students a time limit and watch them go. Be a participant yourself. Any activity of this kind will work better when you are part of it.

- **Name Game:** In the name game, students form a circle with their desks and hang a 3-by-5 card on the front of the desk with their first name printed on it. Pass out magic markers so the names can be written in big, bold letters that can be read from across the room.

The first person begins the game by giving his or her first name plus a rhyme, an adjective, or a nickname

that describes him or her. This part is always good for laughs.

The second person does the same, and then repeats what the first student said. The third person does the same, and then repeats what the second and first students said. By the time the game has gone around the room, the person who is "it" has a lot of names and nicknames to remember, but the name cards on the front of the desks serve as reminders. Class members are directed to quickly supply missing information if a fellow student gets stuck.

As simple as it sounds, this game usually generates a lot of kidding around while it helps students associate names with faces. Of course, the teacher goes last and learns the students' names in the process.

Class Introductions

- **Partner Introductions:** Students pair up and introduce their partners. Structure the interview by providing a list of topics. Interviewers typically get specifics about their partner's family, pets, hobbies, and special interests. Go around the room and have each student introduce his or her partner to the class.

- **Group Sharing:** Have each student share with the group the best thing they did over the summer, their biggest fear, their biggest hope for the new school year, and so on. You supply the list of topics.

Art and Graphics

- **Design a T-shirt:** Have each student design a T-shirt press-on that tells about him or herself. Each student then stands up to display and explain the design.

- **Polaroid Photos:** If you have access to a Polaroid camera, take the students' pictures on the first day of school. Have the students list five things that describe themselves on the bottom half of a sheet of notebook paper. Then, have the students read their lists to the group prior to your mounting their photos on the top half of the paper. Post the photo sheets around the room.

This activity can be extended throughout the first week of school by having each student bring a baby picture. Number the baby pictures and post them on the bulletin board. Have a contest in which points are given for matching current pictures with baby pictures.

Personal Characteristics

• **Guess Who:** Hand out a sheet with ten questions about personal characteristics of the students. Have the students answer the questions and hand them in. The teacher reads the first item on a student's list, and the entire class has to guess who the person is. Additional items on the list are read until the student is identified. The rest of the students follow in turn.

• **Place in the Family:** Have students form groups according to their place in the family (oldest, middle, youngest). The students in each group list the things they have in common and the advantages and disadvantages of their place in the family. Each group makes a list and shares it with the class.

First Impressions

Students will have a well-formed impression of each teacher by the end of the first day of the school year. They

will know if the teacher cares about them. They will know whether this class is a work environment or a place to kick back. They will know whether they have an old pro or a rookie.

The students can always tell what is important just by watching you. Things that are important are worth your time and effort. Things that are not important are simply announced to the class. Nothing will ever be important to them until it is first important to you.

Do not, however, think that this chapter only applies to the first calendar day of the school year. Tomorrow can always be the first day of school.

If you acquire these skills in the middle of the school year at a workshop or from reading this book, don't wait until the beginning of the next semester to use them. You will lose them by then. Jump in and get wet.

Tell your students what you are doing. They will know everything anyway. You might say:

"You know that I went to a workshop (read a book) last week. It was about classroom management. I learned how to use our class time a lot more effectively.

"So, let's imagine that this is the first day of school. As you saw, I met you at the door, and I had a mind bender on the board for you to begin as soon as you got to your seats. This was an example of a Bell Work activity. Next, I would like to..."

Things that are important are worth your time and effort.

Chapter Twelve

Teaching Routines

Preview

- Classroom routines train the students to carry out procedures with a minimum of wasted time.

- Each routine must be taught with the care of any other lesson. This is time-consuming at the beginning, but it pays large dividends for the remainder of the semester.

- By doing chores, students learn to take pride in helping out around the classroom. The rule of chores is, "Never do anything for students that they are thoroughly capable of doing for themselves."

- Structuring communication with parents is crucial. They will either be your allies or your adversaries, depending on the nature of your first contact with them.

- Sending work home on a regular basis with provision for feedback helps involve parents in proactive problem solving.

Rules, Rules, Rules

"You and your stupid rules! I can't do anything!"

Rules have never been terribly popular, particularly among young people. It is not too surprising that young teachers, new to the "parent role," approach making rules for their classrooms with some ambivalence.

"I remember all of the rules my teachers used to have. I thought most of them were dumb. Don't do this, and don't do that."

In fact, rules are typically stated in terms of "Don't do this, and Don't do that." I had

to chuckle recently when I read the rules posted at the entrance to a state park:

- No fires
- No liquor
- No glass containers
- No littering
- No dumping
- No dogs
- No camping overnight

On the bottom of the sign someone had scratched, "No breathing."

This tradition of stating rules in terms of "Don't do this," and "Don't do that" is nowhere more evident than in our school discipline codes. A high school principal friend of mine once told me,

"Our school discipline code is a compilation of every outrageous thing that any kid has ever done on campus and should never be repeated. It takes up four pages of the student handbook. It serves as the oral tradition of our school."

I was consulting at a juvenile corrections facility in a small town in Michigan several years ago, and the administrators and I were trading stories after the workshop. They too had a student handbook that contained an endless list of the things that students should never do. One of them said,

"I got a call last year from some guy at the local airport. One of our kids was over there running around on the runway, and nobody could catch him. So, I drove over there, and the kid finally ran out of wind and gave up. By that time there were four or five Cessnas anxiously circling the place. So I asked the kid, 'What were you thinking?' The kid said, 'Hey, Mr. Donaldson, you didn't say we couldn't do it.'"

There must be a better way to approach classroom rules than making a list of do's and don'ts. These lists have never had a major effect on behavior anyway.

Types of Rules

When we speak of "rules," we are addressing a broad topic that is far more complex than "do's and don'ts." Different kinds of rules serve different functions.

In the classroom, there are two basic types of rules.

- **General Rules:** General rules spell out the teacher's overall expectations for good work and good behavior within the classroom.

- **Specific Procedures and Routines:** Specific procedures and routines spell out exactly how we will do this and exactly how we will do that.

General Rules

General rules deal with broad classes of behavior and are best stated in positive rather than negative language. Typical examples are, "Treat each other with respect." and, "Pay attention when the teacher is speaking to the class."

It is time well spent for a faculty to devise a list of general rules that all teachers can share. The discussion that accompanies this process can produce some important consensus building.

The following guidelines for general rules will be helpful during this discussion.

- There should be relatively few general rules (five to eight is most common).

- Only make rules that you are willing to enforce at any time. (Failing to enforce your rules defines them as hot air.)

- General rules should be simple and clear.

- They should be posted.

These general rules might best be understood as part behavioral guideline and part *values clarification statement.* A discussion of each general rule with the students at the

We traditionally state rules in terms of "Don't do this," and "Don't do that."

NO SPITTING,
NO CURSING,
NO CUSSING,
NO SLACKING,
NO SLEEPING,
NO EATING,
NO PINCHING,
NO BITING,
AND NO GENERAL GOOFING AROUND.

THANK YOU.

beginning of the semester gives the teacher a chance to convey his or her goals and expectations to the class.

Specific Procedures and Routines

As mentioned above, specific procedures and routines describe exactly "how to do this" and "how to do that" in the classroom. As such, they are the nuts and bolts of classroom structure.

Getting the entire class to perform a procedure properly, like handing in papers, getting into small groups, or lining up quietly takes a lot of effort. This is not an effort that a teacher would want to repeat all semester long. The only way to make procedures affordable is to make them a matter of routine. A routine is simply a well rehearsed response to a teacher's directive.

Viewed in this light, classroom routines are one of the teacher's primary labor-saving devices. Their objective is not so much orderliness as *efficiency*.

Classroom routines focus on the predictable – those tasks of management that face the teacher day after day. In a sense, classroom routines deal with the mundane. In another sense, however, the efficient execution of routines saves a huge amount of time for learning that would otherwise be wasted.

Routines must be taught. They must be practiced until the teacher's request produces the desired result with a minimum of milling around and wasting time. Each procedure and each routine, therefore, is a full-blown lesson.

Do it right, or do it all year long.

As a result the teaching of classroom routines is time-consuming. *First*, each routine must be taught thoroughly. And *second*, there are many of them to teach.

Teaching Procedures and Routines

Making the Investment

Research has repeatedly shown that the teachers with the best run classrooms spend most of the first two weeks of the semester teaching their procedures and routines. Teachers who do not make this investment deal with the same behavior problems over and over all semester long. It is a case of: *Pay me now, or pay me later. Do it right, or do it all year long.*

As logical as this might sound, few teachers actually make the investment. In fact, the older the students are, the less investment we make.

The teachers who make the greatest investment are, of course, the primary teachers. They spend half of their time teaching procedures and routines. The investment is still considerable in the middle grades. But by high school, the teaching of procedures has typically become rather perfunctory – often just some announcements on the first day of school.

When teachers of the older students are asked why they do not spend more time on teaching procedures, they typically respond, "They should know how to behave by now." When pressed, these teachers say such things as:

"Spend the first two weeks of the semester on rules – you have to be kidding! I don't have two weeks for that. Do you know how much material I have to cover this semester? I would never make up that time."

or

"I can see doing it with the little kids, but give me a break! How many times do these kids have to go through it?"

Consequently, the teaching of classroom procedures and routines is one of the most neglected areas of classroom management. This lack of proactive management will cost teachers dearly as the semester progresses.

While these teachers' concern with "losing valuable instructional time" is sincere, it is also naive. The students know exactly how to behave in class. They always have. The question is, *do they have to?*

You should know from your own experience that students don't act the same in every classroom. They adjust their behavior to match the standards of each teacher. If their second period teacher lets them talk and fool around while their third period teacher does not, they will act up in second period and cool it in third period.

The standards in any classroom, to put it bluntly, are defined by *whatever the students can get away with.* If teachers do not take the time to carefully teach their rules, routines, and standards, they will get whatever the students feel like giving them.

This is a classic example of *proactive* versus *reactive* management. A wise teacher knows that spending time on procedures early in the semester saves time in the long run. Prevention is always cheaper than remediation.

A Sample Procedure

Let's take a typical procedure as our laboratory for examining the teaching of a classroom routine. By the time you have taught your first routine of the year, the students will know you a lot better.

Imagine that you are a fourth grade teacher, and it is the third day of school. Today, you will take the class to the library to meet the librarian. But, before the class can get to the library, they must pass through the hall. So, today you will give the lesson on *passing through the halls quietly.*

First we set the stage by talking about how noise in the halls prevents students in other rooms from learning. You know this tune.

Next, before you go out into the hall, you must develop visual cues so you can pantomime instructions to the students. A finger to the lips or a zippering of the mouth is standard fare. You will also need "stop" and "start" signals. But one signal you *must* have is the signal to *stop, go back, and start all over.* You probably remember it. The teacher turns solemnly, holds both palms toward the students, and then, with a circular motion, points both index fingers back toward the classroom.

The standards in any classroom are defined by whatever the students can get away with.

double line rather than a single line keeps the group more compact.

Before going out into the hall, you will need to rehearse each of your signals one last time to be sure that you can direct the students with nonverbal cues. Only then are they ready, with a final zippering of the lips, to go out the door. With due seriousness, you check the lines for straightness before giving the signal to "follow me." The little band heads down the hall.

Now, let's interject a note of reality. What do you think the odds are that this collection of fourth-graders will make it all the way to the library in complete silence? If your guess is "zero," you show real promise as a teacher.

Halfway down the hall you hear a giggle from somewhere in the group. Do you care who giggled? No. Do you care how loud it was? No. Do you care whether students in nearby classrooms were actually pulled off task? No.

You turn, hold palms toward the class, make the circular motion with your hands and point back toward the classroom. Brace yourself for a pained look on those little faces. Some show disbelief for a moment before they realize that you are not kidding. Keeping a straight face is the hardest part of this routine.

The class shuffles back to where they began, and you repeat your signals; straight lines, zippered lips, follow me. Off we go again.

This time the class makes it two-thirds of the way to the library when you hear some talking at the back of the line. Do you care who talked? No. Do you care how loud it was? No.

You turn, hold palms toward the class and give your now well-known "about face" signal. This time you see real pain on the faces of students. Several students mouth the

Next, you will have to line the students up. Assign places in line for the same reason that you assign seating. Place the students who disrupt right under your nose, and place the orderly students at the back of the line. Separate best friends to reduce talking. Students should be able to name the person in front of them and behind them. A

... until we get it right.

words, "I didn't do it," with pleading hands and looks of exaggerated sincerity. Keep a straight face.

Back to the beginning. Line straight, lips zipped, follow me. Off they trundle one more time.

This time they *almost make it* to the library when you hear some whispering from behind. You know what to do by now, don't you? Turn solemnly, palms to signal stop, and then about face.

The pain registered on faces the third time around is almost too much to bear. Bite your lip. They shuffle back, some under protest.

Old pros know that this is the only way to play the game. Green teachers need to be reassured that they are doing the right thing.

While the students' faces may register displeasure at practicing until mastery is achieved, your mood is always upbeat. If you were practicing a routine inside of the classroom, like lining up, where you could speak instead of pantomime, you might give feedback in the following manner:

"Class, we did better that time. Gina, Cameron, and Samuel, you walked just as I asked. Now, class, we are going to practice it again, and I want you to focus on facing forward after you line up. We almost have it."

Through simple practice to mastery, you are signaling to the students by your investment of time and energy that this piece of behavior is important. And, you are teaching the students a thing or two about yourself. If they understand that you are the living embodiment of the two timeless characterizations of a teacher; namely: *I say what I mean, and I mean what I say,* and *We are going to keep doing this until we get it right,* the students' testing of you will be greatly shortened.

Establishing Standards

And now, a note about standards. It is easier to have *high* standards than to have *low* standards.

To understand how this works, first realize that most of the reinforcement for deviant behavior in the classroom comes from the *peer group.* A student makes a silly remark, and four kids giggle. The student who made the silly remark was just reinforced for playing the "clown" by four peers.

In the management trade, this peer reinforcement for deviant behavior is called "bootleg reinforcement." As in the bootlegging of liquor during prohibition, the goods are being delivered "around the law."

You will have a hard time putting the lid on any type of disruptive behavior as long as bootleg reinforcement is being delivered by the peer group. The peer group reinforces the goofing off as fast as you can set limits on it, and you get nowhere.

So, here is a piece of advice for the management of disruptive behavior: *Get a monopoly on reinforcement.*

How can you get a monopoly on reinforcement in order to eliminate bootleg reinforcement? First, let me list some things that don't work.

- Nagging
- Pleading
- Preaching

Now, let me list what does work.

- Practice
- Practice
- Practice

Keep doing it until you get it right. *Practice to mastery.* As you practice, practice, practice, a transformation occurs within the peer group.

Typically, "the many" are sheep in the face of the deviant behavior of "the few." After all, criticizing a peer for goofing off is *most* uncool. Consequently, *the many* tend to remain silent and mind their own business in the hope that someone else will deal with the problem.

In the classroom, that someone else is *always you*. But you will have a hard time enforcing standards without the help of *the many*.

Now, let's return to our example of teaching the class to walk quietly through the halls. After you stop and start over for the third time, *the many* start losing patience. They want to get to the library, and they are tired of trekking up and down the stupid hall. When they finally lose patience

with this repeated practice, they also lose patience with the few who are causing them to do it.

The next time down the hall when one of the class clowns begins to do something silly, he or she immediately gets "dagger looks" from fellow classmates. Sensing that it is now "uncool" instead of "cool," the goof-off thinks better of it.

Finally, the class makes it to the library. And, in the process, the students learn that "quiet means quiet," and that when you tell the class to do something, you mean it. Only in this way do the students learn to take you and your standards seriously.

This assessment of you by the students will need to be strengthened through the learning of many routines. But each new routine will be easier to establish.

The next time down the hall when Larry begins to do something silly, he immediately gets "dagger looks" from his classmates.

Words Have the Meaning You Give Them

For those teachers to whom this level of investment seems strange, it is worth emphasizing at this point that *not one word* in any language has any fixed meaning in your classroom on the first day of school. Words will only have the meaning that you give them.

Take, for example, a simple three-letter word: "now." What does "now" mean? Well, in some families "now" means "Now." In other families it means, "Just a second!" In other families it means, "Okay, in a minute!" In other families it means, "Okay, as soon as I'm done with this!" In other families it means, "Okay, as soon as this show is over!" And, in some families it means, "In your dreams!"

Each family is a subculture. The kids in your classroom come from all kinds of family subcultures. As you can see from the above example, words mean different things in different subcultures.

Kids will bring all of these different meanings into your classroom on the first day of school. As a result, a word as simple as "now" means nothing until you teach your students what *you* mean by it. The same could be said of the word "quiet" or the word "walk." None of these things have any fixed meaning until you teach the class exactly what they mean *in your presence.*

Incidentally, don't expect these meanings that you establish at such effort to magically transfer from one setting to another. The students can easily discriminate what

will be tolerated in one teacher's classroom as opposed to another. That is why students can change their behavior so readily when they change classes or have a substitute.

Simplifying Rules and Routines

One way of simplifying rules and routines is to group them into clusters. One primary teacher, for example, had a cardboard stoplight prominently displayed in the front of the classroom where she could place an arrow pointing to the red, yellow, or green lights.

The *red* light condition meant "walk quietly and work quietly." The *yellow* light condition meant that only one person could leave his or her seat at a time, and only one person could talk at a time. The *green* light condition signaled that the class could move about and talk freely.

The stoplight served as a form of shorthand for conveying an entire set of rules and expectations. As usual, the investment in training early in the semester was repaid many times over through sheer efficiency of communication.

Classroom Chores

Certain classroom routines engage the students in helping you out around the classroom. These routines are traditionally referred to as "chores."

Frazzled Parents, Lazy Children

Where do children learn that it is important to help out? It certainly does not come from being waited on hand and foot.

It is easier to have high standards than to have low standards.

Some parents do all of the work around the house. They clean, straighten up, prepare meals, do the dishes, and pick up after the kids all day long. Their only reward is to become exhausted serving a house full of lazy ingrates.

Owning a servant, be they parent or teacher, does not seem to transmit a sense of selfless giving to children. Quite to the contrary, it trains them to expect much and give little.

How often have you heard a parent say, "You know, it is just easier to do it myself." In fact, doing the job yourself rather than supervising a child's doing it *is* easier – especially when the child tries to avoid the work by whining and heel-dragging. It's easier, that is, in the *short run*.

But, what is easy in the short run becomes exhausting in the *long run*. Picking up after a child right now might seem easy, but picking up after them *forever* will not be so easy.

The Value of Being Needed

Effective parents train their children to help and to take pride in helping. Effective teachers do the same.

The adults could use the help, of course. But, more importantly, the children *need* to help.

Children who are neither asked nor expected to contribute to the well-being of the group are, by definition, not needed. They are excess baggage. Being peripheral members of the group tends to bring

Never do anything for students that they are thoroughly capable of doing for themselves.

out the worst in children. It feeds into laziness and dependency while denying them a way of demonstrating their worth.

On what occasions might children feel proud because they have pulled their own weight? To receive a meaningful answer to this question, whether at home or at school, children need jobs that contribute to the social unit. They need "chores."

The Rule of Chores

In the classroom dozens of routine jobs need to be done on a daily basis. Only then will the teacher have time to respond to students' special needs.

Effective teachers delegate. The size and complexity of the teacher's job require that they train the students to carry some of the burden.

Never do anything for students that they are thoroughly capable of doing for themselves.

Since chores are good for both the teacher and the students, I would suggest the following "rule of chores."

Organizing Classroom Chores

I have known teachers, particularly in the upper elementary grades, who had a job for each student in the class. These teachers rarely had to lift a finger to do anything but teach. They had a gift for organization.

If they were teaching a small group and suddenly felt the need for their grade book, they would say to their "grade book monitor,"

"Patrick, may I please have my grade book?"

Patrick would quickly deliver the grade book and return to his seat. What a deal!

Frankly, I doubt my own ability to keep thirty classroom chores straight. A simple way of reducing the complexity of chores would be to group them into four clusters of chores and assign a team of students to each cluster. Rotate the chores every week so that each student does every chore during a four-week rotation.

Of course, the chores will be different in World History than in wood shop. The clusters listed on this page are typical of a self-contained classroom and may serve only as food for thought.

Cleanup

- Clean up paper and litter in the classroom.
- Arrange books and materials on the shelves.
- Clean up work areas and take care of equipment.
- Clean the chalkboard and erasers.
- Clean up a portion of the yard. If all classrooms are involved, the yard can be kept in good shape.

Bulletin board and decoration

- Make bulletin boards. Why do teachers spend so much time making bulletin boards themselves when,

with a little structure, the students can have fun doing it and learn in the process?

- Decorate the classroom. Holidays, special events, and new social studies units provide sources of inspiration.
- Plan art projects for the class.

Enrichment

- Plan enrichment activities and learning games.
- Help construct learning centers.
- Provide suggestions for good TV viewing for the week.
- Present current events on a daily or weekly basis.

Clerical work

- Collect and pass out papers.
- Correct papers and record grades under the teacher's supervision (insofar as you are comfortable with this). Students often take care of recording Bell Work.
- Help with attendance and collecting lunch orders, milk money, paperback book orders, and so on.

The main investment in building routines is simply the practice required for mastery. For example, the first time the students are on the cleanup committee, you will have to teach them how you want your boards erased. And, the first time your enrichment committee presents current events, you will need to rehearse them. As always, the investment in classroom structure is greatest at the beginning, but it yields dividends for the entire semester.

If your first meeting with a parent is about a problem, you have just made an adversary for the remainder of the year.

Helping with Instruction

While most chores have to do with mundane matters, make your students responsible for as much as they can handle. They can help you teach by developing visual aids for lessons and writing lists of test questions. Student learning groups can carry out skill practice, test review, and the editing of written work.

Peer tutoring can be considered part of the group's self-management. You model Praise, Prompt, and Leave as well as Say, See, Do Teaching every day. Teach the class these key instructional skills so they can help each other more effectively. It will make them better tutors.

Communicating Your Standards to Parents

No Second Chance

You will have dealings with the parents of your students sooner or later. The helpful parents will often contact you as soon as the school year begins to volunteer as aides or chaperones. But the parents of the troublemakers tend to avoid contact with the school.

If, however, your first meeting with these parents is about a problem, you have just made an adversary for the remainder of the year. They do not want to own the problem, and they will blame it on you or any other convenient target if given the chance. These are the parents you least want to have as adversaries.

It will be to your advantage to be proactive rather than reactive in getting to know the parents of your students – particularly the parents of the problem students. You will need a plan for structuring your first contact.

A Self-Contained Classroom

I have known elementary teachers who sent out invitations to a barbeque or a picnic at their homes as soon as they received the class list in August. Most of their col-

leagues expressed admiration while declining to do the same. Yet, these teachers had a level of help and cooperation from parents that was on a different scale from that of their colleagues.

Many teachers at the elementary level send out a letter before the school year starts welcoming the parents and their children, listing books to read over the summer, and giving a brief preview of the curriculum for the coming semester. This type of communication can also take place during the first week of school, accompanied by a copy of the general rules for the class and a brief "mission statement" to set the tone.

As a follow-up to this contact, it is extremely important to be proactive in structuring your first personal conversation with the parents of each student. Do it early before problems force you into a negative first contact. Beginning in the second week of school, call the parents of each student. This is a brief conversation of roughly five minutes duration. Call five parents a night.

The structure of the conversation is as follows:

• **Introduce yourself.**
• **Briefly describe the highlights of your curriculum:** When I say brief, I mean *brief*. Just give a flavor of the coming year, as in:

"This is the year the students learn about the age of steam and the industrial revolution, so you will be hearing a lot about that. In addition, we will begin writing essays of several paragraphs in length."

• **Say something positive about the child:** This conversation deals with *good news only*. If there is already a problem with the child, save it for another day.

• **Discuss the classroom standards that you sent home:** You get the opportunity to express a commitment to high standards while answering questions about your classroom rules that you sent home. In addition, you find out which students do not take things home. In such cases, tell the parents that you will send another copy home tomorrow. This level of follow-through often convinces students that messages sent home are intended to get there.

- **Ask about any special needs of the child:** Begin by asking if there are any *medical* problems that you should know about. Asking about medical problems helps the parents relax rather than jumping to the conclusion that you are asking about academic or emotional problems. The sharing that follows will often alert you to things that are not in the student's folder. Perhaps the most significant communication, however, is that you care.

- **Emphasize that you need their help:** Stress the fact that successful students have both their parents' and their teachers' support. You might say something like this:

"As students go through school, there are typically some bumps in the road. It might be something to do with schoolwork, but it might just as easily be something that a classmate said at recess. You might hear about it before I do.

"The kids who do best at school have both their teachers and their parents behind them. If you hear about something that is worrisome, please call me. And if I hear about something that is worrisome, I would like to feel free to call you. If we work together, we can usually iron out these bumps before they become 'real problems.'

"Before I hang up, I would like to invite you to 'Back-to-School night.' I will be sending an announcement home next week. This year it is the evening of..."

As a supplement to this first phone contact, some teachers "randomly" call the parents of one student per week to give a full report. This simple program seems to give the teacher a great deal of leverage over behavior in the classroom since some calls are less random than others.

A Departmentalized Setting

A teacher in a departmentalized setting, such as a high school, may see over 150 students in a given day. Such settings obviously need a different plan for reaching out to parents.

Some schools have highly elaborate outreach programs which include a welcoming picnic or special assembly for the parents of incoming freshmen, faculty ombudsmen assigned to each student, a student body welcoming program (i.e. Link Crew), connections to community churches and service organizations that make regular announcements of students on the honor roll, awards assemblies which include parents, and so on.

The development of such a plan, however, is an issue of *school site* management that involves the *entire faculty* rather than an issue of *classroom* management that you can implement by *yourself.* For your own good, however, you may wish to augment the school site program. It would be a good investment to make a welcoming phone call during the second week of school to the parents of the five students in each class whose misbehavior will most likely produce a parent conference before long.

Ongoing Communication with Parents

Sending Work Home

Sending work home regularly with a provision for parental feedback opens a communication link that will produce increased parental involvement in problem solving. This program takes on a somewhat different form at the elementary and secondary levels.

At the elementary level, send a folder of the child's work home every Thursday. The first writing assignment of the year might be the following:

Dear Mother and Father: This is the folder work that I have done in school this week. It will show you the kinds of assignments that I have been given and the kind of work that I have done. Some of the papers have been graded and some have not been graded. Please look over my work and sign your name in the space at the bottom of the page. If you have any comments, write in the space provided.

The folder system does more than simply send work home so that parents can monitor their child's performance. *First*, it says to the parents that the school wants their involvement. *Second*, it establishes an open communication link with parents. This can serve as an early warning system to the teacher.

At the secondary level, teachers usually send work home when a project or major assignment has been completed. Whatever the occasion for sending home work, the value of regular communication with parents will be no less at the secondary level than at the elementary level.

Commendations

When students do a good job, they need to hear about it, and so do their parents. While commendations are sometimes overdone to the point of being meaningless, they can also be an important part of teacher-parent communication. A personal note is probably the most meaningful form of commendation. For a teacher who regularly sends folders of work home, these communications represent very little additional work.

Preventative Conferences

Teachers and parents will either be allies or adversaries when they meet to deal with a student's problem. A conference with a parent when the problem is *small* can be a

fairly relaxed exercise in problem solving. A conference with a parent whose child is in deep trouble is unlikely to be either relaxed or constructive.

Dealing with problems proactively when they are small can save you angry confrontations later on. Parents almost always perceive a large problem with their child as a failure on the teacher's part to deal with the problem before it became serious.

A Final Note on Being Proactive

Most of us are capable of being either proactive or reactive in our approach to problem solving. Very few people are consistently proactive.

Focusing on potential problems can be disquieting. It is easy to give in to denial and procrastination. When we do, we back ourselves into "reactive management."

Proactive management is more than a set of procedures. It is a mindset. It is the way a person thinks when success is not negotiable, and it just happens to be easier in the long run.

Section Six

Setting Limits

Chapter Thirteen

Understanding Brat Behavior

Our Number One Concern

Nearly every educational poll of parents and teachers over the past twenty five years has placed "discipline" as our number one concern. More recently our focus has shifted toward the more severe end of the discipline spectrum by targeting violence, crime, and drugs.

While sensational topics make the news, typical parents worry most about the every day events in their own children's classrooms. They tend to equate classroom discipline with "fooling around," "wasting time," and "being picked on." Parents ask themselves, "What does the teacher allow, and how does that effect my child's happiness and learning?"

Does Discipline Mean Punishment?

While most people agree that discipline management is a central issue in the life of a classroom, educators typically approach the subject with ambivalence. The terms "discipline," "disciplinarian," and "rule enforcement" have a distasteful ring. They fly in the face of our desire to make the classroom a positive and inviting place.

If you were to ask fifty people on the street what it means to "discipline a child," they would give a very predictable answer. Fill in the blank yourself. *When you discipline a child, you _____ them.*

Indeed, common sense and common usage equate the word discipline with punishment. Disciplining children means "punishing them for doing something wrong."

Parents, teachers, and administrators have traditionally equated discipline in the school setting with negative consequences, such as being kept in from recess, kept after school, sent to the principal's office, suspended, or expelled. Look in your local high school's student handbook under the heading "Discipline Code" to see what form it takes.

The School Discipline Code

The Hierarchy of Consequences
The logic of all discipline codes is timeless – *the punishment fits the crime*. The larger the crime, the larger the punishment.

As a result, consequences for misbehavior are arranged in a hierarchic fashion from small to large. At the lower end of the hierarchy are small penalties for small infractions like staying in from recess for disrupting in class. At the high end of the hierarchy are suspension and expulsion. We all know this system "by heart" because we grew up with it. It is one of the "givens" of school life – background rather than foreground.

In order to get a fresh look at the school discipline code, imagine yourself at a welcoming assembly for freshmen on your first day of high school. This will not be a real assembly, of course. It will be a *mock* freshman assembly to allow us a level of candor that is foreign to such events. Naturally, you would never speak to young people quite like this.

The Mock Freshman Assembly
"Freshmen, welcome to high school. Now that we have taken care of that, let's get down to business. Our business today is the school discipline code. The

discipline code spells out what goes and what doesn't go around here.

"First I want to say that this is one of the finest high schools in the region, and a high school is no better than its faculty. We value our faculty above everything else. Consequently, I will not tolerate the abuse of that faculty *for one moment*.

"Having said that, let me cite a statistic. There is nothing like a good statistic to rivet peoples' attention. At any school site, 90 percent of office referrals are produced by 5 percent of the student body. At the majority of school sites, 95 percent of the office referrals are produced by 5 percent of student body!

"Let me give a name to that 5 percent of the student body so that you may identify yourselves. *Troublemakers!* That's what you are, a bunch of troublemakers! Maybe I've been in education too long, but to me, once a troublemaker, always a troublemaker.

"My message for today is simply this. We are not going to put up with it!

"Of course, I know that some of you jokers are laughing up your sleeves right now thinking, 'Yeah, right. What are they going to *do* about it?' Some of you, for example, think you can use foul language or throw a punch or tell a teacher to do an unnatural act and get away with it. Well, I'm here today to tell you, *you can't*.

"On the other hand, of course, we love children. We are not going to cut you off at the knees right away. So, here's how it works.

"The first time you pull some stunt around here, we are going to give you a *verbal warning*. Our sincere hope is that you will repent right there on the spot. But, I know that most of you troublemakers are thinking, 'Big deal.'

"The next time you pull some stunt, you will be sent to *detention after school*. This is a little honor system we operate around here. We take some troublemaker who told his third period teacher to 'Go ——— your-self and ask him to report to the office at the end of the day to 'do time.' Believe it or not, we have been 'stiffed' with this system frequently over the years. The doggone kid didn't show up.

Do you know what will happen to you down at the office?

PRINCIPAL

OCCUPIED

"Listen up! Quit laughing!

"Now, if you pull another stunt around here, we will schedule a *conference with your parents!* Let me explain exactly what that means. We will spend *hours* of professional time in an attempt to collaborate with those members of the community who have already demonstrated their total *incompetence* by rearing you. I know what you're thinking, 'Oh, yeah, get my old man to come to a conference. That will be the day! And if my mom comes, all she'll say is, 'I can't do anything with him at home, either. Do you have any suggestions that might help?'

"Hey, pipe down and pay attention! This is no joke! If you pull another stunt, I'll tell you what will happen. You will be *sent to the office!* Do you know what will happen to you down at the office? Well, you don't want to find out!

If you get in trouble again, you'll be sent to the office again. And, if you get in trouble a third time, you'll be sent to the office a third time.

"You might be thinking, 'Is that it? All I get is a ticket out of class?' Oh no, it is not!

"If you pull one more stunt here at school, you will be *suspended!* Let me explain *exactly* what that means. For a period of 24 hours, you will be denied all of the following privileges:

- mathematics
- social studies
- English composition
- science
- foreign languages
- gym class

"And don't bother trying to check out books from the library to make up missed work. You have lost library privileges as well!

"Of course, we don't have people on the payroll to supervise you once you've been suspended. So, we must put you under the supervision of your parents. By way of the grapevine we have learned what goes on at home in the place of school:

- sleep late
- watch TV
- play video games
- shoot hoops
- meet your friends
- go to the mall

"After 24 hours of total deprivation, I hope we have brought you up short! But, once a troublemaker, always a troublemaker; At least, that's the way it seems to me. You just keep pushing the rules. You never know when to quit. You think you're *above the law.*

"Well, I'll tell you what will happen the next time. If you pull one more stunt around here, you will be *suspended for three days!* You will have the same loss of

privileges as before, and the same supervision at home.

"At the end of *three* days of total deprivation, I hope you return to this school site with an entirely new attitude toward education. Do I make myself clear?"

Does This Sound Nuts?

Does this sound as nuts to you as it does to me? Let me ask you another question. Am I making this up, or is this pretty much the way the system has functioned since your parents were in school?

I would like you to imagine a particular student. Let's call this student *Larry.*

Larry is the student that you prayed would be home-schooled. Larry is the kind of student who makes a teacher age three years in one. Larry is a royal – well, let's just say that Larry is a difficult child.

Let me ask some deep and probing questions concerning Larry's psyche. Does Larry *like school?* Yeah, right!

According to Larry, school _____. (Fill in the blank.) What is the one thing Larry wants more than anything else in relationship to school? How about, *O,U,T?*

Would you believe that we have a management program whereby Larry can achieve his heart's desire?

> **"I have seen the enemy, and it is us."** *Pogo*
>
> - Larry hates school.
> - Larry would love to get *out.*
> - Larry *can* get out.
> - To get out, Larry must *abuse the faculty.*
> - The management system that reinforces Larry for abusing the faculty was designed and implemented by the people he is abusing.

Larry *can* get out. But, there is one thing that Larry must do first.

Larry must first *abuse the faculty*. However, occasional abuse won't get the job done. It must be *frequent* abuse. In order to get out of school, Larry must be such a constant thorn in the side of education that he works himself all the way up the hierarchy of consequences in order to get the boot. Only then does Larry get, *O.U.T.*

I Have Seen the Enemy

Walt Kelly's cartoon character Pogo once uttered the famous words, "I have seen the enemy, and it is us." *We are* management. The management system that is designed to put the lid on when push comes to shove actually reinforces Larry for abusing *us*.

The problem is systemic. A typical high school of 1500 students has between 3500 and 5000 office referrals per year, and it has been that way for decades. Every year, we place our faith in a management system that has never turned things around in the hope that this year it will finally work. This persistence reminds me of the Chinese proverb that defines insanity as *doing the same thing over and over, and expecting a different result*.

To be technical for a moment, a behavior requires a *schedule of reinforcement* for its occurrence to be maintained over time. Without this schedule of reinforcement, you have, by definition, an *extinction program* that will cause the rate of the behavior to go down. In high school, the same 5 percent of the student body produce 95 percent of the

office referrals for *eight straight semesters!* Who, do you think, is providing the schedule of reinforcement that maintains the misbehavior?

Unfortunately, the more we learn about management, the more we realize that if it is not working, we need to look in the mirror to find the cause. It is *our* management system, and *we* are the managers.

Dysfunctional Social Systems

One of the hardest realities to accept about social systems is the following: *All social systems function exactly as they are designed.* They produce what they are built to produce.

For example, if a social system is designed to produce well-made automobiles, it will produce well-made automobiles. If, on the other hand, a social system is designed to produce poorly-made automobiles, it will produce poorly-made automobiles. Compare the automobiles made by Mercedes Benz, BMW, and Porsche-Audi with those made in the former East German Democratic Republic if you think that excellence resides anywhere other than in the immediate "corporate culture."

The entire technology of quality control focuses on the design of *social* systems that produce excellence. In the final analysis, every level of leadership within an institution manages *people*.

When a social system is not working properly, the first symptom is always *blaming*.

> All social systems function exactly as they are designed.

"If they would do their job right, I could do mine!"

At the school site the teachers say:

"I send a student down to the office, and what do they do down there? I wish I knew! The next day the same kid is right back in my class acting the same way. I need some help, and I'm not getting it. All they have down at the office is the 'revolving door policy.'"

In response, administrators say:

"What am I supposed to do? I have eight students on the bench outside of my office waiting to be seen, and it is only second period. I can talk to them, I can call their parents, but I can't give them brain transplants."

Everybody blames everybody else. But, if a management system consistently fails to live up to expectations, there is a structural reason for that result. The only cure is a redesign of the system.

No Means No

A Story about My Mom

When I was a little kid, we lived next door to a family named Smoyer. Tommy Smoyer was my playmate, and Mrs. Smoyer (his mom, whose first name was none of my business) was dearly loved by us kids.

Not only was Mrs. Smoyer a nice lady, but she was also a compulsive baker. Most afternoons our play would be interrupted by Mrs. Smoyer opening the screen door to her back porch and calling, "Kids, come in now!" This meant that we were about to have a treat – something she

had baked. Maybe it would be cookies or, better yet, brownies! Yeah!

But some days Mrs. Smoyer would open her screen door and say, "Tommy, come in now!" This meant that Mrs. Smoyer had baked a pie and would be serving it to her family rather than to the neighborhood kids.

One afternoon, as we were playing in the backyard, I began to smell gingerbread wafting from Mrs. Smoyer's kitchen. I love gingerbread! I could hardly wait for my piece. As evening approached, Mrs. Smoyer opened her screen door and said, "Tommy, come in now!"

My heart sank. I wanted gingerbread! Why couldn't I have a treat too? Life was unfair! I wanted justice.

So, I ran across the driveway into my mother's kitchen where she was preparing dinner. I opened my negotiations where all children open negotiations, at *whine level number one.*

"*Mom,* can I have something to eat? Tommy's getting gingerbread."

My mother turned from the stove and said,

"Fred, I'm going to have this meal on the table in 45 minutes. Now, I don't want to ruin your appetite."

Naturally, I escalated the negotiations to *whine level number two.*

"But *Mom,* can't I have *something?* I'm hungry!"

Dysfunctional Social Systems

When a social system is not working properly, the first symptom is always blaming.

"If they would do their job, I could do mine."

"But *Mom,* can't I have *something?* Don't we have some ginger snaps? I'm hungry!"

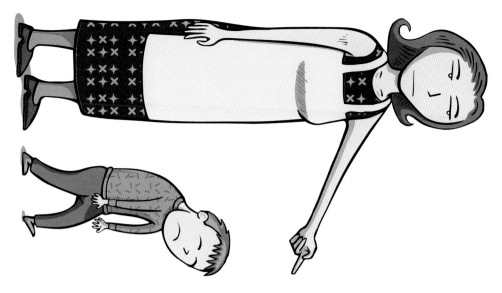

My mother said,

"Fred, I am not going to give you a snack now and then watch you sit at the dinner table and just *peck at your food*."

My mother always used bird analogies when talking about my eating. But, I knew what to do. I went to *whine level number three* without missing a beat.

"But this isn't *fair!* Tommy gets gingerbread. Can't I have something?"

My mother put down her spatula and turned slowly to face me. She looked at me intently as she wiped her hands on her apron and said,

"*Fred*, I said *no*, and *no* means *no*."

I couldn't just let go of it. After all, life had been unfair.

"But why can't I? Tommy gets..."

I was cut off in mid-sentence. My mother, with eyes squarely focused on mine, said,

"Fred, I am not going to stand here and listen to

No means no.

your *yammering*. 'Yammering' was my mother's code for, *You are really pushing it. You may either go outside to play, or you may open your mouth one more time and end up sitting on the stairs until dinner.*"

"But, why can't I..."

Those were the last words spoken. My mother stood before me with eyes fixed and finger pointing to the stairs. I felt something inside me wilt. I knew it was over. I was silently ushered to the stairs to sit.

I must have been there for 45 minutes. Mother finished preparing dinner, and Dad came home from work. My older brother, Tom, came home from playing at a friend's house and was given a quick gesture to leave when he started to ask me why I was sitting there. Mother set the table and called Dad and Tom to the table. When they were all seated, Mother turned to me and, without a trace of upset in her voice, said,

"You may join us now."

I have no idea how many times I was sent to the stairs while growing up, but I am sure that it was more than once. From these experiences, I learned two very important lessons about parent-child relations that served me well in later life:

Rule #1 – No means no.
Rule #2 – I am not going to stand here and listen to your *yammering*.

Weenie Parents

Years later I found myself on the faculty of the University of Rochester Medical Center training interns and postdocs to work with families. While we sometimes dealt with severe psychopathology, the majority of our cases in the child outpatient clinic had to do with "brat" behavior.

A typical case might have a father, age 37, a mother, age 35, and a single child, age 3. Who do you think was running the household?

"Therapy," in these cases, involved training parents in behavior management skills. As you might imagine, one of the cornerstones of discipline management was, "No means no." With practice my clients even became adept at saying, "I am not going to stand here and listen to your yammering."

But, some parents just couldn't bring themselves to set limits. To begin a session, I would ask, "How did it go this week?" Then, with whining, the excuses would start.

"Wellll… We were in a restaurant, and we had already ordered when he started to act up. We couldn't just leave at that point, could we?"

"Wellll… We were in the supermarket, and he kept pulling the cans off the shelf. The faster I put them back, the faster he pulled them off. Then they all fell down. I didn't know what to do."

"Wellll… We were at grandmother's, and I didn't want to make a scene. She is an old woman and easily gets upset."

"Wellll… It was his birthday party, and I didn't know what to do when he started running around and hitting the other children. I couldn't send him to his room in the middle of his birthday party, could I?"

These parents just could not bring themselves to say "No" and mean it. The nickname for these parents around the clinic was "weenies." You will have conferences with many "weenie parents" in the course of your career.

Weenie parents have a hard time setting limits.

Consistency

Kind of Consistent

Consistency is a word that everyone knows but few people understand. We all know that it has something important to do with child rearing. But, exactly how does it work?

One of my weenie parents said, "But, Dr. Jones, I think we are being *pretty consistent*." When I told this to my colleagues, we had a big laugh. We had a bigger laugh when one of my other weenie parents said, "But, Dr. Jones, I think we *are* consistent *most of the time*."

What weenies fail to understand about consistency is that the concept does not permit *degrees* of consistency. There is no such thing as "pretty consistent" or "very consistent" or "extremely consistent."

Consistency permits only *two* conditions. You are *consistent*, or you are *inconsistent*. There is nothing in between.

Building Brat Behavior

Imagine that my mother, instead of being consistent, had been *pretty consistent. Four out of five* times she "cracked." Maybe she had a good excuse – she was busy or stressed or distracted. So, in a moment of weakness, she blurted,

"OK, take some ginger snaps, go outside, and leave me alone! I'm tired of listening to your yammering!"

If my mother had cracked, she would have taught me:

Kind of Consistent?

There are no *degrees* of consistency. Consistency permits only two conditions:

- You are consistent.
- You are inconsistent.

"When the going gets tough, the tough get *yammering*."

"If at first you don't succeed, *yammer; yammer again*."

"Never give up! Have hope! Today might be your *lucky day*."

When parents crack, they teach children that *yammering pays off*. Children learn that they *can* and *will* get their way, but first they must wear down their parents by acting like brats.

Reinforcement Errors

The technical name for cracking is *reinforcement error*. A reinforcement error is a specific error in management that causes the problem to *go away* in the short-term but guarantees that it will *get worse* in the long-term.

As we get more savvy about discipline management, we will become astute at spotting reinforcement errors. How, other than by reinforcement errors, could parents maintain brat behavior throughout the years of childhood? And, how else could the school discipline code maintain Larry's brat behavior for *eight straight semesters?*

The Irony of Consistency

The irony of consistency is that the closer you come to being consistent before you fail, the worse off you are. If the parent cracks easily, the child does not need to be a world-class yammerer in order to succeed. But, if the parent does *not* crack easily, the child must learn to play hardball in order to win.

By making kids work hard in order to win, we train them to be ruthless and persistent. So, if parents are going to be weenies, they are better off being weenies *every time.* The kid will get his or her way in any case, but at least the weenies won't have to suffer as long beforehand.

Thinking Like a Teacher

If you want to *act* like a teacher, you must *think* like a teacher. Effective teachers know that consistency is crucial in a classroom of 30 young people. The teachers who die from stress are, for the most part, victims of their own "weenieism."

In later chapters, we will look at the skills of *meaning business*. But these skills are nothing in the hands of a weenie. They must be used every time, not just most of the time or when convenient.

Anyone who hopes to thrive in the teaching profession would be well advised to think like my mother. Two cornerstones of classroom management are, and always will be: *No means no, and I am not going to stand here and listen to your yammering.*

Consistency and the School Discipline Code

Institutional Weenieism

You would never look at these pathetic weenie parents with their obnoxious brat kids and say, "Oh boy, let's reproduce that system of management at our school site." But, in fact, that is exactly what we do.

Larry hates school. Larry wants out of school. Larry wears us down and gets kicked out of school. This is exactly how to build and maintain brat behavior.

With the management options contained in the traditional school discipline code, we can maintain Larry's brat behavior for as long as he is in school! We might think of

this system as "institutional weenieism" – a monumental collection of reinforcement errors.

The Discipline Task Force

Educators have always known that, somehow, this system doesn't work. From time to time districts and school sites go through spasms of reform. One fairly common exercise is the "discipline task force" – a committee of teachers, administrators, and parents who waste a year attempting to redesign the school discipline code.

While some upgrades might be possible, depending on what was there to begin with, these committees usually end up with a warmed-over version of the system that was in place before they started. After all, there is nothing we can legally do to Larry that every educator has not known about for the past fifty years.

Discipline Code Revisited

If, however, you have concluded by now that I have no use for the school discipline code, you are wrong. The school must be able to say "no" to severe offenses and make it stick.

We will look at the design of the school discipline code in a later section entitled, "Using the Backup System." But before we can produce a result that is significantly different from that of the discipline task force, we must first cover a lot of ground in discipline management.

We will begin in the classroom. The classroom is where big problems begin, where learning time is lost, and where teachers suffer most of their stress.

The school must be able to say 'no' to severe offenses and make it stick.

We will redesign the entire classroom management system so that *prevention* rather than remediation plays the primary role in discipline management. We are already well on our way toward this goal with the implementation of working the crowd, Say, See, Do Teaching; VIPs; and Praise, Prompt, and Leave. These procedures wean the helpless handraisers while replacing passive sitting with active learning.

In the following sections of the book we will explore discipline management in the more traditional sense of dealing with overt classroom misbehavior. We will look at skills of *meaning business* that allow the management of disruptions to be low-key and nonadversarial. We will learn how to make students responsible for their own actions. We will learn how to make Larry into a good citizen. And, we will learn how to deal with severe discipline problems. We will need all of these skills, along with our procedures for managing instruction and motivation, before we can even imagine a school discipline code that might succeed.

Self-Imposed Blind Spots

The equation of discipline management with punishment is one of the most pervasive and damaging stereotypes in our culture concerning the rearing of children. This negative stereotype has historically led both researchers and teacher-training programs to avoid the topic. What professor would want to build a career as the "punishment guru"?

This self-imposed blind spot has unwittingly contributed to today's crisis of discipline management in education. By limiting investigation of the topic, educators have preserved a limited perspective with a limited set of options.

As a result, we have never developed real expertise in discipline management. It is sobering to talk with teachers about their preparation for managing discipline problems in the classroom.

"They didn't give us any of this stuff in college."

"We had a survey course that covered a bunch of different theories."

"I was told that I would pick it up once I was out on the job."

"The subject was never brought up."

"Where were you twenty years ago?"

Mastery of the intricate skills and procedures required for success in discipline management comes neither naturally nor easily. Without extensive training, teachers are left to sink or swim. Perhaps it is not too surprising, then, that over a third of the new teachers quit by the end of their second year on the job.

Chapter Fourteen

Keeping It Positive, Keeping It Cheap

Wanting to Be Positive

Wanting Is Not Enough

As teachers, we want to have a positive classroom atmosphere. We want our students to look forward to coming to school in the morning, to love being in our classrooms, to enjoy learning. Any teacher who does not delight in these things has made a truly bad career choice.

No one enters the teaching profession wanting to nag and criticize, but many teachers end up doing so every day. At the beginning of their careers, these teachers who nag and criticize *wanted* to be positive. But, wanting to be positive and having the skills to pull it off are miles apart.

Think Candidly about Childhood

To put classroom management into a parenting perspective, imagine toddlers, and ask yourself:

- Do they share?
- Do they take turns?
- What happens if they do not get their way?

Children do not begin life civilized. They acquire civilization slowly and at great effort to their parents and to their schoolteachers.

One of the most important variables in child rearing is the effective supervision of children's play. Parents who provide this supervision deal with countless little crises

Preview

- The most common management technique in education is nag, nag, nag.

- The disruptions that cause a teacher to go home tired are the common misbehaviors that occur minute by minute, day after day.

- Talking to neighbors accounts for 80 percent of disruptions in a typical classroom, while *out of seat* accounts for 15 percent.

- Teachers rarely have a plan for dealing with these common disruptions that produce most of their stress and lost learning time.

- Unless you manage these disruptions efficiently, you will become tired and frustrated which will compromise your capacity to nurture.

- Management skills for the common, yet costly disruptions will be described in exacting detail.

of sharing and turn-taking, more than a few "time-outs," and enough tears to float a ship. There will be heart-to-heart talks to explain values, endless comforting of hurt feelings, and days when the parents feel that the stormy willfulness of early childhood will never end. Yet, if they "hang in there," these parents will produce a five-year-old who has the emotional maturity to begin kindergarten.

Contrast the learning described above with the experience of poorly supervised children. In unsupervised play, might makes right. When you crease your little playmate's head with a Tonka truck, it is yours.

The Normal Ability Spread

Are *all* children well-socialized and age-appropriate as they enter school? Yeah, right! On the contrary, you will have *at least* a half-decade of ability spread in your classroom on any variable you wish to name. This is true of both academic ability and social-emotional development, and it is equally true at any grade level.

A high school freshman algebra teacher will have students who are comfortable manipulating unknowns and students who are uncomfortable with their multiplication tables. They will also have students who solve social problems constructively and students who hit.

Some of the more obvious social-emotional variables that teachers encounter on a daily basis are:

- sharing
- turn-taking
- attention-seeking
- dependency
- aggressiveness

The little book, *Everything I Ever Needed to Know, I Learned in Kindergarten* speaks about these things, but its title is

something of a misnomer. Children need to know these things *before* they go to kindergarten, or they will stick out as the "babies" or the "terrors" of the class. Some kids still do not have these traits of maturity by high school.

Now, imagine teaching a classroom containing students with the normal range of social-emotional development. Do they ever gang up? Do they ever goad each other and feed off of each others' antics? Do they ever show off? Do they ever take their anger and upset out on you? Is there a grade level in which students have finally grown up to the point where they no longer do these things?

Nag, Nag, Nag

Have you ever heard teachers use words like these as they deal with everyday student behavior?

"All right class, there is absolutely no excuse for all of this *talking!* When I look up, I expect to see people *working!* There is an assignment on the board, and we have ten minutes until the bell rings, so let's get something *done!*"

or

"Where are you going? Would you please *take your seat?* I am sick and tired of looking up only to see you wandering aimlessly around the room!"

or

"What are you *playing with?* Let me see that! You may have this back at the end of the period. Right

The most widespread management procedure is nag, nag, nag.

now, would you please turn around in your seat, put your feet on the floor, and get to work?"

or

"Would the two of you keep your hands to yourselves and *pay attention* to what is going on in class? If I see any more of this behavior, you will stay after class!"

I have just given four examples of the most widespread behavior management procedure in education: *Nag, nag, nag*. Ask yourself, is this the way I wanted to sound when I went into teaching? Do I like myself when I sound like this?

Typical Disruptions

The Misperception That Drives Policy

When you ask classroom teachers to name their biggest discipline problem, they usually name a *student* rather than a behavior. In the previous chapter we called this student *Larry*. Teachers will say,

"I could deal with the rest of the class if it weren't for Larry. He causes me more grief than all of the other students combined."

Larry tends to be in the foreground of teachers' minds when they think about discipline management. No doubt this is because Larry's antics are highly memorable.

Yet, if we define Larry as our biggest discipline problem, we will end up looking to the school discipline code for our salvation. After all, outrageous behavior requires real consequences.

This logic, however, leaves us exactly where we have always been in discipline management. It opens up no new avenues for solving problems more constructively. To get a fresh start in dealing with classroom disruptions, we must switch perspectives.

Taking a Fresh Look at Classroom Disruptions

Some teachers make discipline management look easy. In an attempt to understand what these highly effective teachers are doing, I have spent hundreds of hours in the back of classrooms observing. I have recorded students' disruptions as well as teachers' responses to them. I scored anything that you might call goofing off – anything that the student was doing other than the assignment.

The data paint a clear picture of classroom disruptions that teachers instantly recognize even though it is at odds with their perception of Larry as being their most costly discipline problem. I will say to a room full of teachers,

"Think about the behavior of typical students. They are supposed to be working on an assignment. Imagine that a few of them are goofing off. If students in your class are doing something other than the assignment, what are they probably doing?"

In unison, the teachers respond: "Talking."

Indeed, the teachers' perception is dead accurate because they deal with this problem every day. Roughly 80 percent of the disruptions in any classroom can be scored during observation as "talking to neighbors."

This percentage is relatively stable and predictable regardless of the setting. I have counted it in elementary and secondary classrooms, inner city and suburban classrooms, regular and special classrooms, and in all subject areas.

Of the disruptions remaining, 15 percent can be scored as "out of seat." This includes students standing at the

pencil sharpener or the drinking fountain when they should be in their seats. But, more frequently I am observing a student that I have nicknamed "the wanderer." Take your eye off of this student for *five seconds*, and he or she will be wandering aimlessly around the room.

Thus, in a typical classroom 95 percent of off-task behavior is either *talking to neighbors* or *out of seat*. The next two behaviors, in order of frequency, are "drawing pictures" and "passing notes."

Getting Tired by the End of the Day

If we were to pick the biggest problem in the classroom in terms of teacher stress and lost learning time, the easy winner would be *talking to neighbors*. While Larry may indeed be memorable, his antics occur only sporadically. In contrast, talking to neighbors occurs minute by minute, day after day.

Talking to neighbors is the mean, median, and mode of classroom disruption – the bellwether of goofing off. No other problem even comes close. If you cannot successfully manage talking to neighbors at an affordable price, you are not even in the game.

Talking

to neighbors

accounts for

80 percent

of disruptions in

a typical classroom.

The Stages We All Go Through

If *talking to neighbors* is your most common classroom disruption, the logical question of management is, *What are you going to do about it?* Your level of stress and your frequency of nagging will be determined by how you answer this question.

Yet, answering this question is something that we are not prepared to do when we enter the teaching profession. Instead, we must figure out for ourselves how to deal with talking to neighbors once we are on the job. Consequently, we all progress through the same learning curve. It is one of the main reasons that our first year of teaching is so exhausting.

Have you ever seen your life pass before your eyes? As we struggle to deal with talking to neighbors, we all pass through four predictable stages. Stage one of this journey is: *As Green as Grass*.

As Green as Grass

Imagine, again, that it is the first day of your teaching career. As the saying goes, you are *as green as grass*. Green teachers are very clear about what they are *not* going to do.

"I am not going to nag, nag, nag. I used to *hate it* when teachers did that! I am not going to criticize or embarrass kids in front of their peers, either."

As is typical of green teachers, you want to be nice to the students, and you want the students to be nice to you. You are in "bonding mode."

Thus, with a smile on your face and love in your heart, the ball game begins. Five minutes into the first assignment of the school year, you look up from helping some student to see two kids on the far side of the room *talking* instead of *working*. As you watch, a question runs through your brain that

The Stages We All Go Through

● As Green as Grass
● Do Something
● Sick and Tired
● Laying Down the Law

was never clearly addressed during your training: *Now, what do I do?*

Most green teachers, not wanting to nag and remembering something about the extinction of behavior, say to themselves: *I'll just ignore that problem for a while, and maybe the students will get back to work.*

Of course, the students keep talking because goofing off is so much more fun than working. Unfortunately, the rest of the class can see that the students are talking and that the teacher is doing nothing about it. Not surprisingly, they conclude: *If they can talk, so can I.*

Soon, other students start to talk, and the noise level rises. Finally, "the wanderer" is up and gone. At this point, you, the green teacher, are finally forced to confront reality. You are losing control of the class. You conclude: *I have to do something!*

But what? As you contemplate what to do next, you graduate from phase one of the learning curve to phase two: *Do Something!*

Do Something!

You swing into action. You stand, turn toward the offending students and say their names.

"Tyrone. Roberta."

They respond with an ingratiating look – that familiar look of mild surprise and total innocence. This is the most basic fake-out move in all of studentdom. We will call it "smiley face."

Green teachers often mistake this look of innocence for genuine repentance. As you watch and wait, Tyrone and Roberta seem to get back to work. You return to helping your student. What do you think Tyrone and Roberta will be doing ten seconds from now?

Tyrone and Roberta are engaging in one of the most basic control moves of childhood. We will call it *pseudo-compliance*. Pseudo-compliance is when children do what you ask them to do just long enough to get you off their case. As soon as your attention moves elsewhere, they go back to doing what *they* wanted to do.

The four phases of pseudo-compliance to look for in successive interactions with the disruptive students are:

- **Smiley face:** They give you the look of the repentant angel as if asking, *Who, me?*

- **Book posing:** They open their books and look back at you as though to ask, *Does this fulfill the requirements of formal education?*

- **Pencil posing:** They get out a pencil and touch it to paper before looking back at you as though to say, *Look, I'm writing.*

- **Pseudo-scholarship:** They start to write with furrowed brow, but look up periodically to see if you are still paying attention.

It certainly looks like compliance from where you stand. You turn away from the disruptors to help your student. Tyrone and Roberta return to their conversation.

How many times will you endure pseudo-compliance before it finally gets under your skin? When you find yourself getting upset by the continuous talking on the far side of the room, you have entered phase three of you apprenticeship: *Sick and Tired!*

Sick and Tired

The students know when you finally become *sick and tired.* You turn with a look of grim determination. You put your hands on your hips, grit your teeth, cock your head forward, raise an eyebrow and draw in a breath before saying the students' names – but with an *edge* on your voice:

"Tyrone! Roberta!"

It sounds as though something *heavy* is finally coming down, but what? You still have no clear answer to that basic question, *Now, what do I do?* Consequently, you are faking it, and the students know it.

When forced to say something when we really don't know what to say, we are likely to engage in "silly talk." The following examples are some of the silliest things that teachers say in the classroom.

"Roberta, what are you supposed to be doing?" (Students know what they are supposed to be doing.)

"Roberta, this is the second time I've had to talk to you." (They are keeping count.)

"Roberta, am I going to have to come over there?" (They know you don't want to.)

Since silly talk does not change behavior, the students' talking resumes as soon as you turn away. How long must you put up with it before *enough is enough?* Sooner or later you will have to go over there to get results. This brings you to phase four: *Laying Down the Law!*

Any time that you are working harder at discipline management than the students, you will lose.

You cannot afford to walk into a classroom of thirty young people and "wing it" with your favorite home remedies contained in a bag of tricks. You will be backed into a corner and, when you sense that you are losing the group, you will do what you have to do to get it back.

To succeed, you will need both *love* and *skill*. Love without expertise is powerless. Unless you manage effectively, you will become tired and frustrated and, ultimately, lose your capacity to nurture.

Mastering Discipline Management

Every teacher is a "disciplinarian" by necessity. Discipline management begins before the students are seated in the morning and does not end until the room is empty in the afternoon.

Any classroom has the potential to become a "problem classroom." Whether the class develops its full potential depends on how it is managed.

No one is born with management skills. Nor will they magically come to you after years of teaching. But, these management skills can be described and understood. They can be taught and learned.

In the following chapter, we will look at one of the most important survival skills of teaching — *meaning business*. We will start with *talking to neighbors*, and we will answer the question, "What do I do next?"

Love without expertise is powerless.

Chapter Fifteen

Staying Calm, Staying Strong

Biology and Behavior

Perhaps the reason that common sense has never gotten us very far in discipline management stems from the fact that the only thing we have in common as a species is biology. And biology only equips us for primitive responses.

The Fight-Flight Reflex

We will begin with the very first thing that happens to us when we look up in the classroom to see some student fooling around. It is a reflex – a very primitive reflex that we share with all other vertebrates.

This reflex is our natural response to anything that we dislike or do not expect. It could be triggered by a clap of thunder, a shadow passing across the window, a big spider on our clothing, or a near accident with the car. We learned about this reflex in our freshman high school biology class. It was called the *fight-flight reflex.*

The fight-flight reflex is synonymous with *upset.* Consequently, it is the teacher's natural response to any disruption in the classroom. A room full of students can trigger this response quite often during a school day.

Managing the Fight-Flight Reflex

Reflexes are immediate and automatic. You do not choose to have them.

Yet some teachers rarely, if ever, become upset in the classroom. Others become can-

Preview

- Any classroom disruption will trigger a mild fight-flight reflex.

- This reflex not only makes you vulnerable to becoming upset, but it also stresses you physically.

- Triune Brain Theory helps to explain how the brain "downshifts" during a fight-flight reflex so that you end up functioning out of your brainstem instead of your cortex.

- The understanding and the complex social skills required for leadership reside in the cortex.

- To lead under pressure, you need to use all of your knowledge and experience. Thus, the fundamental rule of social power is, "Calm is strength. Upset is weakness."

- Remaining calm under pressure is achieved through relaxation. Relaxation is a skill that can be mastered with training.

didates for a burn-out workshop. The teachers who stay cool, calm, and collected have the same reflexes as everyone else, but they manage their stress and upset more effectively.

We will need to find out how they do it. But, before we can, we must become much more familiar with the fight-flight reflex. Many of our emotions are mediated by the fight-flight reflex, and our actions are mediated by our emotions.

Anatomy of the Fight-Flight Reflex

The fight-flight reflex is referred to in more advanced textbooks as a "generalized physiological mobilization response." While this sounds a bit imposing, like most biological terms, it tells us what is happening.

"Generalized" means that it involves our entire body. It is generalized as opposed to being localized. And, it involves the mobilization of our physiology – our heart rate, our blood pressure, our muscular tension. Our body is "revving up" as fast as it can to deal with threat.

This mobilization occurs in two phases. In coming to understand these two phases of the fight-flight reflex, we will come to understand much more about the management of stress.

The Fast (Neuromuscular) Phase

The fast phase of the fight-flight reflex has to do with the tensing of muscles. Within a fraction of a second our bodies begin to mobilize. This tensing of muscles prepares us to move quickly if we need to.

The fight-flight reflex tenses muscles that you can *feel:*

• Eyes open wide (This maximizes the field of vision.)
• Teeth clench
• The diaphragm flexes (This causes us to inhale

deeply to oxygenate the blood.)
• Skeletal muscles tense (This gets us ready to move.)

The fight-flight reflex tenses muscles that you may *not feel:*

• Blood vessels in the stomach contract (This vasoconstriction interrupts digestion, so that blood can be shunted to the muscles. This leaves acid in the stomach while increasing blood pressure.)
• Heart rate increases rapidly (This also increases blood pressure.)

The fight-flight reflex is our natural response to anything we dislike or do not expect.

The fight-flight reflex is crucial to survival – at least, for an animal in a state of nature. But, our species left that state a long time ago to create an alternative – civilization.

Civilization is accompanied by physical crowding and the development of complex social organizations. Civilization requires that we constantly interact with each other in order to solve problems, negotiate conflict, and generally boss each other around.

Some of us even place ourselves in a room full of young people all day long in order to earn a living. In biological terms you might think of this as the petri dish for growing stress – the perfect medium in which it might flourish.

Within the classroom the fight-flight reflex is triggered not every few hours as it might be in nature, but rather, every few *minutes*. In this environment, every aspect of the fight-flight reflex represents a potential symptom of chronic hypertension.

Reflexes are immediate and automatic.
You do not choose to have them.

Observe the ads on television to see what percentage of them are attempting to ameliorate the fight-flight reflex. Will it be aspirin or Tylenol or Advil or Aleve to help with our tension headache? After all, vasoconstriction in the brain is the beginning of that headache. Will it be Tums or Rolaids or Mylanta to help with stomach acid? Will it be Sominex or Nytol or Tylenol PM to help us fall asleep? It is hard to go to sleep when we are tense, you know.

We pay a high price for working in a stressful environment. But, it just goes with the territory, right?

Don't be too sure. It is my personal opinion that nobody pays you enough money to justify donating your physical well-being to the next generation.

The Slow (Biochemical) Phase

The slow phase of the fight-flight reflex has to do with adrenaline. You already know what an "adrenaline rush" is. Adrenaline *intensifies* the physiological mobilization of the fast phase of the fight-flight reflex and *maintains* it over time. It makes sure that the intensity and focus of the fight-flight reflex will stay with us throughout the crisis.

Within tenths of a second our bodies begin to dump adrenaline into the bloodstream. The more upset we become, the more adrenaline enters the blood. The concentration of adrenaline builds for several seconds – slowly enough for us to turn it off, if we know how.

Here are some things to know about adrenaline:

- It increases our metabolism, particularly the rate at which the body burns sugars. This is where "nervous energy" comes from.

- It takes roughly 27 minutes for adrenaline to clear the blood stream. Thus, it takes only two "squirrely" behaviors per class period to keep us chemically "wired" all day long for the remainder of our careers.

It is common for us to operate on "nervous energy" in the classroom. We call it, *being on our toes*. As a result, we build up an "energy debt" all day long due to our increased metabolism.

Do we pay for this energy debt when the kids go home? No, we still have another half-hour on adrenaline before it clears the bloodstream. Consequently, we have energy right after the kids leave as we scurry around organizing books and materials for tomorrow's lessons.

The energy debt hits us about a half-hour *after* the kids go home. A wave of exhaustion comes over us, and we look for a place to sit down. *What a day!*

Recovering from an energy debt that has been building for the past six hours will take us well into the evening. Who then pays for the fact that we are working too hard in the classroom? As the song says, "You only hurt the ones you love, the ones you shouldn't hurt at all."

Our spouse says,

"Honey, we need to talk about something."

and we say,

"Do we have to talk about it *now*?"

Our child says,

"I just broke this."

and we say,

"You broke it *already*? You just got it *last week*."

We can't be very good with our own family when we come home day after day with the tank empty. It is also my personal opinion that nobody pays you enough money to compensate for the happiness of your family life.

Fight-Flight by Different Names

Nag, Nag, Nag

When we have a fight-flight reflex, our mouth tends to open. It may be a scream if our lives are in danger. But in less emotionally charged social situations, like the classroom, it sounds like this:

"All right class, there is no excuse for all of this talking! When I look up, I expect to see people working! There is an assignment on the board, and we have ten minutes until the bell rings, so lets *get something done!*"

"Where are you going? Would you please *take your seat?* I am sick and tired of looking up only to see you wandering aimlessly around the room!"

"What are you playing with? Let me see that! You may have this back at the end of the period. Right now, would you please turn around in your seat, put your feet on the floor and get to work?"

"Would the two of you keep your hands to yourselves and pay attention to what is going on in class? If I see any more of this behavior, we will discuss it together after the bell!"

You remember nag, nag, nag from earlier chapters. Let me give you a *technical* definition of nagging: Nagging is nothing more than a *fight-flight reflex with dialogue*. If you open your mouth when you are upset, you will nag.

> # Nagging is nothing more than a fight-flight reflex with dialogue.

We *all* nag. Nagging is normal biological behavior. If you have a friend who claims that they never nag, you have a liar for a friend.

The question that is relevant to classroom management is simply, "How often do you nag?" For some teachers it is a rarity. For others it happens all of the time.

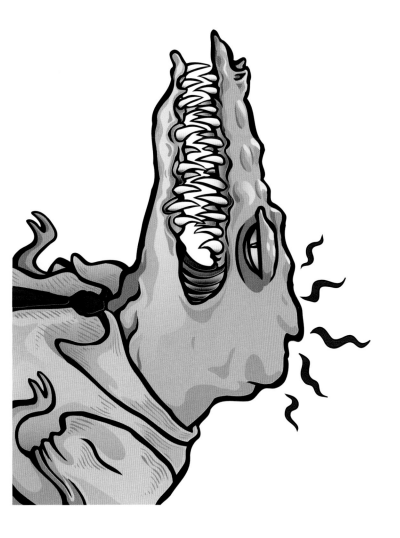

A *common variant of the fight-flight reflex is "snap and snarl."*

Pheasant Posturing

We talk with our *hands* as well as our mouths. When we talk with our hands while nagging, we engage in "pheasant posturing."

Pheasant posturing is a term from anthropology that refers to *a lot of squawking and flapping that produces no damage*. Male pheasants do a dramatic job of squawking and flapping during their mating combat without ever touching each other. In the classroom, the *squawking* is the *nag, nag, nag*. We will focus here on the *flapping*. We do that with our hands.

Most of the time, however, we are not attempting to fly. We just want to kick up a little dust around the barnyard so the chickies know that we are serious. In such situations we only use *one* hand.

The two most common one-wing flaps are the "circular" and the "vertical." We use the circular flap as we motion to students to turn around in their chairs. We use the vertical flap as we motion for students to sit down.

When both wings become involved, the situation is obviously serious. Imagine a teacher, upset and flustered, standing in the front of the classroom with both arms raised announcing to the class,

"The longer it takes all of you to get *into your seats* and *settle down*, the longer I will be standing here with my arms up!"

Snap and Snarl

A trainee from the court schools of Los Angeles (you can imagine the student body in the court schools of Los Angeles) said,

"I have a different name for it. I call it 'snap and snarl.' You snap your fingers and point when you say 'Take your seat' or 'Turn around and get to work!'"

We all had a laugh as we practiced snapping and snarling. It gives you a feeling of primitive power. A dinosaur comes to mind with eyes narrowed, teeth flashing. These thoughts of primitive power made me think of an interaction I had had with my younger son.

Upset Changes Brain Function

Snap and Snarl with My Son

The altercation had to do with backpacks – the kind that kids take to school with their books and stuff inside. Patrick (my older son) and Brian (my younger son) used to drop their backpacks as soon as they came in the back door from school – right at the bottom of the stairs. This was a dangerous place to put backpacks. I had taught the boys (I thought) to place their backpacks out of the way when they came home from school.

One day, when I was jet-lagged from a delayed flight home the night before, I found myself in a rotten mood. I was in the kitchen when Brian came home from school. He waltzed in the back door, dropped his backpack right at the foot of the stairs and started up to his room.

I snapped,

"Brian! Where is that back pack supposed to go?"

Brian snapped,

"Aw, Daaad!"

I must have been in good form to combine snapping and snarling with a silly question. And, I hadn't seen Brian in four days. Some greeting!

I felt bad. After I collected myself, I went up to apologize to my son and have a decent conversation. But later, I could not help but wonder how I could have been so stupid.

Let me put this whole thing into perspective. I have a Ph.D. in clinical psychology. At this point in my life I had spent nearly three decades learning to understand peoples' needs and feelings, to solve interpersonal problems constructively, to structure win-win solutions for people, to be *therapeutic!* Where were all of these skills when I needed them?

Actually, I knew exactly where the skills were. I had studied it in great detail during graduate school.

Triune Brain Theory

Triune Brain Theory explains what happens in the brain when we become upset. It helps to describe why we snap and snarl when we have a fight-flight reflex.

To begin with, the fight-flight reflex is extremely predictable and reliable. Animals that failed to execute it properly over the past 500 million years became someone else's lunch.

Reflexes are made reliable by failsafe mechanisms. So, what are the failsafe mechanisms of the fight-flight reflex? Among other things, Triune Brain Theory explains the failsafe mechanisms of the fight-flight reflex.

For starters, there have been three great epochs of brain development over the eons. These epochs of brain development produced characteristic structures. You can see them in a cross-section of the brain.

Triune means "three in one" ("tri" as in tricycle and "une" as in unicycle). The "three brains in one" are:

1. **Reptilian Brain (Brainstem):** These are the lower brain centers which regulate basic life functions. They include the spinal cord, the cerebellum (muscular coordination), the visual cortex plus ganglia that regulate bodily functions.

2. Ancient Cortex (Paleocortex): These are the mid-brain centers referred to irreverently by graduate students as "doggy-horsey brain." To see what these brain centers do, compare the social behavior of a lizard with your doggy. Your doggy can love you and be loyal. Your pet lizard will just eat and sleep.

3. New Cortex (Neocortex): These are the higher brain centers that are responsible for "higher intelligence." This refers to us! It also refers to Plato and Socrates, Bach and Beethoven, Einstein and Fermi.

When we become upset, the brain "downshifts" from the cortex to the brainstem.

Downshifting

How does the brain insure that, when your life is on the line, you "get it in gear" rather than dithering about what to do? Well, you can't dither without a cortex. So, your brain eliminates its own cortex.

This process is called "downshifting." Under *mild* arousal, the brain shifts from the neocortex to the mid-brain. This change can be disconcerting. Have you ever "blocked" on people's names when you were a little nervous? Downshifting plays havoc with long-term memory.

Under *moderate* to *severe* arousal, the brain downshifts all the way to the reptilian brain and spinal cord – referred to irreverently by graduate students as "going brainstem." We have all "gone brainstem" at some time, haven't we? Have you ever blown up, gone ballistic, flown off the handle, lost your cool?

Now, let me give you a piece of advice about discipline management in the classroom. You will do a much better job *with a cortex*. When you lose your cortex, a classroom suddenly becomes thirty cortexes manipulating one brainstem. These are not even odds.

This brings us to the real issue underlying this discussion of brain function – *power*. Who runs your classroom, anyway?

Social Power

Power and Control

Power is one of those words that leaves a bad taste.

"He is really on a *power trip*."

In fact, power is value-neutral. It simply refers to *control*. But control is another word that leaves a bad taste.

"She is a real *control freak*."

"He is the most *controlling person* I have ever met."

We subconsciously translate these words into "overpowering" and "controlling" – terms that denote threat. Without this "spin," they are just words that attempt to describe what is happening.

Take, for example, the management of a simple disruption in the classroom. You look up to see two students *talking to neighbors* when they should be working. You cruise over to them as you work the crowd, and you ask them to get back to work.

Chances are that they *will* get back to work. This, however, does not signify virtue. It signifies the fact that these students have the brains to cool it when the teacher is standing over them. To find out whether or not the students *really* get back to work, you will have to wait a minute or two.

Imagine that two minutes have passed, and, from the far side of the room, you look up to see these two students *still working*. Who is in control of their behavior?

You are. The students wanted to talk, and you wanted them to work. Now, simply look at what has happened as a result of your interaction with them. Are they doing what *they* wanted to do, or are they doing what *you* wanted them to do? Since they are pursuing your agenda rather than their agenda, you are in control of their behavior.

Power is simply control. Who is controlling whom? Who is controlling whom? Who calls the shot? Who gets their way?

Now imagine that the situation with *talking to neighbors* turned out differently. When you look up two minutes later, the two students who "shaped up" when you were standing over them are talking again.

Now ask yourself, who is in control? Are they doing what *they* wanted to do, or are they doing what *you* wanted them to do?

As you can see, the outcome of this interaction is public knowledge. Any student in the classroom can see whether or not you are able to get two students to shape up. There is no place for you to hide.

The Art of Getting Your Way

Power is control, and control is power. These terms do not, however, denote the "dark force." They simply describe who is leading and who is following. The person with more power leads. The person with less power follows.

When some people try to lead, they rub everybody the wrong way and people resist their leadership. They lack the necessary skills.

Other people are born leaders. They lead gracefully, and people follow. They definitely have the skills.

Leading skillfully is an art form. It is the art of *getting your own sweet way*.

When you lose your cortex, a classroom suddenly becomes thirty cortexes manipulating one brainstem.

Leadership is often described as "getting things done through people." It is the art of employing social power in order to achieve a social objective. In this sense, leadership is synonymous with words like management, parenting, and diplomacy.

In political science, diplomacy is often described as "the art of getting the other person to do what you want them to do and have them *thank you* for it." Skillful diplomacy is definitely the art of social power – the art form by which you earn your living.

All day in the classroom you will be attempting to get students to do what you want them to do and thank you for it. You will take children during their sweetest years of youth and incarcerate them in a school building where you will sit them down and require them to do one assignment after another all day long. And, you will want them to like it so much that they look forward to doing it again tomorrow. This will test your management skills to the limit.

Power Conflicts

Two Types of Power

There are, it would seem, *two* types of power within us – *social* power and *primitive* power. They compete with each other to control our behavior.

Primitive power is the power that we have used since time began in order to insure our survival. It begins with the fight-flight reflex. In a social situation, it quickly becomes up-

set followed by *nag, nag, nag* and occasional wing flapping, or worse.

Social power, in contrast, is not natural – it is learned. It is not instinctual – it is skillful. It is subtle and complex, and it is acquired at great effort. Many people acquire precious little of it during an entire lifetime. It definitely resides in the cortex.

The conflict within us between these two types of power centers around the fact that you cannot do them both *at the same time*. When we downshift to the brainstem during a fight-flight reflex, we lose the cortex. To get cooperation from a room full of students all day long, you will *constantly* need your cortex.

Calm Is Strength, Upset Is Weakness

This competition between two different kinds of power in governing our actions brings us to the most fundamental principle of social power:

Calm is strength. Upset is weakness.

When you are calm, you can bring all of your wisdom, experience, and social skill to bear in solving a problem. When you are upset, none of that knowledge is available to you. As the saying goes, *My life is in the hands of any fool who can make me angry*).

Intimidation Is Exhausting

Yet, while emphasis on calm may be valid, it also seems counter-intuitive at some level. People say to their children when exasperated, "Now, I'm *really* getting *angry!*" as though this reference to impending upset carried great power. Isn't it upset strong too?

Well, yes, if you are attempting to *physically* intimidate somebody. But, you cannot use primitive power all day long to manage a classroom full of young people without

Self Control

You will never be able to control another individual until you are first in control of yourself.

alienating them and *exhausting* yourself. It is too crude of a tool for such complex work.

Who Is Controlling Whom?

To put primitive power and social power into perspective, ask yourself the following two questions:

- If you are *upset*, who is in control of your mind and body? (Trainees respond in unison, "They are.")

- If you are *calm*, who is in control of your mind and body? (Trainees respond in unison, "You are.")

You will never be able to control another individual, much less a roomful of them, until you are first *in control of yourself.* Before we can ever hope to mean business, we must be in control of the situation rather than the situation being in control of us.

One of the hardest lessons to accept about meaning business is that it is first and foremost *emotional.* Unless we can first be calm, our fancy management strategies will avail us nothing. They will be in the cortex while we are in the brainstem.

But the biological game is played very quickly. It is over before most people know that it has begun.

Adrenaline will begin to enter your blood stream in tenths of a second. It will reach a critical concentration in

a few seconds, and then it is too late. You will go to your brainstem whether you want to or not, and you will not return for roughly 27 minutes.

Then, perhaps you may want to apologize as I did to my son. But, that is a far cry from being skillful.

Power Is Control

Primitive Power

- Fight-Flight Reflex

- Force and Counterforce

- Reflex Behavior

- Brainstem

Social Power

- Social Skills

- Leadership and Management

- Learned Behavior

- Cortex

Calm Is a Skill

It's a Matter of Breathing

When you look up in the classroom to see a disruption, you will have a fight-flight reflex. No amount of training will *prevent* it.

However, you can *abort* the reflex. You abort it by relaxing. Breathing in a slow and relaxed fashion is the most direct route to relaxing your entire body.

Practice in relaxed breathing is part of any training program to reduce stress. It is used in prepared childbirth training, therapy for anxieties or phobias, yoga, or the training of baseball umpires. If your job requires relaxation under pressure, you will need to master the art of the "relaxing breath." The practice of relaxed breathing is part of training teachers to *mean business.*

A relaxing breath is slow and relatively shallow. It is the way you would breathe if you were beginning to doze off. It lowers your heart rate and your blood pressure. Your muscles relax, and your face becomes calm and expressionless.

Calm Can Be Learned

Relaxed breathing can be learned like any other skill — with practice, practice, practice. The more skillful you become at relaxation, the more quickly you can relax after something upsetting occurs. With mastery, relaxation can be almost instantaneous.

The quicker you relax, the less adrenaline enters your bloodstream. Relaxation keeps you in your cortex while reducing wear and tear on your body. It is a basic survival skill for any teacher.

Emotions Are Contagious

If you are calm, you will have a calming effect on those around you. If you are upset, you will tend to upset those around you. During training, teachers learn: *Emotions are contagious. You will get exactly what you give.*

Our objectives in managing classroom disruptions are two-fold:

- *Calm* the student.
- Get them back *on task.*

These objectives are two sides of the same coin. You must calm students in order to get them back on task.

Adrenaline makes people jumpy. If you raise your voice to someone, they stay jumpy for quite a while.

If students are upset, they will not be able to concentrate. If they cannot concentrate in order to study, they will probably find something else to do, like goofing off. This goofing off will become your next discipline problem.

Calm is strength.
Upset is weakness.

Our objective is to make problems smaller, not larger. If we remain calm, we contain the problem while preserving ourselves. If we get upset, we become our own worst enemy.

Chapter Sixteen

Meaning Business

Preview

- We instinctively read each other's body language in order to predict what the other person is going to do next.

- Body language "telegraphs" our real thoughts, feelings, and intentions whether we want it to or not. The students read us like a book.

- Since we telegraph the thoughts and feelings that precede action, the students are really reading our minds.

- In this chapter, we examine the body language of meaning business while dealing with the most common of all classroom disruptions — talking to neighbors.

- Our priority at all times is that *discipline comes before instruction*. Until this issue is resolved in our minds, our body language will betray our ambivalence.

Meaning Business Is Body Language

Naturals in Action

Natural teachers make discipline management look easy. We have described many of the skills that they use which include working the crowd, weaning the helpless handraisers, and teaching procedures that embody high standards and expectations.

But one of the most important attributes that the naturals possess is *meaning business*. Meaning business seems to keep the class somehow "in line" without nagging, upset, or exasperation.

During our initial observations, we could not see what these gifted teachers were doing. It was so subtle that it was invisible to

us. Nor were the naturals aware of what they were doing. They could not begin to describe it.

Only after months of observation, hours of brainstorming, and considerable trial and error did meaning business become visible to us. Yet, it was always visible to the students. *Meaning business* is conveyed through body language.

It Is Genetic and Generic

The whole human race has essentially the same body language. Happiness, sadness, anger, and boredom look the same on any continent. The cultural differences in body language are trivial compared to the similarities.

The only thing we all have in common is "human nature." Such uniformity of behavior can only come from its being "inborn." Body language is biology.

To learn about body language, we must study an area of biology known as behavioral biology. Certain behaviors are biological, like a spider's ability to spin a web. In higher animals, these behaviors can be quite complex.

Decoding Body Language

Body Language Aids Prediction
Animals instinctively "read" each other's body language in order to know what the other animal is going to do next. Prediction is a matter of survival.

We also read body language in order to predict behavior. One of the most common examples in everyday life is sports. The offense reads the defense, and the defense reads the offense. What is the other player going to do next? A shift of the eyes, a shift of weight – subtle signs tip us off.

Children Read Us Like a Book
Long before children have language, their eyes follow us and study us. Children not only read our actions, but they also read our emotions in order to predict our actions. They know whether we are calm or upset, happy or sad, pleased or displeased.

Consequently, body language conveys more than just action. It is also the language of *thoughts* and *feelings* and *intentions*.

In a classroom the students study *you*, and they become more astute with each passing year. At any moment of the day, the students will know just how far they can push you. They will know whether or not they need to take you seriously. They will know what they can get away with.

Body Language Does Not Lie
Body language is a constant in our make-up and nature. It has not changed in a million years. Nor, can you change it by an act of will.

It will telegraph to the students your *real* thoughts, feelings, and intentions whether you want it to or not. Do not ever think that you can fool a child. The language of the body does not lie. A skilled athlete might be able to fake going right or left, but you cannot *fake* something as complex as meaning business hour after hour.

You have two choices in relation to body language. You can learn about body language so that you can consciously use it to help students succeed. Or, you can be ignorant of it in which case the students will always be one step ahead of you.

Body language is the language of thoughts, feelings, and intentions.

The Game Plan

Where to Begin
We send and receive body language constantly. There is a body language for meeting and greeting, for courtship, for gaining acceptance, and for dominance and submission.

But, since this is not a textbook on body language, we will narrow our focus to the classroom. More specifically, we will attempt to replace goofing off with time-on-task.

Typically, you will have a couple of students in the classroom talking to each other instead of working, and you will want them to stop talking and get back to work. How do you signal to the students to stop goofing off in a low-key fashion that clearly conveys that "no means no"?

Eighty percent of goofing off is talking to neighbors.

Focus on Small Disruptions

To begin with, we will focus on the small, everyday disruptions such as "talking to neighbors." We will do this for two reasons:

- **Small disruptions are more costly.** As we mentioned in the previous chapter, small disruptions occur at a much higher rate in the classroom than large disruptions. Consequently, they account for most of the lost learning time and most of the teacher's stress.

- **Big disruptions grow from small disruptions.** While a crisis can sometimes erupt from out of the blue, most often big problems are just small problems that have been allowed to fester. When we see an eight-year-old acting like a tyrant, we strongly suspect that this problem did not begin yesterday. Similarly, when we see a child who is willing to be outrageous in the classroom, we might suspect that he or she has been "getting away with murder" for a long time.

The most common disruption in the classroom, as we have mentioned in earlier chapters, is *talking to neighbors*. Consequently, it is the natural candidate for study. When you respond to goofing off in the classroom, you will be responding to *talking to neighbors* 80 percent of the time.

Learning a Language

When we focus upon meaning business in dealing with classroom disruptions, we do so as a means to a greater end. We are not just learning a technique to add to our bag of tricks. Rather, we are learning a new language – body language.

While you have been reading body language since early childhood, you must learn to read it and speak it at a *conscious level* so you can signal to students at any time that *you mean business*. In addition, you must learn to read how students signal that they *will or will not comply*.

We will begin to learn this new language as one would learn any new language – with simple words. Then we will move to simple phrases, then simple sentences, then paragraphs. We will build logically from the simple to the complex.

In the beginning, the "phrases" of body language always look like techniques. This feeds into our natural tendency to look for "quickie" prescriptions for solving problems. But this tendency to interpret fluid and dynamic interactions in static terms is just a stage on the learning curve.

Eventually we will learn enough of the language to express ourselves effectively without the need for verbalization. Body language is, after all, a *conversation*. It is a conversation in which we will participate either knowingly or unknowingly. Our objective is to be *knowing* participants.

Worst-Case Scenarios

When new learning confronts old habits, our defenses go on alert. We tend to confront change before we embrace it.

We usually fend off change with the "Yeah, buts." These *Yeah, buts* typically take the form of worst-case scenarios.

"Yeah, but I have a kid in my class who would..."

"Yeah, but I've tried things like that and..."

"Yeah, but you don't know the kinds of homes our kids come from..."

Before we go any further, let me reiterate that we are learning a *language*. We are not attempting to answer questions that begin with, "Yeah, but what would you do if..." We are not presenting packaged remedies.

Rather, we are using a typical situation with typical students in order to paint a picture of a typical conversation

in body language. The students are unremarkable, and the situation is unremarkable. The only thing remarkable about *talking to neighbors* is the fact that it accounts for 80 percent of the lost learning time during a typical day in the classroom. For that reason, this unremarkable situation is pivotal.

Keep It Cheap

Looking Students Back to Work

Imagine that you are helping a student in class when you look up to see two kids on the far side of the classroom talking when they should be working. What do you do?

Have you ever turned toward disruptive students from a distance and simply *looked* them back to work? Most teachers will respond, "Yes."

It is not as though meaning business was just invented, and it is not as though you have never done it. When you have gotten the result you wanted, chances are that you did a pretty good job of meaning business.

On the other hand, have you ever had to *walk* over to the disruptive students in order to get them back to work? Most teachers will again respond, "Yes."

Now, let me ask you the most important *practical* question concerning your efforts to manage the classroom. Which one of these two responses is *cheaper*?

Obviously, looking the students back to

Body Language Is Dialogue

Body language is a conversation in which we will participate either knowingly or unknowingly.

Our objective is to be knowing participants.

work is much cheaper. It takes very little time and effort. Most of the cost in setting limits on this misbehavior would be contained in the trip across the classroom.

This consideration focuses our attention on the *beginning* of your interaction with the disruptive students – on the *turn* and the *look*. If the turn and the look are convincing, you will often save yourself the trip across the classroom.

It Is a Fast Game

In order to analyze the body language of meaning business as we turn toward the disruptive students, we must slow down the action. Body language is very subtle, and the students read it instantaneously. They will know immediately whether or not you mean business.

By the time you have *turned toward the students*, the game is usually over. An amazing amount of information is conveyed to those students with your turn.

The Turn: Your Commitment

A Difficult Choice

Let's deal with your head before we deal with your body. After all, body language is the language of thoughts, feelings, and intentions.

Let's imagine that you are helping a student named Robert with a complex piece of work, like a geometry proof. He is lost somewhere in the middle of the proof among the theorems and axioms and corollaries.

> **If your turn is convincing, you can usually save yourself the trip across the classroom.**

You have been working with Robert for a couple of minutes, and you are nearing closure. Given another thirty seconds, Robert will be able to progress on his own.

At this moment, out of the corner of your eye, you catch two students on the far side of the room talking instead of working. Be *utterly candid* with yourself as you imagine deciding *what to do next*. Do you want to *abort* the teaching interaction in which you have invested several minutes and in which you are nearing closure? Or, do you want to *finish* helping Robert before you deal with the problem?

During training, a roomful of experienced teachers will respond in unison, "Finish helping Robert." Of course you would like to finish helping Robert, because you have made an emotional and intellectual *investment*. You would hate to waste all of that time and effort, particularly when he almost "has it."

Consequently, teachers will almost always return to helping Robert when this situation occurs in the classroom. But, this situation happens over and over. It represents *80 percent of goofing off.*

Now, let's look at this situation from the *students'* perspective. It is the beginning of the school year, and they are trying to figure out who you are. They just saw you look up to see two students goofing off, and then they saw you return to helping Robert. From the students' perspective, answer the following question: *In this classroom, is discipline management on the front burner, or is discipline management on the back burner?*

Whoops! It is definitely on the *back* burner. You "pulled your punch." They just saw you make a choice, and that choice will cost you dearly. You may as well make a public announcement to the class as follows:

"Class, I have told you that I have high standards. But, you also know that talk is cheap. What you just saw was reality, not talk. In my classroom, when I have to choose between instruction and discipline, I will choose instruction. I would like for there to be no discipline problems, of course, but I find that dealing with them is most inconvenient. Consequently, I will not do it if I do not *have to.*"

You have just made Larry a happy man – along with many of his classmates. Most students would love to talk to their neighbors whenever they feel like it. How nice it is to be in a classroom where nothing stops you!

Your Priority

You are on the horns of a dilemma that was described in an earlier chapter. If you fail to do something about the talking, you have just signaled to the class that talking to neighbors is *not worth your time.* We called this "declaring open season on yourself." But, if you do respond, what do you do?

To begin with, let's deal with your *priorities* before we consider your actions. In the classroom at all times, the following priority must govern your decision making. It is not optional. It is not a suggestion. You live or die by it. Your priority is this: *Discipline before Instruction.*

Discipline *always* comes before instruction. It is not up for debate, so don't *think* about it in the heat of the moment. Instead, lean over gently and say, without hesitation, "Excuse me, Robert." The decision to do this must be made *in advance.*

If you stop to think at this juncture, all of your thoughts will be rationalizations to justify continuing with what you would *rather* be doing, which is *instruction.* Here are some truly *irrelevant* questions that might flash through your mind to cloud your judgement if you stop to debate with yourself:

- **How big is the disruption?** This is irrelevant because there is a disruption, and you must either deal with it or declare open season on yourself. The disruption is typically small – your garden variety *talking to neighbors* in most cases.

- **How important is the assignment?** This is also irrelevant. If the assignment were not important, you would not be teaching it.

Drop the debate and do your job. This is exactly the situation in which *meaning business* usually occurs.

Weenieism versus Consistency

Do you remember in chapter 13 when we talked about *weenie parents?* They just can't say "no" and mean it. In my years as a clinician, I spent a lot of time trying to teach weenie parents to convey to their children that "no means no." Along with a discussion of *no means no* comes the topic of *consistency.* No means no *every time,* or it means less than nothing.

Discipline

before

Instruction

Weenie parents have a hard time understanding consistency. Instead, they are "kind of consistent." Sometimes they deal with the problem, and sometimes they turn a blind eye to the problem, and sometimes they crack. As one of my weenie parents said, "But, Dr. Jones, I think we are consistent *most of the time*."

What weenie parents fail to understand, as we mentioned earlier, is that you are either consistent or not. There are no *degrees* of consistency.

The way you build brat behavior is by being consistent "most of the time" – by following through sometimes and not following through at other times. This forces the child to *continually* test you in order to see if you really mean it *this time*.

Commitment and Follow-Through

It is now time to check your own commitment to time-on-task and high standards. Assuming that the students are not supposed to be talking to each other at this time, are you going to stop and deal with the talking? Or, will you only deal with it *if it is convenient?*

Realize, however, that discipline management is *never* convenient. It is never what you "would rather be doing." It is always an unpleasant intrusion.

But this is the *moment of truth*. Are you willing to do it *now* and do it *every time*? If not, quit kidding yourself and admit that you are a weenie.

> No means no every time, or it means less than nothing.

The Turn: Your Emotional Response

Calm Is Strength

Your commitment to act is instantaneous, and so is your *fight-flight reflex*. Since this is hardly a life-threatening situation, you will not feel a big jolt. You will just have a feeling of *exasperation*. Before you interact with the disruptive students, take a *relaxing breath* and *slow down*.

But slowing down is not easy. During training we spend a lot of time practicing the *relaxing breath* so that we can slow down *instantaneously under pressure*. We practice it with increasing levels of provocation in increasingly complex situations from mild disruptions to nasty backtalk. In lieu of such practice, let me slow down the action and walk you through it.

The Relaxing Breath

When you see the disruption on the far side of the room, lean over and whisper, "Excuse me, Robert." Then stay *down* and take a *relaxing breath*. Your natural tendency is to stand. When you stay down to take a relaxing breath, you do several things at once.

- **You turn away from the problem.** When you excuse yourself from Robert, you typically turn your head away from the disruption. This helps you relax by taking the problem out of your field of vision where it would continue to trigger the fight-flight reflex.

- **You model common courtesy.** It is important to model *common courtesy* whenever possible in the classroom. Many students have little experience with "please," "thank you," and "excuse me" at home.

- **You deliver a closure message.** Excusing yourself from Robert is also a *closure message* interchangeable with, "Just a second." If you do not excuse yourself, poor Robert has no idea as to why you suddenly quit talking to him and turned your back. Consequently, he will often say your name in order to get your attention. Now you have talking coming from two directions.

- **You give yourself time to refocus.** Give yourself a moment to refocus your attention and center yourself before you stand up. After you say, "Excuse me, Robert," *stay down and take a relaxing breath* in order to have some time to clear your mind.

  When you stand and turn toward the disruptive students, it is "show time." Before you even straighten up, one of the disruptive students might say, "What? I wasn't doing anything." If you are not relaxed before this happens, you don't have a chance.

- **You fill your lungs.** If you stand and turn too quickly after excusing yourself from Robert, your lungs will be *empty* because you just spoke. Then you will be forced to *breathe in* as you face the disruptors. When you breathe in, you *flex* your diaphragm. You will not be able to relax peripheral muscles while flexing the most centrally located voluntary muscle in your body.

Speed Kills

Upset is fast, and calm is slow. Students can tell by the speed of your movement how *upset* or *impatient* you are. But, we also move quickly when we are *busy*.

When we are in "instruction mode," we are *very* busy. Our minds are racing as we think about what the student knows, what the student needs, how we will explain the concept, how we will exploit the visual aids, and what is going on in the rest of the class.

When we look up and see a disruption, the fight-flight reflex speeds us up even more. Everything is driving us through the transition from instruction to discipline *too fast*.

The students see this speed of movement and conclude that we will deal with the disruption quickly and return to Robert. Maybe it will just be snap and snarl.

Slow down so that the disruptive students have no doubt that instruction has been interrupted, and that they are the sole focus of your attention. Only when you commit your time and attention to the problem will the students begin to take you seriously.

Mixed messages represent the body language of ambivalence.

The Turn: Your Ambivalence

Beyond Commitment

You have laid the groundwork for meaning business. You have made a conscious *commitment* to dealing with the problem, and you have *relaxed* yourself – not easy things to do. But these events are mostly internal and take only seconds. At most, the students have seen you pause and whisper something to Robert. This is hardly a convincing display of body language to disruptive students.

To be convinced, the students will have to see you actually *do something* – to commit time and energy toward solving the problem. It is at the point of making the actual investment that latent feelings may show through your actions to trip you up. In addition to your *conscious* commitment, we must deal with the *unconscious*. Sometimes we know that we *should* do something when, deep inside, we really *do not want to*.

How will the students discriminate that you are thoroughly committed and that you will *actually follow through*? These questions bring us to an area of learning theory known as "discrimination training."

Discrimination Training

We continually make discriminations in social situations. These discriminations often answer the question, Do they, or don't they? For example, *Do they like me? Do they think my jokes are funny? Do they accept me into the group?*

We also discriminate *change* in people's behavior. For example, we can tell when friends are sad instead of their normal upbeat selves.

How can we tell when a social situation has changed? We look for *signs* or *clues*. We can tell that a friend is sad by a facial expression, a tone of voice, sagging posture, or perhaps by the way he or she walks.

These signs have a name in learning theory. Since they are stimuli that help us to discriminate change, they are called "discriminative stimuli." Their symbol is Sd. They are the signs or "signals" that people read in body language.

Within the present context, how will the disruptive students discriminate that your commitment has changed from instruction to discipline? How will they discern that you intend to deal with the problem – that you *mean business?*

Signal Clarity

Here is how it works. If all of the signals that you give say, "I am *done* with instruction, and I have *gone* to discipline," then even your dog and cat can read it. If, on the other hand, half of your signals say, "I have gone to discipline," and half of your signals say, "I am still at instruction," then no one could be sure of your intention no matter how smart that person is.

As you can see, it all comes down to *signal clarity*. Within the context of meaning business, signal clarity brings us directly to the topic of *ambivalence*.

Ambivalence

When we are ambivalent we are "of two minds." We are *torn* between two choices.

We are torn, for example, when we say to ourselves, "I really want it, but I don't want to spend the money," or "I want to go to graduate school, but I don't want to take that many years out of my life." In Psych 101 we learned about "approach-avoidance conflicts" and "love-hate relationships." All are examples of people torn between feelings that represent *two conflicting choices*.

What are the two choices that confront any teacher when it is time to mean business? It is always the choice between *discipline* and *instruction*.

In the previous section we emphasized that "discipline comes before instruction." That choice sounds simple until we start to deal with our emotions.

Wise veteran teachers have made their peace with the fact that discipline comes before instruction. They have probably done it both ways and been burned when they tried to ignore reality. Live and learn.

But it is a hard pill for green teachers to swallow. They are far more likely to be torn. Perhaps they even know that they *should* stop and deal with the disruption. But if they have not yet made their peace with the choice – if it still galls them to have to terminate instruction in order to deal with discipline – their ambivalence will show.

Mixed Messages

If you are ambivalent – of two minds – your body language will signal *both* states of mind. When you signal two messages at the same time, you send a "mixed message." Mixed messages represent the body language of *ambivalence*.

As always, the ambivalence that teachers confront in discipline management is the tension between *discipline* and *instruction*. We *want* to continue with instruction while knowing that we *should* stop and deal with the discipline problem.

As a result, teachers are very vulnerable to sending mixed messages at the very moment when they need to be clear, unequivocal, and convincing. The consequence will be continued testing by the disruptive students. After all, they need to know how you deal with such situations. It is unsettling to gamble if you do not know the odds.

The following section will deal with *the discriminative stimuli for meaning business* – the signals students read in

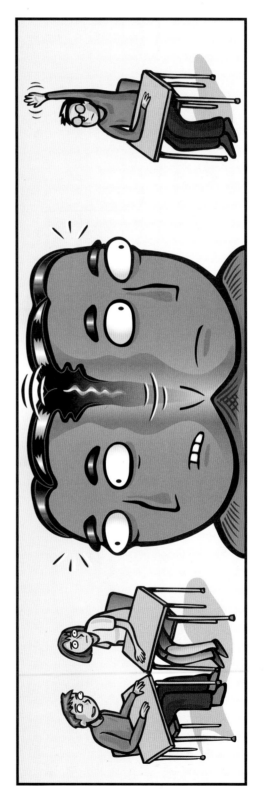

When we are ambivalent we are "of two minds."
In the classroom we are most often torn between discipline and instruction.

your body language that tell them whether or not they need to take you seriously. We will look at both clear messages and mixed messages.

The Turn: Your Physical Response

Turn in a Regal Fashion

After you have committed yourself to dealing with the problem and have excused yourself from Robert, you will, of course, turn toward the disruptive students in order to deal with them. *That* you would turn toward the disruptive students is obvious. *How* you would turn is not.

During training, as an advance organizer for turning toward the disruptive students in a convincing fashion, I demonstrate two different turns. Then I ask the group to choose which one means business more.

The **first** turn takes *three* seconds. I begin by leaning down slowly to say, "Excuse me, Robert." Then:

A thousand and one: I straighten up.

A thousand and two: I point one foot toward the disruptive students and bring my body halfway around.

A thousand and three: I bring my other foot around to complete the turn as I square up to the disruptive students.

After I have completed this turn, the teachers typically look at me as though to say, *Okay, let's see the next one.*

The **second** turn takes *six* seconds. I begin in the same way by leaning down slowly in order to say, "Excuse me, Robert." Then:

A thousand and one: I stay down and breathe in gently.

A thousand and two: I begin to straighten up (about halfway) as I look toward the disruptive students over my shoulder.

A thousand and three: I finish straightening up as I look toward the disruptive students.

A thousand and four: I rotate my shoulders and waist toward the disruptive students.

A thousand and five: I point one foot toward the disruptive students as my hips come around.

A thousand and six: I bring my other foot around to complete the turn as I square up to the disruptive students.

As I am turning slowly, there is almost always a sprinkling of nervous laughter from the group by the time we hit "a thousand and five." It is widespread by the time the turn is finished, and the teacher I have chosen as my target is often laughing or holding up his or her hands saying, "Okay, okay, that's enough."

What is the difference between meaning business and *not* meaning business when you turn toward two disruptive students in the classroom? How about, *three seconds?*

The difference in the effect that these two turns have on both the "target" student and the group as a whole is not subtle. Practice them with some colleagues and see for yourself. This contrast in emotions serves as the first concrete demonstration to the trainees that calm *really is* strength.

What's the difference?

The difference between meaning business and *not* meaning business when you turn toward two disruptive students in the classroom is about *three seconds!*

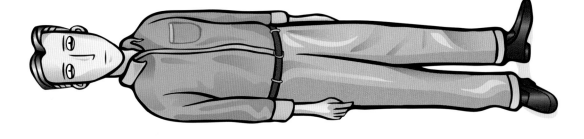

With a partial turn, the teacher has "one foot in and one foot out."

As a means of creating some additional visual imagery to accompany the turn, I have the trainees picture Queen Victoria, the regent of the empire upon which the sun never sets. Then I ask, "Which of these two turns would be right for Queen Victoria?" I repeat the two turns.

The group is unanimous since the slow turn is so clearly "regal" while the faster turn is so ordinary. Consequently, our prompt when we practice turning toward the disruptive students is: "Turn in a *regal* fashion."

However, it is not so easy to turn in a regal fashion. When a drama coach has to train an actor to turn with a regal bearing, there is an entire routine. You turn from the top down in four parts:

- Head
- Shoulders
- Waist
- Feet

This is not the way people would normally turn. Normally, you would lift your foot and turn your body in a single motion. Try doing it this way, and you will find that a six-second turn is nearly impossible. Once you lift your foot, it becomes extremely awkward to stand on one leg for six seconds while trying to turn.

When you slow down in order to turn in a regal fashion, you discover an additional dividend. You have plenty of time to observe the students and to think. In addition, the students have plenty of time to read your meaning. Often, when you slowly turn your head to look at the students, they catch your look and "shape up" before you have to turn the rest of your body.

I have a minimalist approach to discipline management. I want to do the *least work*. If I can turn my body convincingly so that I do not have to walk over to the student,

great! But, if I can turn my head convincingly so that I do not even have to turn my body, better yet!

Point Your Toes

Next during training, I model two additional variations of the turn. Both are done at the proper speed. In both I turn from the top down. The difference is in the *feet*.

The *first* turn is a *partial* turn. Imagine that I am turning toward disruptive students to my *right*. I slowly stand and turn my head, shoulders and waist toward the disruptive students. However, when it gets to my feet, I only pick up my right foot and point it toward the students. I leave my left foot planted as I complete the turn from the waist up.

The *second* turn is a *complete* turn. I do the same turn as before, but I also bring my left foot around so that *both* feet are pointed squarely toward the disruptive students. Once again, there is no doubt among the trainees as to which turn means business more.

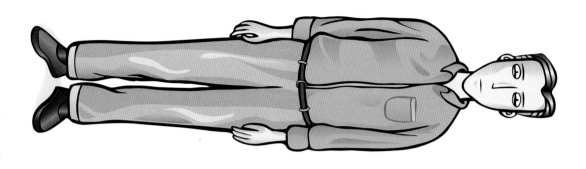

With a complete turn, the teacher has "faced up to the situation."

A partial turn is a classic example of a *tentative gesture*. Tentative gestures bring us back to the topic of *ambivalence*.

Are you *really* done with instruction mentally and emotionally so that you can commit yourself fully to the discipline problem? It is easy to say yes, but the body does not lie. A partial turn leaves the issue of commitment very much in doubt.

Remember, body language allows the other person to *predict what you are going to do next*. In a partial turn your feet are only halfway around. During training, I will relax in this half-turned position and say, "Looking just at my body, predict which way I will move next; to the right (toward discipline) or to the left (toward instruction)." Of course, the group cannot predict. It is a 50/50 call.

Next, I remind the group that there are at least a half-dozen students in any classroom who will have to test you in order to find out whether you will commit to the problem or not. They need to know the price of doing business, don't they?

We have been reading each other's body language for eons. Not too surprisingly, we have many expressions in everyday speech that refer to body language in general and to *ambivalence* in particular. Here is a figure of speech referring to ambivalence that is particularly relevant to the present discussion.

"Well, he has one foot in and one foot out. I wish he would make up his mind!"

With a partial turn, teachers become a living embodiment of this old expression. They literally have one foot in instruction and one foot in discipline. You might say that they are, "riding the fence" or "neither here nor there."

With a complete turn, teachers resolve any ambiguity concerning their commitment. They then embody this old expression:

"It is time to face up to the situation."

In sports terms, your body *telegraphs* your next move. As you can see, it also telegraphs tentativeness. It signals any *ambivalence* you might have toward dealing with the problem.

A partial turn is one of the most common tentative gestures that I observe in the classroom. It almost always accompanies nagging and pheasant posturing. Make it a rule in your classroom *never* to use a partial turn when dealing with a discipline problem. If you do, you will be dealing with the same problem again very soon.

Get a Focal Point

Next, during training, I model two additional variations of the turn. These two variations are differentiated only by the degree of eye contact with the disruptive students.

During the first turn, my eyes glance around the room at other students. My head does not move – only my eyeballs. And, the glances are quick – nothing exaggerated. I am just "checking things out" in the rest of the room as I turn.

During the second turn, I make fixed eye contact with *one* of the disruptive students throughout my standing and turning. Once again, there is no doubt among those trainees in my line of vision as to which turn is more convincing.

Have you ever talked to someone who would not look you in the eye? Typically, furtive eye movement is interpreted as anxiety. In a given situation we might conclude that the other person is lying or is worried about something

In the classroom, such body language usually means that the teacher is worrying about the rest of the classroom while attempting to deal with the disruptive student. The teacher's attention is *split*. The resulting fragmentation of eye contact undermines the perception by the student of cool resolve on the part of the teacher.

With poor eye contact, the disruptive student usually just looks at the teacher impassively as though to say, "What?" Sometimes the student actually says it out loud.

With good eye contact, there is a tension between the teacher and the student that builds with each passing second. This tension represents an expectancy on the part of the teacher. The student almost always understands this expectancy. The teacher, of course, expects the student to *get back to work*.

When the tension builds to the point where it finally dawns on the student that the teacher is serious, the student typically breaks off eye contact and gets back to work. Once again, by clearly signalling commitment, teachers who *mean business* save themselves a trip across the classroom.

Hands Down

When we flex our biceps, we raise our forearms. If we are sick and tired, our hands usually end up on our hips or folded across our chest. If we gesture with our hands while agitated, our gestures are typically animated and waist-high. We have to "go ballistic" before our hand gestures become shoulder-high.

If you relax your body, your hands will be *down* at your side. However, many people feel awkward with their hands just "dangling." You need to have a plan, or those hands will be on the hips before you know it.

You could put them in your pockets, of course. This is a relaxed-looking gesture. For women, however, many items of clothing, such as pleated skirts, lack pockets. Pick a gesture that will be constant and predictable rather than one that must be altered depending on your dress for the day.

There are some advantages to simply putting your hands behind your back. *First*, this is a semiformal posture

Check Your Jaw

Some teachers inadvertently signal tension by setting their jaws, while others smile. Smiling can be a sign of ambivalence as the teacher is torn between "good guy" and "bad guy" roles that have never been sorted out. Their body language says,

Please forgive me for meaning business.

rather than a casual posture and, therefore, more in keeping with setting limits on disruptive students. *Second*, you turn your palms away from your clothing, which reduces cleaning bills due to chalk dust and paint. And *finally*, the students cannot see your arms. This is particularly helpful in the beginning when you are still learning to relax since the last vestige of nervousness is usually some fidgeting with the fingers.

Jaw Down

As the final step in relaxing after trainees have turned in a regal fashion toward the disruptive students, I will give the prompt, "Check your jaw." Setting our jaw or clenching our teeth is one of the most predictable signs of tension in the body.

Nervous tension tends to remain in the jaw muscles even after we have relaxed the rest of the body. Unfortunately, the students can see this gesture from the other side of the gymnasium.

While some teachers will set their jaws while setting limits, others will *smile*. Sometimes this is a sign of ambivalence as the teacher is torn between "good guy" and "bad guy" roles that have never been sorted out. This body language says, *Please forgive me for meaning business.*

When you are relaxed, you have no facial expression at all.

But there are other reasons for many of us smiling when our jaws should be relaxed. We often smile without knowing it because the disruptive students *cause us to smile.*

Smiling is what biologists call a "trigger mechanism." When a person smiles at us, it triggers our smiling back. It is a mild version of submission behavior known as "greeting behavior."

When we catch students goofing off, they typically look up and give us *smiley face* — that ingratiating mixture of mild surprise and feigned innocence that all children use to "get off the hook." "Smiley face" tends to trigger a mild smile from us in response. You may not feel this smile. It is often just a softening of the face around the mouth and eyes that says, *Everything is okay.*

The last thing you want to do while attempting to mean business is to signal students that everything is okay. Rather than shaping up, they *relax.*

This brings us to a well known story about Queen Victoria, our model for *regal* behavior. As the story goes, someone at the royal dinner table told a slightly off-color joke. Since Queen Victoria had little patience for such humor, she looked impassively at the would-be-comedian as the table fell silent. Then she coldly stated to the offending guest the immortal words, *"We are not amused."* That was the "Royal We," of course.

You would do well to think of yourself as Queen Victoria when attempting to mean business. *Relax your jaw.* This is no time to give tacit approval to misbehavior by a softening of the face. Nor, does upset serve any constructive purpose. As students go through their little antics to get off the hook; relax, wait, and give them your best Queen Victoria look that says, *We are not amused.*

Only when the students realize that their antics are getting them nowhere will they consider an alternative strategy. The alternative that you are waiting to see is well understood by students: *Get back to work.*

As a footnote, you should know that "smiley face" is only the beginning of a *series* of ingratiating gestures that have gotten kids "off the hook" since time began. Here are the "three phases of cute." Watch kids play them like a violin.

- Smiley face
- Raised eyebrows
- Head tilted to the side

Have you ever had students in your class who thought they could skate through life just by being cute? Obviously it works for them at home. You will need to help them clearly discriminate that this game does not work in your classroom.

Commitment and Power

The Strength of Our Convictions

Calm is strength, but it is not the only form of power conveyed by you. Commitment is also power. We speak of people having "the strength of their convictions."

During training, teachers will often wrongly attribute the power that comes from commitment not only to their facial expression, but also to irrelevant aspects of their facial expression. They will refer to "the turn" as giving students "the look." Trainees will even refer to the whole process as "staring them down."

You convey *the strength of your convictions*, however, not by your facial expression but, rather, by the *totality* of your body language. Having committed, you simply relax and wait to see what the students will do next. You have no facial expression whatsoever.

Mental Relaxation

Staring them down and *the look* represent the active voice – the language of confrontation. Relaxation is the passive voice. If your thoughts and feelings are adversarial, your body language will show it.

Relinquishing adversarial habits of thought seems to be more difficult than learning to relax the muscles. The fight-flight reflex has a voice of its own that competes with the voice of calm and reason. It shouts into your ear, *You can't just stand there. Do something.*

Teachers often struggle with the notion that *calm is strength.* It may seem sensible at an intellectual level, but it runs against our nature in the heat of the moment.

Yet, until you fully internalize calm, your relaxing breath

Mental Relaxation

Relinquishing adversarial habits of thought seems to be more difficult than learning to relax the muscles.

"Staring them down" and "the look" represent the active voice – the language of confrontation. Relaxation is the passive voice.

will be nothing more than a pause before you return to upset.

Mastery of Meaning Business

Practice Makes Perfect

Body language can only be mastered through practice, practice, practice. Mastery through practice is the main difference between this book and a workshop. Nowhere is this difference greater than in learning the body language of meaning business.

With practice, the many facets of thought and movement described in this chapter become integrated and fluid. As we approach mastery, the delay between the *fight-flight reflex* triggered by the disruptive students and the subsequent *relaxation response* triggered by us becomes shorter and shorter. At mastery the delay approaches zero. At that point we become truly *unflappable*.

Some lucky teachers achieve this level of mastery without formal training. Perhaps it was modeled by their parents throughout their childhood. They are congenitally resistant to stress.

The rest of us must learn to be naturals. However, it won't come just by your trying it a few times. With no more practice than that, you will be one of those teachers who says, "It doesn't work for me."

With adequate training and practice, however, mastery will come, and you will no longer feel the pieces

of performance separately. Instead, you will feel the whole. What once seemed awkward will become second nature.

Meaning Business on the Fly

When you master meaning business, you can do it "on the fly." I can remember a few teachers from my school days who could mean business in the middle of a sentence.

I have a clear picture in my mind of my fifth grade teacher, Mrs. Haines, describing something to the class in an animated fashion. Larry (who was actually in my class) did something disruptive on the far side of the room. In mid-sentence Mrs. Haines stopped and turned her upper body slowly toward Larry as though to say, *I beg your pardon.*

All eyes turned to Larry whose face seemed to say, *Whoops.* As Mrs. Haines waited, Larry came around in his chair and faced forward. After a pause, Mrs. Haines continued as though nothing had happened. Queen Victoria would have been proud.

Mrs. Haines had *finesse.* She was able to say "no" to Larry's behavior in no uncertain terms with very little effort. She was one of the only teachers I had in elementary school who did not want to kill Larry by the end of the year.

The Voice of Upset

The fight-flight reflex has a voice of its own that competes with the voice of calm and reason. It shouts into your ear.

You can't just stand there. Do something.

Chapter Seventeen

Following Through

Preview

- With pseudo-compliance, students give you just enough compliance to get you "off their case."

- Pseudo-compliance is all about cutting deals. It is how disruptive students establish the price of doing business with parents and teachers.

- The question in the minds of disruptive students is *Do I have to?* The asking of that question and our answering it constitute the conversation in body language that we call *meaning business.*

- This chapter takes us beyond "the turn" in dealing with disruptive students who are playing games at every opportunity.

- When done properly, the body language of meaning business is invisible. Consequently, it protects disruptive students from embarrassment in front of their peers.

Beyond "The Turn"

No Guarantee

The conversation in body language described in the preceding chapter was complex but brief. The teacher has done nothing more than terminate instruction, relax, turn, and commit to dealing with the disruption.

Let's assume that the students see "the turn" and respond by looking at the teacher – usually with a bit of "smiley face." Often they will get back to work. Or, at least, they may *appear* to get back to work.

But discipline management is an indoor sport. Basketball players know how to fake, and poker players know how to bluff.

Students know how to do both at the same time.

Maybe the students would just like you to *think* that they are getting back to work. How could you know what the students *really* plan to do next? You must be able to see into the future.

Fortunately, you *can* see into the future. You can predict the students' behavior by reading their body language just as they read yours.

The Conversation Continues

"The turn" is only the beginning of a conversation in body language. If the students decide to test you, the conversation may become quite lengthy and complex.

In this chapter we will assume that the students *do not* intend to get back to work. We will also assume that they know how to *appear* to get back to work. They would love to fake you out so that you would leave them alone.

This little battle of wills between teacher and student is part of everyday classroom life. It will provide a vehicle for analyzing the complex dialogue in body language that often accompanies meaning business.

Predicting Noncompliance

Look at the Feet

In the two pictures to the right, both students in each picture have gotten back to work after *the turn*. Can you tell which pair will keep working and which pair will start talking again as soon as your back is turned?

It's not much of a mystery, is it? When I have two teachers model these positions during a workshop, the whole room will pick the students on this page as having no intention whatsoever of getting back to work.

What is the critical feature of body language that allows every teacher in the room to predict the future? It is the lower body – *knees and feet.*

The body language above the desk top is called "window dressing" – a pretty display that is intended to impress potential "consumers." In this case, the students are *faking* compliance with their upper bodies while their lower bodies signal their true intent.

In sports such as basketball and football, every coach and player knows that you *fake* with the upper body and *commit* with the lower body. After all, the body must follow the feet. That is why the coach tells the players to *watch the body, not the ball.* Discipline management is an indoor sport, and savvy teachers will watch the body.

Pseudo-compliance

In the picture of window dressing below, the students are giving you the *appearance* of compliance while actually *withholding it.* In previous chapters we have called this partial compliance *pseudo-compliance.*

Pseudo-compliance lulls you into a false sense of closure so that you prematurely terminate supervision and abort follow-through. By way of review, the four phases of

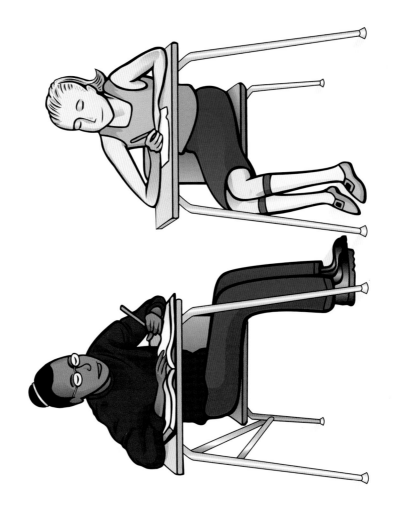

If the students intend to continue talking, their body language will usually give it away.

pseudo-compliance to look for as you observe students getting back to work are:

- **Smiley face:** They give you the look of repentant angels asking, *Who, me?*
- **Book posing:** They open their books and look back at you as though to ask, *Does this fulfill the requirements of formal education?*

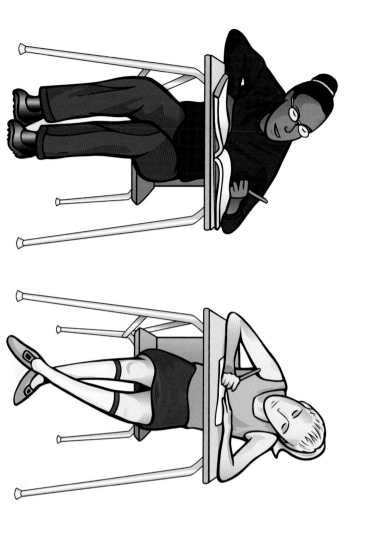

- **Pencil posing:** They get out a pencil and touch it to paper before looking back at you as though to say, *Look, I'm writing.*
- **Pseudo-scholarship:** They start to write, but they look up periodically to see if you are still paying attention.

Let me emphasize that I do not care how students sit in class while they are working. Rather, the topic being addressed here is how you as a teacher discriminate *change* in the students' behavior from goofing off to time-on-task.

The present chapter is an extension of the discussion, begun in the preceding chapter, about *reading pseudo-compliance.* Now that you have turned toward the disruptive students and they seem to have gotten back to work, how can you tell whether they will continue to work? Have you accomplished your objective yet, or are the students still playing with you?

Cutting Deals

Children love to *cut deals* with adults. Pseudo-compliance is all about cutting deals. You might say that pseudo-compliance is how children establish the price of doing business with their parents and teachers.

Imagine, for example, that you ask your four-year-old daughter to pick up the blocks. She picks up *half* of the blocks and then stops and turns to you as though to say, *Is this good enough?*

If you say, "Thank you for helping. Let's go have lunch," you have just defined with your actions the meaning of the phrase, *Pick up the blocks.* And you have given your daughter a good idea of what "finishing a job" entails. The next time you ask her to do a job, you will be *lucky* if she does half of it.

Imagine, instead, that you persist, aware that you are teaching your child what it means to *do a job.* "Now, pick

If the students are focused on the assignment, their body language will telegraph that too.

...Until We Get It Right

> Turn a blind eye to a half-finished job because it is not worth your time and effort to follow through, and you will have a child who believes that half-baked is just fine.

up the rest of the blocks," you say. Your daughter, of course, will protest the higher cost of doing business with some fussing and whining.

But if you keep your toes pointed and your mouth shut at this critical juncture, the protestations will slowly die down. Eventually, your daughter will grudgingly pick up some more blocks.

Imagine that, with two-thirds of the blocks picked up, your daughter again stops and turns to you as though to ask, *Is this good enough?* As always, pseudo-compliance has to do with cutting deals. In body language your daughter is saying, "I have just done you a *big* favor by picking up some more of these stupid blocks. This is a deal I only cut for preferred customers. You should be thrilled. I recommend that you take this offer."

If you say, "Oh, good. That is enough for now. Let's go have lunch," you have just defined two-thirds finished as the equivalent of "done." This child knows she has a sucker for a parent.

Children are little power junkies. They want their way. Call it "infantile omnipotence." And, if they cannot get *all* of their way, they will fight to get at least *some* of their way. If you persist until your daughter does 90 percent of the job, but she withholds doing 10 percent of the job, in her

little child's mind, "She didn't *have to*." Do not be surprised if she "steps over the line" as soon as your back is turned just to prove to herself that she didn't have to.

But what if you hang in there until *all* of the blocks are picked up? It takes time, of course. And, you will need a few relaxing breaths to get you through the fussing. But, your daughter will eventually learn that, when you ask her to do a job, you expect it to be done *right*. Life in this household embodies those timeless elements of parenting wisdom:

I say what I mean, and I mean what I say.

and

We are going to keep doing this until we get it right.

Doing it *right* is, in fact, an act of *submission* on the part of the child – submission to the will of the parent. As such, it is the end of the struggle. Over time, your daughter's fussing and whining when asked to do something will weaken as she learns that such efforts are futile. You will have to go through this process more than once before you teach your child to help around the house without a lot of fussing.

But if you want your child to be a fusser and whiner, all you have to do is *crack* once or twice. Be a *weenie*. Turn a blind eye to a half-finished job because it is not worth your time and effort to follow through, and you will have a child who believes that half-baked is just fine.

As we continue our conversation in body language with disruptive students in the classroom, we will learn a lot more about pseudo-compliance. The disruptive students continually ask, "Is this good enough?" as they attempt to cut deals. Their asking and our answering constitute the heart of the conversation in body language.

Move the Body, Not the Mouth

Your Next Move

Let's imagine that, after committing to the disruptive students, you see only window dressing. You rightly conclude that the students have no intention of continuing to work. What next?

Actually, the next move is no strategic tour-de-force. You will have to go over to the disruptive students in order to deal with the situation.

As obvious as this response may seem, it is very common for teachers to act *tentatively* at this critical point in the "conversation." No doubt this is because walking over to the students is both distracting and time-consuming.

Beware of Silly Talk

"Silly talk" is our label for silly things that parents and teachers say to wayward children instead of swinging into action. It is a form of *pheasant posturing*. It is very tempting for adults to try to talk their way out of meaning business. After all, talk is cheap. Maybe the students will repent in response to some hot air?

We described silly talk in chapter fourteen. By way of review, here are some time-honored examples:

"Billy, what are you supposed to be doing?"

"Billy, this is the second time I've had to talk to you."

"Billy, am I going to have to come over there?"

Walk, Don't Talk

If we could do discipline management with our mouths, all children would be nagged to righteousness before their third birthday. Shut the mouth, take two relaxing breaths, and walk over to the disruptive students.

Now, let me ask you a question. Have you ever started to walk toward disruptive students only to have them turn around in their chairs and face forward before you had even taken three steps? What just happened?

As you might imagine, you have just communicated with the students in body language. The question for the students was, *Do we have to?* In their experience, parents often do a little pheasant posturing in situations like this and then turn away. Inquiring minds want to know, *are you like those other adults, or do you have to be taken seriously?*

Obviously, the only way to find out is to test you. They will give you a little pseudo-compliance to see if it will get them off the hook. If it does, they now know that they can "blow you off" with impunity.

When you keep your mouth shut and walk toward the students, you answer the question that they were asking with pseudo-compliance. They asked, *Do I have to?* and you answered, *Yes*. When they turned around in their chairs to face forward, they said, *That's all I wanted to know. I'm not in this for high stakes.*

The Body Language Poker Game

Students Are Gamblers

The best analogy to the conversation in body language between the teacher and the disruptive students is a *poker game*. Poker, as you know, is a form of gambling. You do not have to condone gambling to understand the analogy.

Students are born gamblers. When they disrupt, they are betting that they can get away with it. But, they have to test the teacher in order to find out the exact odds in this classroom.

If the students can win easily, they will gamble like bandits all year long. But if they cannot easily "get away with it," they must gamble conservatively. As a teacher, you want a roomful of very conservative gamblers.

Basic Rules

Poker is a simple game. You are either *in* or you are *out*. If you are in, you either match or raise the bet. If you are out, you fold.

In the body language poker game, the teachers fold when they *turn away* from the disruptive students *before the students have folded by giving up the game and getting back to work.* When this happens, the students immediately return to goofing off.

Bluffing

Pseudo-compliance is bluffing on the part of the students. They may not want to stay in the game until the stakes get high, but they can afford a modest raise to see if you are ready to fold. You will have to stay in the game and meet raise with raise if you ever expect to see the students give up the game and return to work.

Nagging and pheasant posturing represent bluffing on the part of the teacher. The teacher seems to be doing something about the problem when, in fact, nothing of any consequence is being done.

A note to the uninitiated. You cannot fool a child. Children can smell a bluff a mile away, so don't try.

You play this game *straight up.* You raise with your time and effort. Talk is cheap. It gets no respect at the poker table.

Moving In

We will slow down the action as the teacher walks over to the disruptive students. We will examine the moves of the poker game in their logical sequence as we give them labels.

As in "the turn," the conversation in body language as the teacher walks toward the disruptive students is very rich and subtle. The analogy of the poker game holds up quite well as both the teacher and the students make decisions to raise or fold.

For this generic walk-through, we will, as usual, imagine typical students who are engaged in *talking to neighbors.* Students with histories of child abuse whose "personal space" is quite large will have a "hair trigger" in response to a teacher approaching. We will deal with those students in a later chapter. For now, think "typical child."

Say Their Names

Imagine that you are "moving in" on the two students pictured earlier, call them Tameka and Kathy. Sometimes the students are so consumed with their conversation that they fail to notice you. In this case, say their names. Use a flat tone of voice, neither sweet nor upset.

Shrewd gamblers, however, keep an eye out for the teacher. When you look at them, they will usually catch you out of the corners of their eyes. However, do not get hung up on direct eye contact at this point. Cultural norms vary.

Nagging and pheasant posturing represent bluffing by the teacher.

Smiley Face
Imagine that, in response to seeing your turn or hearing their names, Tameka and Kathy give you smiley face

*Students know when to hold 'em,
and they know when to fold 'em.*

followed by the pseudo-scholarship pictured earlier. You instinctively check the knees and the feet, and you realize that you have so far accomplished *nothing*.

Walk

Take two relaxing breaths, omit silly talk, and walk slowly over to Tameka and Kathy. Pick one of them as your focus, preferably the instigator. In this case it happens to be Kathy.

Walk to the edge of her desk so that you can barely touch her desk with your legs. Stand relaxed but upright and take two relaxing breaths. Check your jaw.

It is now Kathy's move. She has two choices. She can either fold by turning forward and getting back to work, or she can continue to play.

Half a Loaf

We will imagine throughout this example that the students continue the game by raising the teacher. However, we will look at the subtle, incremental raises of the shrewd gambler rather than the clumsy play of the student who becomes easily rattled. Clumsy players make rash moves like backtalk.

The next move of the shrewd gambler is pseudo-compliance. Kathy raises you by scooting her chair *half-way around*. We will call this move "giving the teacher half a loaf." Rather than giving you what you want, Kathy has given you only *part* of what you want. In the language of negotiations, she just said, *I will give you half of what you asked for. I am gambling that you want out of here badly enough to take my offer.*

Imagine that you, also being shrewd, notice this partial gesture, even stepping back to look under the desk to see feet if necessary. Rather than being satisfied with "half a loaf," you realize that you have just been raised.

Raising with Pseudo-compliance

By now, you probably see the pattern emerging. The way in which students typically up the ante is with *pseudo-compliance.* Pseudo-compliance is a less risky strategy than defiance. For this reason, we must become astute observers of *partial gestures.*

Visual Prompt

Seeing a raise rather than a fold, you instinctively up the ante. You *raise* Kathy in this situation by giving her a prompt. A prompt is simply a message that tells her what to do next.

Lean over gently, resting your weight on one palm, and gesture with your other hand for Kathy to bring her chair around. Stay down, wait, maintain eye contact, and take a relaxing breath.

Begin with a *visual* prompt because it is safer than a *verbal* prompt. Speech, like smiling, is a *trigger mechanism.* The most predictable way of getting someone to speak to you is by speaking to them. Consequently, a verbal prompt by you raises the odds of a verbal reply by the student. This would make the situation unnecessarily complicated.

Another Partial Turn

Typically, the student would bring his or her chair all of the way around. But we will assume, for the sake of analysis, that Kathy once again gives *partial* compliance. Her chair comes three-quarters of the way around.

You could, of course, repeat the visual prompt. Let's assume, however, that after one or maybe two visual prompts, you are still looking at partial compliance. Seeing this, you up the ante once again.

Verbal Prompt

You now *tell* Kathy to bring her chair *all of the way around.* Speaking to Kathy increases the risk of backtalk, but you have little choice. A simple sentence in a kindly tone of voice is sufficient.

"Please bring your chair all of the way around."

Usually, the student complies. The specificity of the teacher's prompt leaves her very little room for "playing dumb." To stay in the game with one more raise, the student must engage in a blatant act of *noncompliance.* The student has pushed *pseudo*-compliance about as far as it can go.

Student Choices

Blatant noncompliance in this situation usually takes the form of backtalk.

"I wasn't doing anything."

"He was talking to me."

"Hey, leave me alone."

With backtalk, the price of playing poker escalates dramatically. Instead of pennies, nickels, and dimes, backtalk gets us into serious betting.

Backtalk will be the subject of the next two chapters. It is a sufficiently taxing subject to be worthy of its own space.

For now, it is enough to realize that most students, even the mouthy ones, are penny-ante gamblers. They just look brave because they have been winning with penny and nickel bets for so long.

The way in which students up the ante is with pseudo-compliance.

Teacher Choices

We will assume that Kathy has concluded, as most students do in this situation, that discretion is the greater part of valor. She has turned all of the way around in response to your prompt, and she is working.

You can probably remember teachers when you were a kid who told you to bring your chair *all of the way around.* That teacher knew a thing or two about pseudo-compliance. You may have "made a face" as you complied, realizing that the teacher was on to your game.

Returning to our scene with Kathy, it would seem at this point that you have achieved your objective and that the game is over. Far from it, you have just arrived at a crucial juncture, one which dooms the efforts of many teachers.

Palms

Rest your weight on both palms and lock your elbows as though to say, *I have all day.* Relax your hands, making sure that you are neither up on your fingertips (I want out of here) or making a fist (I am anxious). Take two relaxing breaths as you *watch* and *wait.*

Watch the student work long enough to see a *stable pattern of work that represents a commitment to time-on-task.* Wait long enough, for example, to see Kathy write a few sentences or do a math problem.

It is not too late for pseudo-compliance on the part of the student. Kathy may actually get to work, or she may just *appear* to get to work. As you watch and wait, look for signs that the student is still "gaming" you.

> When students finally give up the game, they will focus on their work instead of the teacher.

Eyes Up – Eyes Down

If Kathy is still more concerned with you than with the assignment, she will keep checking to see what you are doing. When Kathy finally gives up the game, she will focus on the work and quit worrying about you.

The most predictable sign that the student is still "playing off of the teacher" is *eyes up – eyes down.* Kathy looks up briefly as though to say, *Oh, are you still here?* When she sees that you have not budged, her eyes go back down to her work.

As you watch and wait at "palms," Kathy may check you out several times. Each time she does, her behavior tells you to *hang in there.* The game is not over yet.

Eye Prompts

A variation on *eyes up – eyes down* is for the student to look up and *not* look down. This could mean any of a number of things from defiance to simply waiting for another prompt. It is hard to tell. However, this leaves you and the student eye to eye. The situation becomes more awkward the longer you are locked into looking at each other.

Finesse the situation by giving the student an "eye prompt." The simplest eye prompt is to look down at the student's work. You have said, in effect, *All I care about is the work.*

To make an eye prompt more convincing, turn your upper body if you are in front of the student so that you can read his or her work right side up. This more clearly says, *All I care about is the work.*

Thank the Student

After the gaming has stopped and Kathy is fully engaged in working, thank her for getting to work. A simple sentence is sufficient, and touching is optional. Your emotions go from neutral to warm as you thank the student so that your tone of voice is gentle.

"Thank you for getting back to work."

After you thank Kathy, *stay down* and take *two relaxing breaths* as your emotions again become neutral. Watch and wait until Kathy once again demonstrates a stable pattern of work.

The most common error is to thank the student and then *stand up*. If you do this, do not be surprised if the student quits working. Thanking the student is not only common courtesy, but it is also a *closure message.* It says, *That is what I wanted.*

Many students, unfamiliar with both common courtesy and closure messages, misinterpret this closure message. They think it means, *You have done everything that you need to do, and I am now finished dealing with you.* Consequently, I have seen students look up with a relieved smile and lay down their pencils.

Therefore, after you thank Kathy, *stay down.* Watch and wait until she *recommits* to the task. Her behavior then says, *Oh, I guess I had better keep working, huh?*

Repeat the Process with the Second Student

Give both students equal time. If you do not, the first student feels picked on, and the second student feels as though he or she faked you out.

Move gently to Tameka and stay at palms. Watch her work for a while until you get the definite feeling that she is "into the assignment."

"Second students" are usually in compliance when you get to them since they are trying to disappear. They rarely need a separate prompt. But reprompt Tameka if she is not facing all of the way forward.

Finally, thank Tameka and *stay down* just as you did with Kathy. Wait until both students are fully at work.

Typical Error

The typical error in "moving in" is for teachers to *leave too quickly.* As you can see from the preceding example, the greatest investment in "moving in" is *staying after you arrive.*

It takes time to wait out the gaming. The students are struggling with the issue of submitting their agenda (socializing) to your agenda (time-on-task). They do not want to submit their entire agenda, so they test to see how much of it they can retain. There is no way to speed up this process of testing.

Moving Out

The Game Continues

Even after the game *appears* to be over, it may continue. Pseudo-compliance can be reformulated into the question, *How long do I have to keep working?* As any parent knows, it is not uncommon for children to go back to what they *were* doing as soon as your back is turned.

We will choreograph your "moving out" just as carefully as your "moving in." Moving out is straightforward in this simple scenario.

Testing The Limits

Pseudo-compliance can be reformulated into the question,

How long do I have to keep working?

Stay Until You Make Your Point

When teachers go to the trouble of "moving in" only to leave too quickly, they literally undo what they just did.

breath and wait until it is clear that everyone is working.

Walk and Buttonhook

As you leave Kathy and Tameka, you may momentarily turn your back toward them as you walk away. Before you become involved with another student, however, turn *fully* and "point your toes" toward the two disruptors. Should they glance up, they will see a teacher quite willing to return.

As you begin to help the next student, buttonhook so that the students you just left are in your *direct line of vision*. It is not uncommon to get "eyes up – eyes down" at this late stage of the game. This should serve as a reminder to you to continue tracking Tameka and Kathy. You are not done with meaning business. You will probably remain on alert for a resumption of goofing off for the rest of the period.

Slowing Down

Slow Is Difficult

After practicing "moving in" and "moving out" during training, I will ask the teachers, "Did you feel that the entire process took a *huge* amount of time – much more than you are used to giving it?" They will respond in unison, "Yes!"

Stand and Wait

Stand slowly after thanking the second student, and take two relaxing breaths. If you get "eyes up – eyes down," take an extra relaxing breath and wait until it is clear that everyone is working.

It does not get complicated until the next chapter when we deal with back-talk and "cheap shots."

The contrast between our normal speed of movement in the classroom and the speed of meaning business is so great that it must be appreciated. Of course, this perception only lasts until we get our internal clocks recalibrated. With the detailed description provided above, you could structure some practice with a colleague fairly accurately.

While slowing down is difficult, the relaxing breaths *pace* you. Relaxed breathing, however, is the *first* skill of meaning business to be *lost* after training as forgetting takes its toll on learning. The result is a gradual increase in the speed of performance. For this reason, follow-up practice is as important as the practice of initial acquisition in creating a stable pattern of performance.

School site trainers are taught to look for the following comment from trainees in the weeks immediately after training.

"You know, I am using body language to set limits, and it works. But, I have to keep doing it over and over with the same students."

When teachers go to the trouble of *moving in* only to leave too quickly, they literally undo what they just did. The students look up to see the teacher gone and think, *Gee, that wasn't as big a deal as I thought it was going to be.*

Slow Is Expensive

It is impossible to practice the limit setting sequence without realizing how *expensive* it is. More than the effort involved, it takes *time!* It is natural, therefore, to want to *economize.* Discipline management, after all, must be cheap to be affordable.

How can something so expensive ever be cheap? The way in which we achieve the necessary economy will determine whether or not we are successful at meaning business in the long run.

False Economies

Nag, Nag, Nag

The most common way in which teachers save themselves the time and effort of "moving in" and "moving out" is *nag, nag, nag.*

"Phillip and Peter! Would you please quit talking and turn around in your seats?"

Nagging doesn't work in the long run, but it can be cathartic in the short run. Maybe that is why we keep doing it.

Speeding Up

Another false economy is to *speed up*, often done unconsciously in order to get the whole thing over with. As we just discussed, this naturally occurs following training unless we continue to work on our skills.

However, continuing to work on newly acquired management skills is the exception in education rather than the rule. Our natural impatience combined with poor follow-up for training at the school site makes speeding up fairly common.

True Economies

Training

Meaning business is a matter of both skill and consistency. We must be highly predictable.

Let us imagine, for example, that it is the first day of school, and Larry is in your class. Larry, naturally, will be the first student to test you. All of the other students know this. Consequently, Larry serves as their "point man."

Larry is looking for answers to important management questions. Will you see me goofing off? Will you pretend that you do not see me? Will you do anything about it?

Will you do anything effective? Everybody wants to know who you really are, and Larry wants to know right now.

So, early in the day, you look up to see Larry goofing off by talking when he should be working. Larry may not even be tracking you as he begins to fool around, making a show of nonchalance. Consequently, after the turn you might have to say his name. Larry looks up as though to say, *Who, me?*

To make a long story short, you set limits exactly as we described earlier in the chapter complete with *moving in* and *moving out*. Larry cools it for now. Yet, while Larry was impressed, he is far from repentant. He will have to give you another try.

Later on, Larry pulls the same stunt, and once again, you commit, willing to pay whatever price it takes. You "turn in a regal fashion" and say his name. Larry looks up to see a familiar sight. He is beginning to understand that the first time was no fluke.

Larry must now make a choice. Does he want you to stay where you are, or does he want you to walk over to where he is? At this point, the fact that children are power junkies comes to your aid. Larry wants you to stay where you are. What is the only possible way in which these objectives can be achieved? You guessed it - *get to work!*

When Larry finally wises up enough to make this decision, you have saved your-

---

The Fruit of Consistency

If Larry knows that he cannot win with any of his tricks, all he eventually needs to see is a sign that "the inexorable process" has begun in order to know that it is time to fold.

self the trip across the classroom. The size of your response is getting smaller. It has gone from a *physical* response (moving in and moving out) to *verbal* response (saying his name and waiting). This is a major economy.

But, Larry, being Larry, will have to try you again. Only, this time he is tracking you visually. You have made yourself "significant," so to speak. When you see Larry, Larry sees you.

This time, you can dispense with saying his name as you just turn in a regal fashion and wait. Since Larry folded on this raise the last time, chances are he will fold again this time. Your response has now gone from *physical* to *verbal* to *nonverbal*. You have looked Larry back to work.

The time may come when you can look Larry back to work without even standing and turning. But your ability to do this is predicated on Larry's *belief* that you will pay whatever price you need to pay at any time in order to create time-on-task.

Larry's behavior, therefore, is based not so much on what you are doing now, but rather on your *history* with him. You have taught him to *believe that you will pay* – any time and anywhere. Shrewd gamblers do not throw good money after bad. Larry is learning to fold early.

As you can see, there is no mystery to this process. It is straightforward training. Once you shape the response you want, you can fade the prompts without losing the response.

> **Larry's behavior is based not so much on what you are doing now, but, rather, on your history with Larry.**

As a dividend to your willingness to pay up front *every time* in order to make a believer out of Larry, the amount of work required on your part steadily decreases. If Larry knows that he *cannot win* with any of his tricks, all he eventually needs to see is a sign that "the inexorable process" has begun in order to know that it is time to fold.

The time will eventually come when the unwavering enforcement of your standards becomes synonymous with *your physical presence.* In effect, showing up for work is body language for, *The entire management system is now in effect because it just walked into the room.* This is when *meaning business* truly becomes *cheap.*

Only through this process of training does meaning business finally become *invisible.* A green teacher observing your classroom would, unfortunately, learn nothing about your skills because you are not obviously using them anymore. More accurately, the skills required to train the class are now needed only intermittently in order to maintain the training. As far as the observer is concerned, however, you were once again assigned all of the good kids.

Working the Crowd

An entirely different way of thinking about making meaning business cheap is to realize that *moving in* and *working the crowd* are related. Walking toward a student who is disrupting is always a powerful intervention. That is why students so often "shape up" before you even get there.

You might think of *working the crowd* and *moving in* while meaning business as the *preventative* and *remedial* versions of the same thing. The more you use your body language to prevent disruptions by working the crowd, the less often you will have to stop what you are doing to mean business.

Camouflage

The Big Shootout

As a closing thought, let's imagine moving in on a couple of tough kids, maybe seventeen years old, with reputations and a few buddies in the class. After you turn in a regal fashion and say their names, you walk slowly toward them.

Can you imagine their buddies chiming in as you walk closer?

"Hey Larry, here he comes."

Does this remind you of "The Shootout At The O.K. Corral?" Are you getting uncomfortable yet? You should be.

You have just made discipline management into *theater*, and Larry's peer group is the *audience*. Larry cannot back down now. You have just violated one of the most basic rules of meaning business:

Don't go public if you can help it.

You need *camouflage.* Camouflage allows you to mean business without making it into a public spectacle.

How can you mask what you are doing so that you do not embarrass Larry and back him into a corner? Fortunately, you have all of the camouflage you need. The natural cover for moving in is *working the crowd.*

Moving in with Camouflage

Imagine that, as you are working the crowd while helping students, you catch Larry goofing off on the far side of the room. He catches your eye as you look up.

You excuse yourself, stand slowly and turn in a regal fashion. Larry has seen this before. But as you begin to cruise toward Larry, you stop casually and look at another student's work. You may not care about that student's work right now, but you act as though you did. For now, you are spending a moment with that student is camouflage. It is your normal pattern of interaction as you work the crowd.

After looking at the work for a moment, you turn and stroll toward Larry, maintaining eye contact with Larry for an extra split second as you move. You are talking to Larry with your body language, and, chances are, Larry is reading it very accurately. You are saying, *I see you fooling around, and it is the main thing on my mind right now. I am coming over there as I normally would in working the crowd. Is there something better that*

---

you might be doing by the time I get there?

You walk a few steps more and casually interact with another student. As you turn to leave, you once again point yourself toward Larry a little more directly than usual and maintain eye contact for an extra split second. You are asking Larry the same question that you asked a moment earlier. Perhaps you interact with yet another student before you finally get to Larry.

Now, ask yourself, how stupid would Larry have to be to get "caught" fooling around? He can see it coming *a mile away.* To get into trouble, he would have to *want* to get into trouble.

Most students, even Larry, do not *want* a hassle. They just want to play a little. It is penny-ante gambling. They do not want to constantly run the price of poker up to the point where gambling becomes serious business.

By the time you get to Larry, the problem, in all likelihood, will have evaporated. When you get to Larry's desk, the two of you share a knowing look. Enough said.

Win-Win or Lose-Lose

Larry has played this game long enough to appreciate what you just did. Your skill and finesse allow you to teach that "no means no," while protecting him from embarrassment.

Over the years I have come to appreciate a simple truth about discipline management. At the level of everyday fooling around, there is no such thing as a "win-win" or "lose-lose." It is "win-win" or "lose-lose." If you embarrass students in front of their peer group, they will embarrass you in front of the same peer group to get even. And, you will not have to wait until tomorrow.

Natural teachers have *finesse*. They have the social skills to get their way without upsetting students. Most of that finesse comes from the subtle body language of meaning business.

Win-Win Management

At the level of everyday fooling around, there is no such thing as a "win-lose" situation.

If you embarrass students in front of their peer group, they will embarrass you in front of the same peer group to get even. And, you will not have to wait until tomorrow.

Chapter Eighteen

Eliminating Backtalk

Setting You Up

Fight-Flight Reflexes Again

Imagine that you walk over to Larry who is goofing off, and you give him a prompt to get back to work as described in the preceding chapter. Instead of facing forward as most students would, Larry looks up at you and says:

"I wasn't doin' anything. Why don't you just get out of my face and leave me alone?"

All eyes in the class immediately snap toward you. On every student's face is an expression that says, *Wow! What are you going to do about that Mr. Jones?*

To say that you feel *vulnerable* right now is probably an understatement. Larry has just "gone public" – exactly what meaning business tries to avoid. He has made *theater* out of discipline management, and his classmates are all eyes and ears.

There are very few things that a student can do more calculated to upset the teacher than backtalk. By challenging you in front of the entire class, the student says, in effect:

"Hey, you guys! Look over here! This teacher is trying to tell me what to do. I want you all to know that he can't because he isn't in control of this situation. I am!"

Preview

- To understand the management of backtalk, think in terms of two time frames — a short-term response and a long-term response.

- The short-term response is measured in seconds. It has to do with the fight-flight reflex. If you go to your brainstem instead of relaxing and staying calm, all is lost.

- Backtalk is sudden and threatening and public. Both the fight-flight reflex and the fact that speech is a trigger mechanism set you up to speak.

- The Cardinal Error in dealing with backtalk is to speak. The student will play off of whatever you say in order to create a melodrama.

- If you keep your mouth shut in the short-term, backtalk will usually die out. In the long-term you can do whatever you think is appropriate.

If you fail to have a fight-flight reflex under these conditions, you may need to consult a mortician. The rest of us will be sucking in a breath.

Setting You Up to Speak

If you have a fight-flight reflex, you are predisposed to speak. Nagging, pheasant posturing, and snap and snarl are common classroom examples. In addition, as we mentioned in the previous chapter, speech is a *trigger mechanism*. The most predictable way of getting someone to speak to you is for you to speak to them.

When students confront you verbally, everything they are doing seems calculated to *get you to speak*. Could there be a method to this madness?

The Cardinal Error

Having the Last Word

Let's begin with an example of the *garden variety wheedling* that is most common in the classroom. This will be a less emotionally charged situation than the one described above.

The simplest form of wheedling is denial. Denial requires perhaps three neurons.

"I wasn't doin' anything."

"Was not."

"He was asking me a question."

To denial we will add its companion, blaming.

"She started it."

Finally, to this display of garden variety wheedling, we will add a teacher who is committing the *Cardinal Error*. The Cardinal Error when dealing with backtalk is *backtalk*. Taking the scene from the top, it might go like this:

Teacher: "Vanessa, I would like you to bring your chair around and get some work done."

Student: "I wasn't doing anything."

Teacher: "You have been talking this whole period, and I want it to stop."

Student: "No I wasn't."

Teacher: "Every time I look up, I see you talking to Serena."

Student: "She was just asking me a question."

Teacher: "I don't care who was asking who what. When I look up, I expect to see you doing your own work."

Student: "Yeah, but..."

Have you had enough yet? Who do you think will look foolish by the time this conversation winds down?

When you were four years old, you already had the social skills required to have the last word in an argument if you wanted it badly enough. All it takes is perseverance.

The First Rule of Backtalk

Two children arguing is a fairly common sight to a parent. But watching a child and a teacher argue is a bit disconcerting – which brings us to our *first rule* of backtalk:

It takes one fool to backtalk.

It takes two fools to make a conversation out of it.

It takes one fool to backtalk.

It takes two fools to make a conversation out of it.

The first fool is the *child*. Children will be foolish sometimes, but the normal immaturity of children does not worry me. What worries me is the *second* fool. The second fool is always the *teacher*. It is the teacher's backtalk that will get this student sent to the office.

One of the most common scenarios for a student being sent to the office is the following:

- The student mouths off.
- The teacher responds.
- The student mouths off.
- The teacher responds.
- The student mouths off.
- The teacher responds.
- The student mouths off.
- The teacher responds.
- The student mouths off.

Open your mouth, and slit your throat.

By this point in the conversation, teachers will realize that they have dug their hole so deep that the only way out is to "pull rank." That is why backtalk is the most common complaint in office referrals.

Roles in a Melodrama

Think of backtalk as a melodrama which is written, produced, and directed by the *student*. In this melodrama there is a speaking part for *you*.

If you accept your speaking part in the melodrama, it is "show time." But if you do not, the show bombs. This brings us to our *second* rule of backtalk:

Open your mouth, and slit your throat.

Imagine the conversation between teacher and student described earlier if the teacher had had the good sense to keep his or her *mouth shut*.

Teacher: "Vanessa, I would like you to bring your chair around and get some work done."

Student: "I wasn't doing anything."

Teacher: (silence)

Student: "Well, I wasn't."

Teacher: (silence)

Student: "But,"

Teacher: (silence)

Student: (silence)

Students may try to keep the show going for a while, but they cannot keep it going *all by themselves*. When they run out of material, embarrassment sets in. When students begin to feel foolish, they usually fold. Getting back to work suddenly becomes the quickest way to disappear.

If you talk, you actually *rescue* backtalkers from their dilemma. It is like throwing a lifeline to a drowning person. By playing off of whatever you say, he or she can keep the show alive and avoid "going down for the third time."

A Comedy Routine

Think of backtalk as a comedy routine – a classroom comedy duo. There are many duos in the history of comedy: Laurel and Hardy, Abbot and Costello, Burns and Allen, Martin and Lewis.

Comedy duos all have a predictable format. There is a "clown" and a "straight man." The straight man sets up the jokes by delivering "straight lines" like:

"How bad was it?"

"Then what happened?"

"Why did you do that?"

In the classroom comedy duo, the student is the clown and the teacher is the straight man. The clown plays off of the lines delivered by the teacher.

Ironically, no matter how much you may hate backtalk, when you speak, you become the disruptive student's *partner*. This brings us to our *third* rule of backtalk:

If the students want to backtalk,
at least make them do all of the work.
Don't do half of it for them!

Think of backtalk as self-limiting. You have to feed it to make it grow. If you do not feed it, it will starve. Or, think

of it this way. Opening your mouth is like throwing gasoline on a fire. Do you want it to die down or blow up in your face?

Types of Backtalk

Few things trigger a fight-flight reflex more predictably than surprise. The backtalk itself is usually a surprise, but what the student says can also be a shock.

If we can reduce the surprise factor inherent in backtalk, we can reduce the probability of a fight-flight reflex. For that reason, it is useful to know exactly what to expect.

Fortunately for us, backtalk is one of the *least* creative endeavors of the disruptive student. Mouthy students have been saying the same things since little Babylonian kids went to school.

With adequate preparation, you can respond to backtalk with emotional nonchalance. When you completely relax your jaw in this situation, you look *bored* – a lack of expression described by trainees as "withering boredom." Backtalkers find this lack of response most disheartening.

We will look at the types of backtalk that students use. Backtalk can be grouped under three general headings:

- Switching the agenda
- Whiny backtalk
- Nasty backtalk

If the students want to backtalk, at least make them do all of the work.

Switching the Agenda

Seducing the Teacher

There are three agendas in classroom management; discipline, instruction and motivation. As you know from previous chapters, these three agendas represent very different management procedures. While these procedures compliment each other, they do not greatly overlap.

Consequently, if students can seduce the teacher from discipline into either of the other two agendas, discipline management is left behind. This is a very shrewd move for students since they get off the hook with little risk of provoking the teacher.

Switching to Instruction

The most common switch is from discipline to instruction. It delivers maximum benefit at minimum risk.

Have you ever prompted a student who is *talking to neighbors* by saying,

"I would like you to turn around and get to work,"

only to have the student respond,

"But, I don't understand how to do this problem"?

You ought to give the student extra credit for knowing how to play the game.

It's over! You lose! You may as well say to the class,

"Class, let me explain what just happened so that you will all understand. Go ahead and talk to your neighbors. If I see it, and if I walk all of the way over to you in order to deal with it, this is what you do. Look up innocently and say, 'But, I don't understand how to do this problem.' The worst thing that will ever happen to you in my classroom is that I will do part of your assignment for you."

Not too surprisingly, over 70 percent of backtalk in the classroom is switching the agenda to instruction. Switching the agenda to instruction is such a cool plan that I sometimes wonder why students would use anything else. It is a no-lose strategy. Even if students do not get off the hook, they run no risk of getting into trouble because teachers never identify *switching the agenda* as backtalk. Teachers seem to think that backtalk has to be obnoxious. It does not.

At this point you may be wondering, *Well, then, what is backtalk?* Let me give you a simple answer to save you confusion. The way you recognize backtalk is by the fact that the kid's mouth is open.

So, *what should I do?* you might ask. This is a very tricky question, which is another reason why students love to use this strategy.

Let me give you the easy answer first. Take two relaxing breaths, check your jaw, clear your mind, and keep your mouth shut as you kill time. When the backtalker runs out of gas, take two more relaxing breaths and then, if you need to, give a nonverbal prompt to get back to work.

Now, let me show you a naive teacher biting on the bait. In response to the student's help-seeking, the teacher says,

"What part don't you understand?"

Sometimes this actually works. Chalk it up to finesse and luck. But, if the student wants to up the ante, all he or she has to say is,

"Well, I don't know how! What am I supposed to do? Are you just going to look at me?"

This move exposes the vulnerability of our previous strategy. Maybe the student really *does not* know how to do the problem. Or, maybe the student *does* know how and is just "messing with you." How would you know?

The student has you over a barrel, and the student knows it. Consequently, teachers who have not caved in by now usually fold at this point by saying,

"What part don't you understand?"

Remember, students think like lawyers. The lawyer's question is, "Do I have a case?" This student obviously has a good case. How can *you* say to them that they *do* know how to do the problem when *they* say that they *don't*?

The only satisfactory answer to this question lies in all of the instructional procedures described in the first half of the book – *weaning the helpless handraisers*, plus *Praise, Prompt, and Leave*, plus *Visual Instructional Plans (VIPs)*, plus *Say, See, Do Teaching*. With them, you know very well that the students were approaching mastery before you made your transition to Guided Practice.

Consequently, the students don't have a leg to stand on when making a case for genuinely needing help. They know it, and they know that you know it. As a result, they will not even try to switch the agenda. Or, if they do, they will lack the self-righteous zeal required to withstand a dose of withering boredom.

In contrast, if you teach in the Bop 'til You Drop style, you will not have a clue as to what the students know after your transition to Guided Practice due to a lack of Structured Practice. The students know this too. The students therefore have a good case for pleading ignorance, and you may expect them to pursue their case.

Let's add another level to the student's game playing. Students know *why* we went into teaching. We want to see students *learn*. We love students who *want* to learn.

Clever students will use this insight to get off the hook when they get cornered. They will look you in the eye and, with utter sincerity, give you exactly what you want to hear. They will ask for help, as though to say, *This is the magic moment. I am burning with curiosity. Teach me! Teach me!*

When a teacher says, "What part don't you understand?" the visual image that comes to mind is a fish with a hook in its mouth being reeled in.

Switching to Motivation

While not as common as switching the agenda to instruction, switching to motivation has one big advantage. It gives the student *control.*

"I'm not doing this."

"This is dumb."

"We did this last year."

As a simple issue of power and control, you cannot *make* students work. You cannot make them think. You cannot even make them pick up a pencil. The students control their own nervous systems. Students will think and write when they direct their own bodies to do so.

Therefore, *forcing* unmotivated students to work is a dead issue. You cannot intimidate them. You can only flunk them, and they don't care. Not caring gives them their power.

Switching to Instruction

Even if students do not get off the hook, which they almost always do, they run no risk of getting "into trouble." It is a no-lose strategy.

Switching to Motivation

As a simple issue of power and control, you cannot *make students work.* You cannot make them think. You cannot even make them pick up a pencil.

In the long run, if you want students to do schoolwork, you must give them a *positive* reason to do so — something that they *choose.* You will have to answer the question, "Why should I?" This will require some real expertise in the technology of incentive management. (See chapters 9 and 10.)

In the short run, in lieu of incentives, you can always cut your losses. Whisper privately to the student,

"If you are not going to do your work, we can talk about that later. For right now, I will at least expect you to allow your neighbors to do *their* work."

Most students will take this opportunity to cut their losses. Escalating at this point represents a student who is looking for an altercation.

Whiny Backtalk

Whiny backtalk is what I referred to earlier as "garden variety" backtalk. It is the common, unremarkable, everyday self-justification that students most often employ when they are trying to get off the hook. These are the types of backtalk that "good kids" have used since the beginning of time. The main types are as follows:

Denial

"I wasn't doin' anything."

"We weren't talking."

"I'm not chewing gum."

As you can see, this is a *very* simple strategy. It does, however, raise an important question. That question is, *Are you blind?* If you are a sighted individual, there is nothing to debate. You *saw* it.

Take two relaxing breaths, kill some time, and *keep your mouth shut.* This too shall pass.

Blaming Your Neighbor

"She was talking, not me."

"They started it."

"He was just asking me a question."

Blaming, also known as "ratting on your neighbor," is where students go when denial is not working. You can hear the absurdity of a lame excuse if you *paraphrase.*

"Gee, teacher, we weren't goofing off when we were talking. We were operating a peer tutoring program to further our education."

Seeing the humor in backtalk is a wonderful defense against having a fight-flight reflex. Instead of thinking, *Say, what? you think, Yeah, right.*

Blaming the Teacher

If you can't blame the person sitting next to you, blame the teacher. After all, the teacher is handy.

"I had to ask him because you went over it so fast."

"I had to ask her because I can't read your handwriting."

"I had to ask them because you didn't make it clear."

The student always blames the teacher for the same shortcoming — professional incompetence. Now, the absurdity of the excuses is palpable.

"Gee, teacher, we weren't goofing off back here. We were operating a peer tutoring program in order to compensate for your methodological deficiencies in the area of instruction."

An accusation of incompetence can make a person defensive. I have seen teachers bite on this bait.

"I went over this material step by step not ten minutes ago. It is written right up there on the board if you would care to read it. Now, I am sick and tired..."

The hook is firmly set. Reel them in.

Excusing You to Leave

With this version of whiny backtalk, the student is telling you, in effect, to go take a hike. Of course, only a high-roller would say, "Hey, teacher, go take a hike." With whiny backtalkers, the message takes the following variations:

- **Short Form:** "All right, I'll do it."
- **Long Form:** "All right, I'll do it if you just leave me alone."
- **Nasty Form:** "All right, I'll do it if you just get out of my face! I can't work with you standing over me like that!"
- **Emotionally Handicapped Form:** "Geez, what are you, some kind of pervert? Leave me alone!"

As always, relax, be quiet, and wait. Do not allow yourself to be suckered into the Cardinal Error. If you succeed in the short-term, you can do anything you want in the long-term.

Compliment

Sometimes a student will give the teacher a "goodie-two-shoes compliment." This student is attempting to get off the hook while scoring a few brownie points by diverting the teacher's attention. Think of it as just another flavor of baloney.

I have seen teachers thrown off by this tactic. I remember one fourth grade girl who said,

If denial doesn't work, you can always try ratting on your neighbor.

"Oh, Mrs. Johnson, what a beautiful pin."

Mrs. Johnson stood up, looked at the pin and said,

"Why, thank you, dear. I got that for my birthday."

Mrs. Johnson wandered off with a contented smile on her face. Before long the student was talking again.

Nonverbal Backtalk

This may sound like an oxymoron, but it is an apt title for control tactics that function like backtalk without the risk of "lipping off." Here are some of the more common variants:

Cry

If all else fails, try blubbering. If crying gets kids off the hook at home, they may try it at school. Some parents start apologizing as soon as the tears flow.

Stay down, relax, and wait. If you hang in there, blubbering students will eventually dry up. Then they will look up to see if you are still there. When they realize that the gambit did not work, the cheapest way for them to cut *their* losses is to get back to work.

While the whole process may take some time, consider it a good investment. If the tears are interminable, however, you can always cut *your* losses. Similar to cutting your losses when a student plays the motivation card, lean over and whisper gently,

"We can talk about your crying later. For right now, the least I will expect from you is that you get your work done."

Leave, but return as soon as the student's head comes up. Rather than getting rid of you, the student who used crying to get off the hook receives some follow through and "instructional supervision" from close range.

Push You Aside

Sometimes students will push your arm away if you lean on the desk. Is this a big deal or not?

You could, of course, make a big deal out of it. It was, after all, a rather impudent thing to do. But, chances are, it was more reflex than strategy on the part of the student. No point in making a mountain out of a molehill.

Try "rubber arm." Relax the arm that has been pushed aside and stay down. Hang in there and wait without backing off.

Students, confronted by an immovable object, must now finally deal with your presence. At this point, they usually realize that getting back to work is the cheapest way out. You can always talk to the student later if you want.

A Kiss on the Nose

This has only happened once to my knowledge, but it is a good story for highlighting the power of doing nothing. It comes from a first-rate female junior high teacher in a suburb of Minneapolis who was a trainer for me in her school district.

She had the original "Joe Cool" in her classroom – three sport letterman, good looking, liked by the girls and a bit of an imp. He was talking to his buddy to the extent that the teacher finally moved in to "palms" on his desk. He looked up at the teacher, leaned forward, and *gave her a kiss on the nose.*

We had not practiced this move during training, of course. But, she remembered to take two relaxing breaths, stay down and do nothing. Joe obviously expected to get a "rise" out of the teacher. All eyes were on him. It came as a surprise when nothing happened. It became embarrassing when nothing *at all* happened.

Some classmates giggled. Joe blushed. The teacher just looked at him and waited, but her lack of emotion came across as nonchalance, as though to say, "This happens to me all of the time."

Joe wilted. He looked for a place to hide but had to settle for getting back to work. I am told that he never tried anything like that again.

This story highlights a general strategy for dealing with the unexpected,

When in doubt, do nothing.

This may not seem like much of a strategy, but, in the heat of the moment, it can be a life-saver. Would you rather commit from the brainstem or have some time to think?

Basic Short-Term Moves

What do you do with your body in the short-term when a student backtalks? Imagine that you are giving a prompt or are at "palms" when the student mouths off. Also, imagine typical kids and whiny backtalk. We will deal with nasty situations later.

The simplest thing to do, of course, is nothing. Just remain at palms. This provides enough proximity for the student to "feel your presence." Kill some time and wait.

However, if the student keeps talking in order to gain the upper hand or "back you off," you may wish to signal to him or her that this is a foolish strategy. The easiest way to signal this is by *moving closer.*

Camping Out in Front

In response to continued backtalk (i.e., the student's *second sentence*), bend one elbow and gently move down so that your elbow is resting on the table. This gets you closer to the student and improves eye contact.

Take two relaxing breaths, keep your mouth shut, and wait. This move usually dashes the student's hopes.

In response to continued backtalk, bend one elbow and gently move closer.

In the classroom, therefore, do not be surprised if backtalking students try to go two-on-one if you fail to rise to their bait. When the backtalkers' game plan is failing, they may turn to an accomplice in order to "double team" you.

"Jennifer was just asking me a question, (turning to Jennifer) right?"

Often, the second student will "cool it" because he or she would rather disappear than up the ante. If you hang in there and wait quietly in this situation, the first student almost always folds.

But, if the second student chimes in, you have two-on-one. You have a more serious problem if they start to feed off of each other. Kill some time in order to check it out. Often, the gambit will fizzle after a few whiny self-justifications.

If, however, the gambit takes wings so that the two students are working you over, you will have to switch strategies. You need to reestablish "one-on-one" with the backtalker, and you *cannot separate* the two students with your *mouth*.

Rather, you will need to *separate* the students with your *body*. Stand slowly and walk slowly around the desks so that you are standing behind and between the two students. Then, slowly move down between them so that your elbow is on the table and you are facing the first student. This isolates the backtalker.

Once isolated, the backtalker usually folds. Stay down and wait until you have a stable commitment to work. Thank the student as you normally would, and then stay down to ensure that he or she keeps working. Then, turn toward the second student and repeat the process. Next, stand between them for two relaxing breaths before moving around to the front. From there, move out as usual.

Camping Out from Behind

In sports (and discipline management is an indoor sport), offensive strategy can be summarized as follows: *Two good athletes can beat one good athlete.* Consequently, successful offense is synonymous with "two-on-one," "overloading the zone," or "the power play." Different sports have different names for it.

You may prefer Camping Out from Behind if you want to isolate the backtalker.

Camping out from behind actually happens most often as a low-key interaction when you are working the crowd. If, for example, you were standing *behind* the disruptive students, you would probably just stroll over and stand between them. You might even lean down to give a prompt just to make your presence felt. I can remember teachers doing this when I was a kid. Camping out has been around for a long time.

Curve Balls

Sometimes, just as you relax, thinking that the backtalk is over, a student hits you with something that you did not expect. If your relaxation is less than it should be, this jolt may send you over the edge. As always, to be forewarned is to be forearmed. The two most common curve balls are: *the last hurrah* and *the cheap shot*.

The Last Hurrah

After the backtalk dies out and the disruptive student returns to work, you would thank him or her as a closure message to indicate that the "incident" was over. But, sometimes the student does not want the "incident" to be over. At such times, your "thank you" may trigger a "snotty" come-back by the student that I have named "the last hurrah." See if you recognize any of these examples.

Teacher: "Thank you, Donna."

Donna: "Yeah, right," *or*

"You didn't help me any," *or*

"Just leave me alone," *or*

"Whatever," *or*

"Thank you, Donna." (mockingly)

This mouthy student would love to have the last word, and if you were to "lose it," that would be just icing on the

cake. Instead, stay down, take two relaxing breaths, and deliver some withering boredom as you wait.

If the kid had kept quiet, you would be gone. Instead, you are still at "palms," or "camping out." As always, if backtalk fails to get a "rise" out of the teacher, it backfires.

After the student once again returns to work and shows a stable pattern of work, thank him or her once again just as you did before. The student will most likely remain silent this time. This "thank you" is rich in meaning. In addition to placing you above the student's pettiness, it also says:

- *That* is what I wanted;
- You can relax now;
- We will do it my way, won't we?

As always, finesse allows you to be gentle while being powerful.

The Cheap Shot

Sometimes as you turn your back to walk away after thanking the disruptor, the student hits you with a parting "cheap shot." It is usually just a word or two muttered under the breath, such as:

"Big deal," *or*

"Ooooh," *or*

"I'm scared."

You need a plan. If you are trying to figure out what to do as classmates giggle, you will probably overreact.

Naturally, you cannot allow the student to have a mocking "last word." On the other hand, it would be nice to keep your response cheap. The most efficient response, called "Instant Replay," simply repeats *moving in and moving out* with a few slight alterations.

Stop when you hear the *cheap shot*, take a relaxing breath, and turn slowly to face the student. The student already knows at this point that the gamble has backfired. The gamble was that you would pretend not to hear the remark and *keep walking* while showing off.

It is just as foolish to turn a 'deaf ear' to disruption as it is to turn a 'blind eye.'

It is just as foolish to turn a deaf ear to disruption as it is to turn a blind eye. You will have to deal with the *cheap shot*, and you will have to invest enough time to convey that it is serious.

Walk to the edge of the student's desk so that you barely touch it with your legs as you normally would in *moving in*, and take two relaxing breaths. Then, slowly move down to "palms." Now, just kill time from close range. The longer you stay, the higher the cost of *the cheap shot* becomes. Had the student remained quiet, you would be gone.

After you get a stable commitment to work, thank the student and stay down. Then, stand, take a relaxing breath or two, and move out. It is extremely unlikely that the *cheap shot* will be repeated. You have made your point. Cheap shots are *not cheap*.

One wrinkle in this plan occurs when the disruptive students are of the same gender so that you cannot tell from the voice who made the remark. Never overplay your hand by pretending to know more than you actually do. The students know that you couldn't tell who spoke.

Finesse the situation by going to palms between the two students so that you camp out "in the general vicinity." Then, when you thank the students for getting back to work, just say,

"I appreciate you getting back to work."

If one of them says, "I didn't do it," relax and give them a dose of withering boredom.

Post Script

As a post script to this detailed discussion of camping out, you should know that having to camp out is an extreme rarity. I felt obligated to go into detail so that you would not find yourself in the middle of an altercation thinking, "Oh great, Dr. Jones! Now what do I do?"

If you do a good job of working the crowd and have established that you mean business, subtle gestures signal your intent to the students. One of my trainees spoke for many others when she said,

"I finally went to camping out just to see what it felt like. When you are using the rest of the system, you almost never even have to walk over to the students."

Nasty Backtalk

Nasty backtalk definitely increases the price of playing poker. We will refer to it as "high-rolling." The student is risking all in order to get control.

What separates nasty backtalk from whiny backtalk is not so much the words but, rather, the fact that it is *personal*. The backtalker is probing for a nerve ending. If you take what was said personally, you are very likely to overreact. If you do, the student has succeeded.

There are two major types of nasty backtalk: *insult* and *profanity*. Once again, to be familiar with them reduces the element of surprise.

the question of power boils down to a question of *control*. Who controls the classroom? This in turn boils down to the question of who controls *you*.

Can a four-letter monosyllable control *you* and determine your emotions and your behavior? If so, then the student possesses a great deal of power packaged in the form of a single word.

Relax, tune out, and make the student do all of the work.

Insult

There are a limited number of topics that students can use for insults. The main ones are:

• Dress

"Say, where did you get that tie, Mr. Jones? Goodwill?"

"Hey, Mr. Mickelson, is that the only sport coat you own?"

• Grooming

"Hey, Mr. Gibson, you have hairs growing out of your nose. Did you know that?"

"Whooa, Mrs. Wilson! You have dark roots! I didn't know you bleached your hair. Ha ha ha."

• Hygiene

"Hey, don't get so close. You smell like garlic.

"Hey, Mrs. Phillips, your breath is worse than my dog's!"

Are you ready to ring the kid's neck yet? That is the point, after all. Take two relaxing breaths, check your jaw, and stay down. The kid will run out of gas sooner or later.

When the sniggering dies down, the kid is still on the hook. If you are in your cortex, you can make a plan. Right now I am not so much concerned with your plan as I am with the fact that you are in your cortex.

Profanity

There are a limited number of swear words that students can use in the classroom. Chances are, you are familiar with all of them. There are your everyday vulgarisms, and then there are your "biggies."

Now, ask yourself, what is the real agenda underlying this vulgarity? As always, it has to do with *power*. Naturally,

If you give a student this much power, it will be used. And, if control comes quickly and predictably, the student will probably use it again and again.

Responding to Nasty Backtalk

To understand the management of backtalk, and especially nasty backtalk, you must conceptualize your response in terms of *two* time frames, *short-term* and *long-term*. The short-term time frame is *very* short; two or three seconds.

Short-Term Response

The correct short-term response, as you might imagine, has to do with the fight-flight reflex. Take two relaxing breaths, remain quiet, and deliver some withering boredom.

If you are in your cortex, you can use good judgement and choose a long-term response that fits the situation. If, however, you are in your brainstem, judgement is out of the question. Consequently, if you succeed in the short-term, you will probably succeed in the long-term. But, if you fail in the short-term, all is lost.

Your *lack* of an immediate response is very powerful body language. It tells the student, among other things, that you are no rookie. You have heard it all a thousand times.

If the student runs out of gas and takes refuge in getting back to work, you have "finessed" the incident (and gotten somewhat lucky). Count your blessings, and consider getting on with the lesson. You can always talk to the student after class.

The Clinical Dimension

Imagine a situation in which a student says some ugly things in the middle of class, and you finesse the situation

It is hard for students to blame anyone else when they are the only ones 'out of line.'

dents to blame anyone else when they are the only ones "out of line."

Do not worry that students will think, "Mr. Jones didn't do anything about Larry's profanity." Give them some credit for social intelligence. They just saw Larry try "the big one" and fail. They saw you handle it like an old pro. And they learned that profanity is useless in this classroom as a tool for getting the best of the teacher.

They will certainly know that profanity is not taken lightly when, on the way out of class, you say, "Larry, I would like to speak with you for a moment." Of course, you need to be standing in the doorway when you say this.

Long-Term Response

Your short-term response does not foreclose any management options. It simply gives you time to think while avoiding the Cardinal Error.

In the long-term, you can do whatever you think is appropriate. You know what options are available to you at your school site. If in your opinion the student should be sent to the office, then *do it*.

Whatever you choose to do, if you are calm, your actions come across with an air of cool professionalism. You are above the storm. This calm helps students accept responsibility for their own actions. It is hard for students to blame anyone else when they are the only ones "out of line."

so that the student falls silent and returns to work. Imagine also that you keep the student after class for a talk. What do you say?

For starters, let's consider the context. When the student used insult or profanity, was he or she acting in a typical or an atypical fashion? Let's imagine a student who was acting *atypically*.

If you take the student's remarks personally, your upset will get in the way of your thinking. If, on the other hand, you are in your cortex, you can engage in problem solving. With even some simple clinical skills, you can do a lot of good.

The student is upset about something, but that something is probably not you since you have not seen this student for the past 23 hours. Chances are, they are upset about something that has occurred outside of your class.

I would certainly want to know what that something was before I locked myself into using the Backup System. Otherwise, I would run a very high risk of heaping one hurt on top of another.

A Therapeutic Conversation

When you have a conversation with the student after the others have left, you become a clinician. Being a clinician can be straightforward in a simple situation like this one.

People seek therapy for one reason: they are in *pain*. They seek one outcome: the *alleviation* of pain. These two

simple realities give you your starting point for a conversation about the inappropriate behavior in class.

"Vanessa, what you said in class today was not at all like you. Tell me, what has you so upset?"

Take two relaxing breaths and thwart the desire to say anything else. This is called "wait time." You do not know what will happen next. You can open the door, but you cannot make Vanessa walk through it. She might say,

"Nothing! I just want to leave!"

But, before you go to "consequences," play for time. Silence is truly golden since young people have a very low tolerance for it. If you wait calmly, the whole story will probably come spilling out. Do not be surprised if the lip starts to quiver. Have some tissues handy.

After Vanessa spills her story, you may want to give her a pass to the nurse's office so that she can pull herself together before reporting to her next class. Make sure she knows that you will be available after school. Do not be surprised if she shows up.

A Different Relationship

Over the years, I have had more than a few trainees who, when faced with exactly this situation, had the presence of mind to "open the door." One teacher spoke for them all when she said,

"I would be lying if I were to say that I was relaxed after what that student said to me in class. I kept him

---

Minimizing Stress

While there are many types of backtalk, fortunately, there is only one immediate response.

Take two relaxing breaths.

You protect yourself from stress while you protect the student from making matters worse.

back as you suggested, but part of me just wanted to send him to the office. I forced myself to ask him what the 'real' problem was. I took some semi-relaxing breaths. Then, he began to spill the beans.

"I kept the next class in the hall for a minute while he pulled himself together. That was the turning point in our relationship. He has been a different child in my class from that day until now."

Young people need adults to look up to. Sometimes, all they get from the adults at home is verbal and physical abuse. They become hard and cynical before they leave childhood. But they still need adults to look up to.

Vanessa was upset in class today, obviously enough. But, she was also instinctively testing you to see if you were as uncaring as other adults in her life. She probably expected the worst – an angry teacher and a trip to the office. It would not have surprised her.

What does surprise students in this situation is to find a teacher who says, "I can see that you are hurting. Tell me about it." It catches them off guard. Sometimes their defenses crumble because they are so unaccustomed to anybody caring about whether or not they hurt.

Sometimes, healing is mediated by simply taking the time to ask and to listen. Without going that far out on a limb, you answer the defining question in your relationship with the child. Do you even care?

Reconciliation

Power is not the goal of meaning business. Power is a means to an end. It is simply a tool that can be used for good or ill.

The goal of meaning business is reconciliation. Our calmness and skill allow us to say "no" to backtalking while potentially *strengthening* the fabric of our relationship with the student rather than tearing it.

An interaction with another human being is more pregnant with possibilities the more intense it is. A student's crisis in class presents us with this emotional intensity. Depending upon our calmness and skill, we can often turn this crisis toward a constructive end.

If we react from our brainstem as the student's parents might, we confirm the student's worst expectations. But if we have the presence of mind to simply ask and listen, we can open the door to a different way of relating.

In everyday child rearing, the heart-to-heart talks that are remembered usually come on the heels of a crisis of some kind – usually accompanied by tears. These heart-to-heart talks are some of the most precious moments between adult and child. They teach important lessons within a context that says that being "bad," while it leads to real consequences, cannot threaten the bond of caring.

> The ultimate goal of meaning business is reconciliation.

Chapter Nineteen

Adjusting As You Go

Preview

- Sometimes with body language you get the opposite of what you expect. You may think, *It's not working.* But body language is always "working."

- People act in a bizarre fashion for a reason. Atypical responses to *meaning business* can teach us a great deal about the student if we know how to read the message.

- This chapter examines the paradoxical responses that you get from both extremely needy students and explosive students plus a variety of other classroom characters.

- This chapter also examines the situations in which *meaning business* might fail. Understanding the natural limitations of body language will help us transition seamlessly into other procedures when they are better suited to the task.

Strange Responses

The Opposite of What You Expect

It was the first week of school, and the first grade teacher was just getting to know her students. She was working the crowd as the students did an art project at their desks. One little boy, who seemed quite immature, was fooling around at his desk, off in his own little world. The teacher stood at the child's desk for a moment waiting to be noticed.

When the child failed to look up, the teacher bent down and rested one hand on the desktop in order to give him a prompt. When the student looked up and saw the teacher's arm in front of him, he wrapped his arms around her forearm and rubbed his face against her sleeve. He continued to do this for over five seconds.

Sometimes in body language you get the opposite of what you expect. This teacher certainly did not get the response she expected from "moving in."

If you only know the basics of body language, you may think, *It's not working.* But body language is always "working." Sometimes, however, it does not say what you expect.

In the preceding chapters we have examined typical disruptions with typical students. We have gained a sense of the subtle gamesmanship inherent in even an ordinary conversation in body language. In this chapter we will broaden our understanding of *meaning business* by examining the atypical.

A Neon Sign

Israel Goldiamond, a psychologist at the University of Chicago, used to have a saying concerning the symptomatology of clinical disorders. He would say, "A symptom is a neon sign pointing to its own cure." To our group of young psychologists he explained, "If a person is acting in a bizarre fashion, it is for a reason. What do they get for this behavior? Whatever it is, they must want it very badly. Find out what it is, and make sure that they can only get it by acting appropriately."

Dr. Goldiamond's analysis proved unerringly true. You would do well to take it to heart.

When a child in your classroom acts in a bizarre or atypical fashion, the child is telling you a great deal about his or her life. If you can decode the message, you can understand what would otherwise seem inexplicable. And you will have the beginning of a treatment program.

Needy Students

Terry Cloth Mothers

When the child described above wrapped his arms around the teacher's forearm and rubbed his face on her sleeve, the image that came to my mind was of baby monkeys and their terry cloth mothers. This image is embossed in the memory of any student who has ever taken Psychology 101.

Baby monkeys who were deprived of their mothers' presence made surrogate mothers out of the softest object in their cages. That object was a terry cloth towel. They would curl up on it and rub against it in an effort to derive the touch that they were being denied.

Like the baby monkeys, children who are socially deprived often act in ways that we might consider bizarre. For one thing, they read body language differently than normal children do.

Indiscriminate Responding

To understand the behavior of the needy first-grader in our example, think of him as being "starved for attention." Starvation provides us with the perfect analogy.

Imagine yourself going to a new restaurant. Have you ever read through the entire menu two or three times before finally making your selection? This is the behavior of a well-fed person. You are *highly discriminating*.

Imagine, in contrast, that you had not eaten in ten days. Someone offers you some food – the only food available – a turkey sandwich. Can you imagine yourself saying, "No, thank you. I prefer roast beef."?

To the contrary, you would probably "wolf it down" caring only that it was food. Under conditions of severe deprivation, we become *indiscriminate* consumers.

When children suffer from severe neglect, they become indiscriminate consumers of adult proximity and attention. They fail to read the nuances of body language that would signal approval versus disapproval – something that normal children do automatically. Rather, they "wolf it down" caring only that an adult is close enough to provide touch.

Dealing with Extreme Attention Seeking

Getting the opposite of what you expected is part of life in the classroom, although when things go completely awry, it makes even the most experienced teachers feel as

---

Goldiamond's Rule

"A symptom is a neon sign pointing to its own cure."

though they have somehow done something, wrong. However, these situations are laden with information that can give us a more effective way of responding to that situation the next time.

Our little boy's strange body language tells us much that is sad about his life. His extreme neediness has neglect written all over it. As Dr. Goldiamond said, "People are bizarre for a reason."

Understand the reason, and you will have the beginning of a treatment program. Unfortunately, the treatment program is not always pleasant for us.

When we perceive the extreme neediness of deprived children, we instinctively want to heal them. We want to somehow give them the attention and love that they have been denied in order to make them whole. This is *magical thinking* on our part, and it is not how the game is played.

Since these children are so needy of human interaction, literally any interaction that you have with them will be reinforcing. It will reinforce whatever was happening at the time of the interaction.

If, for example, you interact with the child because they are hitting other children, you inadvertently reinforce hitting. The intent of your interaction is irrelevant, because these children are indiscriminate consumers of your proximity and attention.

Personal Space

Some students have an atypically large personal space. They go on "alert" before you even reach their desks.

Consequently, rather than giving your attention to these children unconditionally, you must be *very guarded* – especially in situations which involve dangerous or aggressive behavior. Not being able to discriminate disapproval, the child may act inappropriately *more often* in the future in order to get the proximity that comes with your limit setting.

Teachers, particularly at the primary level, are reporting more and more extremely needy students like the one described above. As the students get older, their attention seeking often acquires a more antisocial flavor. Yet, whether clingy or acting out, extreme attention seeking will probably be present in any classroom in which you teach.

Since meaning business can produce a paradoxical response from such children, you will need some way of setting limits on misbehavior that does not rely on body language, especially proximity. Your options will be the subject of subsequent sections of this book.

Explosive Students

Invading Personal Space

Meaning business could be seen as an invasion of the student's personal space. This invasion is subtle when you lean down to give the student a prompt, but it is beyond subtle by the time you go to "camping out."

In previous chapters we've been imagining a typical student. When you give this student a prompt or go to "palms," you are operating on the edge of that student's personal space – an area that verges on being uncomfortable. In body language you are saying, *If you want to up the ante, I can increase the price of your foolishness by simply moving closer and staying longer.*

However, some students have an atypically large personal space. They go on "alert" before you even reach their desks. Put any child with a history of physical abuse into this category.

If you go to "palms" with these students, they get extremely agitated to the point of "losing it." Your use of physical proximity has now become a liability rather than a useful tool.

Parry Reflex

Fortunately, you can usually tell when you are dealing with students who have a history of physical abuse because their body language warns you. When you get too close, they exhibit a *parry reflex*. Parry reflexes have a lot to do with children being hit.

To parry a blow is to deflect it so that it misses you. A parry reflex is a characteristic human reflex to ward off a blow to the head. Raise your arm suddenly so that your forearm shields your head as you duck, and you will have mimicked a parry reflex.

The beginning of the parry reflex usually consists of clenched fists and a flexing of the pectoral and shoulder muscles, particularly on the dominant side. The student's facial expression is typically grim with eyes fixed on you. If you are right-handed, you can mimic this part of the response by bringing your right elbow into your side and raising your right shoulder slightly as you tense the muscles across your chest.

While you rarely see the student's hands as you *move in* because they are under the desk, you can usually see tensing in the chest and shoulder area, especially if the student is wearing a T-shirt. This preparation to raise the arm in defense should serve as a warning to you. This student will get highly anxious if you get much closer.

Adjusting Your Proximity

You do not *need* to approach the edge of the student's desk, nor do you *need* to bend down to give a prompt, much less stay at "palms." These are choices that you make.

You could stand a foot away from the student's desk as you take your relaxing breath. And, you could prompt from a standing position. You could even turn your body slightly to make the interaction less confrontational.

Remember, body language is not a technique that must be repeated in the same way every time. Rather, it is a form of communication that must be tailored to the needs of the specific situation.

Proximity is simply a tool in body language. Any human interaction is more intense the closer two individuals are to each other. If the interaction needs more intensity,

The parry reflex wards off a blow to the head.

proximity is a good way to get it. Getting a "typical student" to quit playing games and get to work is a case in point.

If, however, the intensity of the interaction is already higher than you want, you can limit the intensity by limiting your proximity. Time is on your side even though less intense interactions take a little longer to get results.

Rude Surprises

Imagine that you lean down to give a young man a prompt only to have him bolt out of his chair and yell, "Get out of my face!" His chair clatters across the floor as he fixes you in his stare.

You don't always see it coming. Some students can stifle their emotions up to the last moment. A situation can sometimes blow up in your face without the warning that body language usually provides.

What do you do? Actually, this is a simple question, and, by this point in the book, you can probably give me the answer. Take two relaxing breaths, stand slowly, check your jaw, and wait. Follow the general strategy for dealing with the unexpected, *When in doubt, do nothing.* Your emotions are contagious. If you are calm, you will have a calming effect.

As you relax and wait, the young man will give himself the extra space that he needs. He will typically pace nervously as he settles down. At some point the student usually begins to feel awkward as he stands in the middle of the room with everyone watching. You may wish to reduce the awkwardness by gently motioning toward his seat.

Of course, the student could just bolt out of the room. Who can predict?

Do not feel as though you have done something wrong. Bolting and running is simply a primitive coping mechanism. The choice of coping mechanisms reveals the level of the student's social-emotional development. You have just received a lot of diagnostic information about this particular student.

Initiate the school policy for a student running in the halls, and continue to take your relaxing breaths. You can assess your long-term strategy in a minute.

No amount of experience can prevent some rude surprises over the years. The needy student and the explosive student are two of the more predictable types that will require you to make adjustments in the heat of the moment. Making adjustments in the middle of a play is just part of being a seasoned player.

When Meaning Business Fails

A Focus and a Range of Effectiveness

Meaning business as we have described it in the preceding chapters is only one element among many in an effective discipline management program. It is not a cure-all.

In spite of our eternal desire to find a panacea for our management problems, successful classroom management will always require a system. This system must have different procedures that do different jobs.

Each element of the system has a *primary focus* and a *range of effectiveness* around that focus. Any element of that

What Do I Do When…

In any surprise situation, the answer is always the same: *Slow down, take two relaxing breaths and remember,*

When in doubt, do nothing.

system, such as meaning business, will perform beautifully when asked to do what it is designed to do. However, as you reach the edge of its range of effectiveness, it will begin to fail.

It is just as important to know the limitations of a procedure as it is to know its strengths. When you reach the edge of a procedure's range of effectiveness, you will want to transition seamlessly into a new procedure rather than riding the old one into the ground.

Limitations of Meaning Business

The following list provides some of the situations in which meaning business might fail. These "failures" simply define the natural limitations of body language in management while signaling the need to switch procedures. Some of these limitations are familiar to us by now. We will list them under three categories: *Teacher Characteristics, Student Characteristics,* and *Setting Characteristics.*

Teacher Characteristics

• **Angry and Upset:** Failure to relax thoroughly produces a parody of meaning business. The damage is greatest when the students are emotionally handicapped since they amplify the teacher's upset.

• **Poor Relationship Building:** The effectiveness of any discipline management procedure relies to a considerable degree upon the preexisting goodwill between teacher and student. At some point in your limit setting, the disruptive student must decide to "go along with you" rather than fight you if the scene is to have a satisfactory resolution. No management technique can carry a teacher who has failed to create a personal bond with his or her students.

• **Inadequate Classroom Structure:** Go back to the example of the teacher training the class to walk quietly through the halls in chapter 12, *Teaching Routines.*

Considerable time was invested in training the class to mastery. The dividend of this investment is a class that responds efficiently to the teacher's cues.

Many teachers simply do not want to make this investment in teaching routines. The net result will be disorderly behavior.

Any management problem that is not *prevented* with effective classroom structure will have to be *remediated.* The first level of remediation is meaning business.

Without the habits of rule-following that routines produce, having to mean business will occur at a high rate rather than at a moderate to low rate. Consequently, teachers who have economized at the level of classroom structure will spend all of their time setting limits. Teachers locked into this cycle tend to say, "I didn't go into teaching to be a policeman!"

• **Immobility:** Teachers who Bop 'til They Drop in the front of the classroom instead of working the crowd will have no end of problems with students disrupting. These problems will come not only from students in the green zone, but also from any student on cognitive overload.

However, some lesson formats preclude working the crowd. *Small group instruction* is the most common example. Imagine that you are seated with a handful of students at the reading table.

Students *not* in the reading group usually become very talkative and noisy as soon as you sit down. In order to

System Design

Know the strengths and limits of each element of the system. It is important to be able to transition seamlessly to a new procedure instead of riding the old one into the ground.

Tailored to the Situation

Body language is a form of communication that must be tailored to the needs of the specific situation.

mean business, you would have to interrupt the reading group and stand up before you could even turn toward the noisy students. The disruptive students would, of course, "cool it" as soon as you turned toward them. Eventually you would sit back down. As soon as you did, the noise would resume. We call this "yo-yoing the teacher."

You are in a no-win situation. Any attempt to mean business is so expensive and inefficient that it encourages the students to gamble like bandits. You are at the edge of the range of effectiveness for meaning business.

You need an entirely different procedure that allows you to manage the classroom *from a seated position.* That procedure will be described in the following section, *Producing Responsible Behavior.*

Student Characteristics

• **Multiple Disruptions:** Sometimes a student makes a wisecrack, and then everybody tries to get in on the act. In seconds, laughter and wise remarks are coming from all directions. What do you do?

This dilemma does not fit neatly into any management niche. If the banter is good-natured, which it often is, you can afford to "go with the flow." Then you might try the following gambit which is cheap, although a little unorthodox.

Before you get into setting limits, try disrupting the disruption by *talking over it.* Simply place your body in the middle of the action and start expounding in some intelligent-sounding way.

"What you said was pretty funny, Mark. And, it looks like the group thought so, too. But, your remark made a point. You'll remember, class, that we were talking about..., and the issue before us was...Let's go back to the point Jennifer made just a minute ago...."

By the time you have finished with this intelligent-sounding *blah, blah, blah,* you probably have everyones' attention. Having wrestled the attention away from Mark, you can then direct it to whichever topic or student you choose.

Do not confuse the situation just described with a teacher who tries to keep a discussion going in spite of interruptions by individual students. When one student interrupts another, it is time to stop and deal with the interruption. Otherwise, interrupting becomes the most efficient way of being heard.

• **Angry and Upset:** If a student is sufficiently angry or has a big enough chip on his or her shoulder, a management situation may continue to spin out of control. At the very least, your calm is keeping *your* blood pressure down, even though it may not be enough to calm the student. More importantly, your calm will allow you to decide what to do next from the cortex.

• **Repeat Disruptions:** Some students are what I will call "repeaters." No matter how effectively you deal with the disruption in the short-term, they start up again as soon as your back is turned.

These kids typically come from homes in which no *never* means no. Rather, the parents say "no" and then go about their business without tracking the child's response or following through.

These children learn to simply pause for a moment until the parent turns away before resuming their activity. With such training, children can reach early adulthood without ever internalizing the notion that they actually have to *stop* what they are doing because another person asks them to.

When you have to set limits on a student a second time for the same behavior, a warning flag should go up in your brain. When you see it for a third time, you have a pattern. you do not need to fail a half-dozen times before you have the picture. Meaning business is obviously not working. It is time to switch strategies.

The next section of the book entitled *Building Responsible Behavior* has some answers to this dilemma. The following section, entitled *Using the Backup System*, has more expensive but more definitive solutions.

• **Praise Makes Worse:** Part of meaning business is the common courtesy of a "thank you." However, some children predictably act out soon after they have been praised. What do you make of that?

This paradoxical response has to do with self-concept and cognitive dissonance. If a child has been raised in an environment of negativism and criticism, the child will tend to have a negative self-concept, and he or she will expect criticism as the validation of that self-concept.

Praise disrupts this pattern. It creates cognitive dissonance between the *feedback* (You are a good person) and the *self-concept* (I am a bad person). Cognitive dissonance is uncomfortable, and the brain automatically seeks to resolve it.

The brain can reduce this dissonance in one of two ways. It can change the entire self-concept, or it can validate the one that already exists. Which of these two operations do you think is easier for the brain to perform?

Taking the path of least resistance, the brain seeks to *invalidate* the dissonant input as a means of *validating* the pre-existing pattern. The child, therefore, immediately acts out in order to get into a hassle which reestablishes life as he or she understands it.

Be patient and keep trying. Improvement will be slow. In the short run, however, dump the verbal praise.

Setting Characteristics

• **Open Field Situations:** Meaning business requires physical proximity, and achieving that proximity may be impractical in an open field situation. For example, a physical education teacher or coach may have students goofing off on the far side of the playing field.

Part of this dilemma has traditionally been dealt with through structure. Physical Education teachers have had squads and squad leaders long before cooperative learning groups became fashionable in the classroom. This decentralization of the leadership role extends the teacher's authority over a greater area.

However, structure and body language have severe limitations in this setting. Most of the slack will have to be picked up with *Responsibility Training*, the subject of the next section of the book. In general, Responsibility Training does the management jobs that meaning business cannot do.

• **Heckling from Behind:** Imagine that you are at palms with a disruptive student when you hear heckling from behind you.

"Hey, what are you picking on her for? She wasn't doing anything."

This situation may seem outrageous, but it is really just a variation on a theme. Two students are double-teaming the teacher. The accomplice who is going two-on-one just happens to be somewhere in the room other than sitting next to the backtalker.

We described your response to being double-teamed in the previous chapter. Your response was to isolate one of the students so that you could go one-on-one. Then, you deal with the two students in sequence, one at a time.

Use the same strategy with heckling from behind. Rather than responding to the heckling when it occurs, stay with the first student until you have closure, complete with "thank you" and some additional monitoring. Then, stand slowly and turn in a regal fashion toward the second student.

In most cases the second student will have already fallen silent because the strategy to "divide and conquer" failed. When you face the second student, relax and wait to see if he or she will return to work. Usually the heckler will return to work since there is nothing to be gained by upping the ante at this point. If the heckler returns to work, you can afford to simply cruise in that direction as part of working the crowd rather than "moving in" to set limits.

Playing with Finesse

Adjustments

Analyzing the body language of meaning business in terms of two typical students who are *talking to neighbors* as we have in the preceding chapters is both illuminating and limiting. While we get a clear picture of the give-and-take inherent in body language, this picture of classroom life is overly simplified.

The present chapter deals with some of the adjustments that you must make with the generic pattern of meaning business. Adjustments are part of playing any game — just as a football or basketball player must continually adjust to changes in the other team's offense or defense.

As you master the body language of meaning business, these adjustments become easier until they finally become automatic. They will be based on your immediate understanding of the *student* and the *situation* — things that only you will know.

Prescriptions

As always, my objective is to solve the problem and get the student back on task at the lowest cost to the teacher. But the choice of procedures is always related to a specific student in a specific situation — one which you will witness and I will not.

Consequently, this book, and this section of the book in particular, are free of *prescriptions*. Most other discipline management programs are comprised of prescriptions. "If the student does *this*, you do *that*."

Instead of laying the groundwork for good decision-making, prescriptions preempt decision making by dictating consequences. They actually prevent adjustments to the specifics of the moment. As a result, prescriptions will always lack the precision and finesse that characterize the management of highly effective teachers.

Fundamentals and Basic Plays

Rather than being a series of prescriptions, effective discipline management is subtle and dynamic. It typically involves a complex give-and-take that we have characterized as an indoor sport.

This book clarifies the fundamentals of the game and some of the basic plays. But, during the game you must act and adjust as the game unfolds.

Crucial choices cannot be made from the sidelines. I certainly cannot sit in my office a thousand miles away and prescribe exactly what you should do with a student I have never seen in a classroom I have never visited. It will ultimately be your call. If your management system gives you an adequate range of options, and if you are in your cortex, it will probably be a good call.

Section Seven

Producing
Responsible Behavior

Chapter Twenty

Building Cooperation

Teachers Need Cooperation

Starting versus Stopping Behavior

Behavior management is conceptually simple. There are only two things you can do with a behavior. You can *increase* it, or you can *decrease* it. If you consistently increase the behaviors you want and consistently decrease the behaviors you do not want, sooner or later you will be left with what you want.

Getting students to *stop* disrupting, therefore, is only half of discipline management. Getting students to *start* doing what they *should* be doing is the other half.

This section of the book will focus on getting students to do what they should be doing. We will examine the building of responsible behavior. Irresponsible behavior costs the teacher as much in terms of stress and lost learning time as does goofing off.

Teachers Need Cooperation Often

Imagine that you want all of the students in your class to:

- Show up on time
- Walk as they enter your classroom
- Bring pencils and paper
- Bring books and lab manuals
- Be in their seats when the bell rings
- Be working when the bell rings

Teachers Need Cooperation

Preview

- A teacher needs cooperation many times a day from every student in the class. Whenever students fail to cooperate, the teacher's job is made more difficult.

- Cooperation is voluntary — a gift. Before students will give the teacher all of the cooperation that is required during a school day, the teacher must repeatedly answer the question, "Why should I?"

- The answer to the question, "Why should I?" is called an incentive. Teachers will need incentives that teach the entire class to be responsible — even the oppositional and highly irresponsible students.

- This incentive system must increase learning time while costing the teacher nothing in terms of time and effort.

- This incentive system is called Responsibility Training.

You have just made six requests for *cooperation* from thirty students, and the class period has barely begun.

Imagine that you are a high school teacher with thirty students in each of five instructional periods. Before beginning instruction in all of these periods on a single day, you will have made *nine hundred* requests for cooperation. By the time these class periods *end*, you will have made thousands of additional requests for cooperation.

Teachers Need Cooperation from Everyone

You need cooperation from *every* student in the class, not from just the few difficult students. And, the nicest kid in your class can be far from perfect when it comes to cooperation.

Sometimes good kids are just a little flakey. Maybe when they were in the third grade and they forgot their lunch money, a parent ran it to school. And when they were in the fifth grade and forgot their homework, a parent ran it to school. They are nice kids, but they often show up without homework or lab manuals or pencils. These students collectively can cause you just as much stress and extra work as Larry.

Teachers Need Perfection

Simply improving the level of cooperation from students is a hollow victory. What is the practical difference to you in terms of stress and lost learning time between *four* kids showing up late and *two* kids showing up late? This may represent a 50 percent reduction in the problem behavior, but, as far as your work load is concerned, it represents very little improvement. You still have to deal with interruptions just as you are starting the lesson. You still have to deal with the added paperwork of tardies. And, you still lose the first five minutes of the class period.

For your life to be significantly improved, you need to eliminate the problem. Only then can you relax and start the

class on time without hassles. Consequently, in the building of cooperative behavior, I am not much interested in *improvement*. I am interested in *every* student in the class being responsible.

Remedial Child Rearing

Consider the Starting Point

To gain a perspective on the scope of your job in training the class to be responsible, take a quick mental survey. Before your students came to school this morning, how many of them, do you think, did the following?

- Made their beds as soon as they got up
- Hung up their pajamas
- Helped set the breakfast table
- Cleaned up their breakfast dishes
- Hustled getting ready for school so they would not make themselves or their parents late

After your students get home this evening, how many of them, do you think, will do the following?

- Hang up their jackets
- Do chores without having to be reminded
- Help set and clean up the dinner table
- Start their homework without an argument
- Head up to bed on time
- Put their dirty clothes in the hamper

Let's See You Do Any Better

You may be getting a sinking feeling as you tally the odds. Even the best parents in the neighborhood nag and sometimes just give up.

But keep in mind that *half of the human race is below average*. This statistic applies to the *parenting skills of the par-*

ents of the students in your classroom. Some of these parents are *way* below average. Some parents can't get the kid to the dinner table without an argument, even though the kid is already hungry and the parents are using food as a reinforcer.

On the first day of school, the entire community will bring all of its childrearing imperfections into your class, dump them on your desk and say, in effect,

"Let's see you get that kid to do something. I can't even get him to make his bed!"

You, in contrast, will be expected to get that child to do something. Six assignments per day to the best of his or her ability, on time, and with legible handwriting. Lots of luck!

The Joys of Irresponsibility

Cooperation Is a Gift

If students do something as simple as showing up to your class on time, do not take it for granted. They have cut short several pleasurable activities in order to do it. They have cut short joking around in the lavatory. They have cut short talking with their friends at their lockers. They have cut short saying goodbye to their boyfriends or girlfriends for the fourth time today.

They have cut short all of these innocent pleasures so that they could show up to your class on time where you will *put them to work*. You should be grateful.

The difficult thing about managing coop-

eration is that cooperation is *voluntary*. It is a gift. You cannot *force* someone to cooperate. If you tried, you would get *coercion*, the opposite of cooperation.

Cooperation requires a *decision* to cooperate on the part of the student. The management of cooperation in the classroom, therefore, focuses on supplying the students with a good reason to make that decision.

Is Virtue Its Own Reward?

Are you familiar with the saying, *Virtue is its own reward?* I simply want to impress upon you the fact that this statement *does not apply to classroom management.*

Quite the opposite is true. *Goofing off* is its own reward. Goofing off is always the easy, pleasurable alternative to being "on the ball."

Consider the problems that teachers face in getting students to do something as simple as bringing pencils to class. Put yourself in the students' shoes.

Remember on the first day of the semester when your English teacher said,

"Class, we do writing every day in this class, and I do not want a constant stream of students going to the pencil sharpener. One of my basic expectations is that you bring *three sharpened pencils* to class each day."

Now it is the second day of class, and the teacher says,

"Class, let's all get out pencil and paper."

A hand immediately goes up.

"Yes?"

"I don't have a pencil."

"Do you remember yesterday when I asked you to bring three sharpened pencils to class every day?"

"I loaned my pencil to a friend last period."

"Well...here. You can borrow mine, but I want it back at the end of the period."

Is this teacher ever going to see that pencil again? The teacher may as well kiss it good-bye before giving it to the student.

Supplying pencils is nothing compared to the management of pencil *sharpening*. Imagine Larry sitting in first period on his first day of high school. Larry knows what he has gotten into. At the welcoming assembly the principal made it abundantly clear:

"Freshmen, let me explain high school to you. We expect you to sit in your seats for the next four years and pay attention to everything because it might be on the test."

Larry has been sitting in first period for *twenty minutes*, and he is already in pain. Larry suffers from multiple quasi-neurological deficits like "ants in the pants." Larry looks at the clock and says to himself,

I won't make it. I want to move. I have to move! I have 3 years, 179 days, 5 hours and 40 minutes to go. I need to move now! How can I get out of my seat and move without getting into trouble?

Larry casts his eyes upon the lead of his pencil, and a light goes on.

"May I please sharpen my pencil?"

The teacher responds,

"Use one of your other pencils."

Larry responds,

"I don't have another pencil."

Larry casts his eyes upon the lead of his pencil, and a light goes on.

The teacher says, pointing to the pencil sharpener,

"Well then, hurry!"

This is not looking good. On the first day of school the teacher was *telling* the class to bring three sharpened pencils. It is only the second day of school, and the teacher is already *begging* students to hurry.

Does Larry hurry? It is a comedy routine.

Larry may have the state record in the 100 meters, but the speed with which he moves toward the pencil sharpener is known in Hollywood as "slo-mo." On his way to the pencil sharpener, Larry forgets his goal in life and stops to whisper to a friend.

"Larry, would you please leave him alone and simply get your pencil sharpened and get back to your seat?"

"What?"

Have you ever looked at the work kids turn in these days and wondered, *What will happen to this country in the next 50 years?* When you watch Larry sharpen his pencil, you know that the future is in good hands. It's inspirational.

He cranks the handle, and then holds the pencil up to the light to check the point. He sharpens it some more. He checks it again. Larry is working to tolerances of 1/1000th of a centimeter. He could go to work building jet engines tomorrow.

He's Not Stupid

Why would Larry bring three sharpened pencils to class if it meant that he would no longer have an excuse to stretch his legs whenever he felt like it? Larry may not be a whiz in school, but he is not stupid.

When the pencil lead finally passes rigid quality control standards, Larry heads back to his seat – by the most circuitous route imaginable.

"Larry! Would you get away from the window and return to your seat?"

"What?"

When Larry finally takes his seat, watch how long it takes him to get going. The shoulders need to be stretched. Every knuckle needs to be cracked. The writing hand makes several passes over the paper as though on a reconnaissance mission. Finally, he begins to write. It has been *five minutes* since Larry asked to sharpen his pencil.

Now ask yourself, why would Larry bring three sharpened pencils to class if it meant that he would no longer have an excuse to stretch his legs whenever he felt like it? Larry may not be a whiz in school, but he is not *stupid*.

Why Should I?

If Larry and all of his classmates are to give you all of the cooperation that you need class period after class period, day after day, you must answer one simple question. That question is: *Why should I?* As you may remember from chapter 9, "Creating Motivation," the answer to the question, "Why should I?" is called an *incentive*.

In the classroom, you will need incentives for *work productivity*, and you will need incentives for *rule following*. Chapter 9 dealt with incentives for work productivity, and this section will deal with incentives for rule following. (Since the fundamentals for both are the same, this would be a good time to reread chapter 9.)

Incentive systems for rule-following that you would currently find in classrooms have changed very little since the 1970s. These management programs typically require a lot of effort from the teacher while accomplishing very limited objectives.

If we want to answer the question, "Why should I?" for the *entire class* throughout the *entire school day*, we must become far more sophisticated in the design and implementation of classroom incentive systems. These incentive systems must accomplish *multiple objectives* simultaneously, and they must be *cheap*. The entire program must represent a *reduction* of the teacher's workload.

To achieve this level of cost-effectiveness, we will need to break new ground in the design of classroom incentive systems. In order to gain a fresh perspective, let's think for a moment about raising responsible teenagers.

A Model for Building Responsibility

Learning to Be Responsible with Money

Imagine that you have a teenage son, and you want him to be responsible with money. After all, soon he will have to manage his own affairs. What is the first thing that your teenager must have before he can learn to be responsible with money? When I ask this question to a roomful of teachers, they respond in unison,

"Money."

Indeed, in order to learn money management, you must have money to manage.

Where does the teenager get the money? In fact, that is the *least* critical aspect of the incentive system. Your teenager can work after school, or you can give him money in the form of an allowance. Both will work just fine if critical aspects of the incentive system are in place.

My parents gave me an allowance when I was in high school. They said,

"Your job is going to school. With your extracurricular activities, you barely have enough time for homework as it is. We will give you an allowance. Payday will be Sunday. You will have to pay for school lunches, dates, burgers with your buddies, and tux rental for your winter and spring formals."

When my wife, Jo Lynne, and I had teenage sons, we used the same system. It worked fairly well, but not without a few glitches. Imagine the following scene. One Friday after dinner our older son Patrick approached me with a proposition.

"Dad, can I have ten bucks until Sunday? I'm just a little short this week. I'll pay you back, I promise. You can just take it out of next week's allowance."

To the uninitiated, this sounds like a reasonable proposition. My son was shocked at my response.

"I'm sorry son, but I don't lend money. I *give* you money, but I don't *lend* money."

With apparent disbelief and imploring hand gestures, Patrick said,

"But, Dad, you don't understand. It's only until Sunday."

A teenager's first assumption at times like this is that you are stupid.

"I *do* understand, son. But I still don't lend money."

"But, Dad, there's a party at Tracy's house after the game tonight, and he just told me about it today. I need to help with food. Monique really wants to go."

What's a poor guy supposed to do when things come up at the last minute?

"Sorry, son. I don't *lend* money."

"Aw, Dad...Then what am I supposed to do?"

A teenager's desperation tactic is to get you to prescribe

"I have no idea."

Traditional classroom incentive systems have been a lot of work for only limited benefit.

the solution to the problem. Then you become responsible for how things turn out.

"Aw, man! I can't talk to you about anything."

Now I have a communication deficit.

"Yes, son. You *can* talk to me about anything. In this case, the answer is, 'No.'"

As you might imagine, we shared a rather grumpy weekend with our son. "Grumpiness" is often a by-product of confronting an inconvenient reality.

Incentives Teach Lessons

Before we attempt to train a roomful of young people to be responsible, we must be clear about how to train *one* young person to be responsible. To begin with, the only thing that young people take seriously is *reality*.

You can preach, you can teach, you can beg or cajole. You can share your personal experiences or the wisdom of the ages. It will all be met with body language that says, *Yeah, right.* Before young people will take it upon themselves to act responsibly, they must confront a reality that demands responsible behavior.

Effective parents and teachers do not leave this reality to chance. It is possible for us to construct a somewhat artificial reality that teaches responsibility quickly and efficiently. This somewhat artificial reality is called an incentive system. It can teach teenagers to be responsible with small bills during high school, for example, rather than having them learn the same lesson with thousands of dollars worth of credit card debt years later.

Learning to Live within a Budget

Let's return to my son and the learning of money management during high school. In addition to understanding the pitfalls of lending, I also knew a thing or two about Patrick's spending habits.

My son's high school had an "open campus." Many students left campus for lunch. My son and his buddies were spending their money at "Jack's Burger Shack" rather than slumming it in the far more economical school cafeteria. To my son's youthful mind, taking out a loan to subsidize "Jack's Burger Shack" seemed reasonable.

Only when this line of reasoning "hit the wall" was my son forced to develop a new plan. The following week when his buddies said, "Hey, Pat, let's go to Jack's," my son had to consider more factors than he had the week before, not the least of which was tux rental for the upcoming winter formal.

What is crucial in money management is learning to live within a *budget*. Few people will learn to live within a budget until they have to. It can be very inconvenient. Having no choice but to live within a budget forces responsible decision making concerning money.

We Are All Incentive Managers

Almost everything you do as a parent or teacher creates some kind of incentive. The example of my son hitting me up for a loan is a case in point. If I say "*yes*," I create one set of incentives. If I say "*no*," I create another set of incentives.

If, for example, I had given Patrick an extra ten bucks on Friday, I would have:

- spared him from experiencing any new "mind-altering" reality that might lead to long-term planning; and

- paid him for running out of money early as a means of increasing the money supply.

I may have a soft heart, but I don't have a soft head.

As you see from this example, we can exploit incentives to do two things at once. The *first* is to supply the children with something that they want and which we feel that they should have. The *second* is to teach a lesson. The better the incentive system is designed, the quicker the lesson is learned.

To learn money management, you will first need money.

Classroom Objectives

Students Waste Time

Students are expert time-wasters. They waste time all day long. They stroll into class at the last minute rather than being in their seats when the bell rings. They sharpen pencils during class time rather than sharpening them during the break. They use hall passes rather than going to the bathroom between classes. They make stretching a lesson transition into an art form.

Students could easily save enough time during a day to allow you to teach an extra lesson by doing two things:

- being in their seats when the bell rings instead of "settling in"

- reducing the duration of lesson transitions from five minutes to one minute

But students have no vested interest in saving time. If they were to save you enough time to teach an extra lesson, they would get an extra lesson. Who wants that?

Teaching Time Management

What is the first thing that students must have in order to learn to manage time? Using money management as our analogy, the answer is, of course, *time*. The students in your class cannot learn time management until they have *time to manage*.

We must, however, teach time management to the *entire* class. Any one student can waste time for the group. It is hard to get started, for example, until everyone is seated.

The students in your class cannot learn to manage time until they have time to manage.

Consequently, we must devise a system of *group management*. Furthermore, it must have sophisticated fail-safe mechanisms that give *every* student a reason to cooperate, *especially* Larry. We will name this system of group management *Responsibility Training*.

Preferred Activity Time

We Give an "Allowance" of Time

In order for the class to have time to manage, we must give the class an "allowance" of time. As with money management, the purpose of this allowance is to teach a lesson. If we structure the incentive system properly, we will be able to teach time management quickly and efficiently.

Our incentive will, of course, be built around a reinforcer – something that the students want. The time that we give them must be desired or, "preferred" by the students so that, as a group, they will work for it. The only type of reinforcer that fills time is an *activity*. The allowance of time that we give to the class will, therefore, be referred to as "Preferred Activity Time" or PAT.

One question that is always asked by someone in a workshop at this point is, "What do the students have to do in order to *earn* PAT?" This question is conditioned by decades of classroom incentives that are built around Grandma's Rule: *You have to finish your dinner before you get your dessert.* It seems wrong to give the "dessert" without first seeing some work.

We have used the analogy of teaching a teenager to be responsible with money in order to get enough distance from Grandma's Rule to allow us to see incentive management through new eyes. In the design of an incentive system, sometimes you *give* in order to *get*.

I *gave* my son his allowance. He did not earn the allowance by being paid, for example, for doing chores around the house. I did not want to train him to think, "What will you pay me?" every time I asked for a little help. Chores were handled separately from the allowance.

The allowance was given for two reasons: *first*, teenagers need money, and *second*, I could exploit that need to teach money management. But the money itself was a *gift*. It was a gift with an educational purpose – as is PAT.

PAT Increases Learning Time

I have no intention of losing learning time as the price of supplying the students with PAT. Quite the opposite, I am supplying the students with a PAT in order to *increase* learning time.

As I mentioned, you can gain nearly a full instructional period during the day by simply training the class to manage two routines more responsibly: starting class on time and hustling during lesson transitions. You can gain additional instructional time during the day by eliminating traditional forms of foolishness such as showing up without pencils or sharpening pencils during class. There are many additional chores and routines during a school day that can increase learning time and reduce teacher stress if done quickly and responsibly by the group.

All of the time that you set aside for PAT, therefore, is "found time." You will *not* relinquish *one minute of time* from your instructional program. Quite the contrary, if you do not *give* the class PAT in order to teach them time management, they will *waste* the time as usual, and you

will have *nothing to show for it.*

There is a second dividend to be gained from giving PAT, lest you think that this program will cost you anything. The PAT itself will *not* be time *away from* learning. Rather, you will use PAT *for* learning.

In subsequent chapters you will find that you can teach any lesson as a PAT – from skill drill to test review to vocabulary. In addition, since I cannot give you an extra planning period, it must require no extra planning or effort.

How Much PAT?

How much time does your class need for PAT? To put it simply, you need enough time in order to do something worthwhile. Teachers might begin with 10 to 30 minutes depending on how often they had PAT during the week.

How often should you have PAT? Let's begin by defining a *time frame* for Responsibility Training. The time frame for the program runs from the *beginning* of one PAT to the *beginning* of the next PAT. Consequently, the students are always on the program, even during PAT.

The time frame for students of a given age is keyed to the amount of time that they can *delay gratification* and *exert impulse control.* It is, therefore, a function of *social maturity* rather than chronological age. Consequently, the following norms should be thought of as general guidelines that you may need to tailor to the social maturity of your particular students.

- **Kindergarten:** Kindergarten students usually have to get up and move every 15 to 20 minutes, and their level of impulse control is nothing to write home about. Consequently, a kindergarten teacher may want to have PAT every 20 minutes or so.

The very notion of having PAT that often would be overwhelming if PAT required much planning and effort. It is apparent from the outset that PAT must be cheap and easy for the teacher to implement.

- **First Grade:** To be conservative, you would probably want to start the first grade year with three PATs in the morning and two PATs in the afternoon. However, by midyear most first grade classes only need three a day – mid-morning, end of morning, and end of afternoon. Do not attempt to get by with only one in the morning before lunch, or you will find that the students "lose it" after 10:30.

- **Second and Third Grades:** At some time during second or third grade, most classes can go to two PATs a day – one before lunch and one at the end of the day. Fading the schedule of PATs, however, is always a judgment call. You can tell if you have been premature in thinning the schedule if you find the students "losing it" during the hour prior to PAT.

- **Fourth and Fifth Grades:** At some time during fourth or fifth grade, most classes will be ready for a single PAT at the end of the day. While PATs become less frequent as the students mature, it would be inaccurate to think that we are attempting to reduce the amount of PAT.

As PATs become less frequent, they become longer. While a first grade teacher might set aside 10 minutes for

each PAT three times a day, a fifth grade teacher might set aside 30 minutes for a single PAT at the end of the day.

- **Middle and High School:** While sixth grade often retains the same pattern as fifth grade, sometime before high school most classrooms go to one PAT per week. As an interim pattern, teachers may have PAT twice a week, on Wednesday and Friday.

An alternative pattern in departmentalized settings is to have 5 to 10 minutes of PAT at the end of each class period. As such, it is typically an integral part of that day's lesson. Often, students play a learning game to review what was just taught.

Learning to Give

Cooperation is a gift. In order to learn cooperation, children must be taught to give. A teacher cannot teach giving except through giving.

This giving by students usually takes the form of being considerate of others. When students waste time, they not only make the teacher's job more difficult, but they also take time from their classmates, most of whom are just sitting and waiting for activities to begin.

To say that children tend to be self-absorbed is something of an understatement. For children to consider the needs of others, they must be taught to consider the needs of others. Maturity does not come from the simple passage of time.

As teachers, some of the most important lessons we teach are lessons about life. If we understand how to design incentive systems, these lessons about life can be learned reasonably quickly and with a sense of joy. The following chapter will focus on the nuts and bolts of the design of Responsibility Training.

Found Time

If you did not give the class PAT in order to teach them time management, they would waste the time, and you would have nothing to show for it.

Chapter Twenty One

Teaching Responsibility

Nuts and Bolts of Training

This chapter will focus on the nuts and bolts of implementing Responsibility Training. But, for Responsibility Training to succeed, the other elements of the classroom management system must also be in place. In this chapter, therefore, we will see how the pieces of the system fit together to produce success.

The Teacher's Role

A Giver

In training students to be responsible, the teacher is first and foremost a *giver*. We give in order to teach giving – the giving of cooperation.

We will give generously. If we err, we will err in the direction of giving. If we give a little extra, no damage is done. But if we do not give enough, we can starve the program.

The teacher will give three gifts:

- **PAT:** The *first* gift that the teacher will give is *Preferred Activity Time* (PAT). PAT does not change behavior. Rather, it sets the stage for the use of bonus PAT. Think of PAT as a "pump primer."

- **Bonus PAT:** The *second* gift that the teacher will give is *bonus PAT*. Bonus PAT changes behavior while empowering students. Bonus PAT is the heart of Responsibility Training.

Preview

- While Preferred Activity Time (PAT) lays the groundwork for Responsibility Training, it is the bonus PAT that empowers students to increase the duration of PAT.

- Hurry-up Bonuses produce hustle. The time that students save by hurrying during lesson transitions and other routines is added to the PAT.

- While students can earn time by hustling, they can also lose time by excessive dawdling. This causes students to become active in managing each other's behavior.

- Automatic Bonuses eliminate the time wasting of "settling in" by giving students extra PAT for being in their seats ready to go when the bell rings.

- Responsibility Training gives teachers an effective means of managing the class during small group instruction when they are seated.

- **Structure for PAT:** The *third* gift that the teacher will give is *structure for PAT*. PAT is structured time, not free time. PAT is time that is structured for learning. Its objective is to make learning fun.

A Timekeeper

Responsibility Training teaches students to be responsible with everything they do in the classroom from bringing pencils to hustling during lesson transitions. However, all of these various forms of responsible behavior can be organized under a single heading: learning to be responsible with *time*.

As mentioned in the previous chapter, students are expert time-wasters. If students were to use their time efficiently, much of the goofing off in the classroom would immediately disappear. Responsibility training, therefore, achieves many different management objectives simultaneously by training students to manage time wisely.

As part of time management, the teacher must keep track of time. In all cases it will be *real* time – time that any student in the class could read off of the wall clock.

The Students' Role

Making Choices

The teacher gives the students time, and the students decide how the time will be spent. Students learn to take responsibility for their actions by making choices about the use of time and then living with the consequences.

Squander or Save

While students are given the power to choose how their time will be spent, their range of choices is very limited. They can:

- **Squander and be selfish:** Students can squander time by being out of their seats when the bell rings, by

sharpening pencils during class, or by dawdling during lesson transitions. These various forms of time-wasting constitute little vacations from work that students take at will.

But, these mini-vacations are not shared by the class. Rather, they are taken by individuals while the rest of the group waits. This is very selfish.

- **Save and share:** Members of the group can always choose to forego the selfishness that squanders class time, but they must have a reason to do so.

What if the students got to *keep* the time that they usually squandered so the *whole group* could use it for something they enjoyed? This would create a vested interest in saving rather than squandering.

The time that the students save is called "bonus PAT." It is the bonus PAT that empowers the students to increase PAT by saving time.

Hurry-up Bonuses

Learning to Hustle

Hurry-up Bonuses achieve one of the most difficult objectives in all of behavior management: training kids to *hustle*. Training kids to hustle is particularly difficult when work can be avoided through dawdling.

To get a sense of how difficult it is to train kids to hustle, consider the varsity basketball team at your local high school. These kids are dedicated to basketball. They love to play.

Yet, coaches throughout the country are routinely reduced to yelling in frustration,

"Come on, hustle! Let's go! Let's go! Let's go! You're just going through the motions out there!"

If you think it is difficult to get the varsity to hustle, try gym class. Try math class. Try social studies.

An Analogy from Family Life

Hurry-up Bonuses are familiar to most of us from everyday family life. Moms and dads have used them since time began.

The most common example of a Hurry-up Bonus around the house is *the bedtime routine*. In chapter 9, "Creating Motivation," I described the bedtime routine that my parents used when I was a little kid. My mother would say:

"All right kids, it is 8:30 – time to get ready for bed. Wash your face, brush your teeth and get your pajamas on. As soon as you are in bed, it will be story time. But lights out at nine o'clock."

My brother and I well understood that the faster we moved, the more time we would have for stories. And we also knew that dawdling reduced the length of story time.

Teaching Responsibility through Empowerment

In the bedtime routine the PAT is, of course, story time. But, during the bedtime routine, who is in control of the

> ## People will only take responsibility for things that they control.

amount of story time that the children receive? During training, teachers respond in unison, "The children."

Indeed, the children are in complete control. If they choose to hustle, they will maximize the duration of story time. But, if they choose to dawdle, they will reduce the duration of story time. My brother and I got into the habit of being ready *before* 8:30 so that we could have a full half-hour of stories.

Understanding the nature of a simple choice made by children at bedtime teaches us one of the most important lessons about learning to be responsible: *People will only take responsibility for things that they control.*

Making choices implies that we have some control over our destiny. If we do not control the outcome of our actions, then choice is a sham since our efforts are to no avail. Before people will learn to make wise choices, therefore, they must:

- have power
- know how to use it

Our job as teachers is *first*, to empower the students to make choices, and *then*, to teach them to make good choices. Responsibility Training, therefore, is a teaching paradigm.

Lesson Transitions

The Mechanics of a Hurry-up Bonus

One of the greatest hemorrhages of time-on-task in any classroom is the lesson transition. A lesson transition usually takes about five minutes.

During these lesson transitions students move in a most unhurried fashion as they hand in papers, sharpen pencils, get drinks, move furniture into or out of groups, and get out materials. There is utterly no sense of urgency. Obviously, students like nice big, unhurried breaks with brief lessons sandwiched in between. They know that, as soon as the transition is over, it will be time to get back to work.

Your average lesson transition can easily be accomplished in half-a-minute if the students choose to hustle. But, why would the students hustle if hustling only puts them back to work sooner?

In contrast, let's walk through a lesson transition that contains a Hurry-up Bonus.

"Class, before you get out of your seats, let me tell you what I want you to do during this lesson transition. First, hand in your papers by laying them on the corner of my desk. Then, if you need to sharpen your pencils, this is the time to do it. If you need a drink of water, this is the time to get it.

"I want my clean-up committee to erase my boards and straighten up the books on the shelf. I want everybody to pick up any paper you see laying around the room and get your desks back on their marks.

"I will give you two minutes to get this done. But you know from past experience that you can get it done in half-a-minute. So, let's see how much time you can save. All of the time you save will be added to your PAT.

"Let's check the clock. (Pause until the second hand passes the six or twelve.) Okay, let's begin."

Being Generous with Time

While it takes students half-a-minute for a typical lesson transition if they hustle, in the preceding example I gave them two minutes. As I mentioned earlier, be generous in the giving of time. If you err, err in the direction of generosity. My rule of thumb for determining the amount of time allotted for the completion of a routine is to:

Socializing is a bootleg incentive that competes with your incentive system.

- Estimate how long it would take if they hustled.
- Round that number up to the next minute.
- Double that number.

If it would take 2 to 3 minutes to clean up after a project, round up to three minutes and then double it to six.

Bootleg Reinforcement

As the students get up from their desks, you immediately begin to *work the crowd*. Your primary objective as you work the crowd is to eliminate the "bootleg reinforcement" that is part of any lesson transition.

As described in chapter 12, "Teaching Routines," bootleg reinforcement is an incentive for goofing off that is delivered by the *peer group*. Imagine, for example, three students standing around the pencil sharpener talking. The reinforcer for socializing is socializing. It is a self-reinforcing behavior.

This bootleg incentive system is competing with *your* incentive system, the Hurry-up Bonus. In this competition, the bootleg incentive usually wins.

One of the main characteristics of a reinforcer that determines its power is *immediacy of delivery*. The bootleg incentive usually wins the competition because it is being delivered now, whereas the PAT will not be delivered until much later.

One of your primary objectives in classroom management is to get a *monopoly on incentives*. This is done by suppressing the goofing off that is self-reinforcing. If you fail to do this, the students' bootleg incentives will constantly neutralize your management program.

Teachers get a monopoly on incentives primarily through "management by walking around." "Just walk up to the students who are chatting and wait patiently. The stu-

By working the crowd, you disrupt the disruption.

dents, well aware of what they should be doing, typically give you a self-conscious grin accompanied by some silly talk.

"I was just going to sharpen my pencil."

As the students "get on the ball," you stroll over to the drinking fountain and four students standing around repeat the drill. As always, by working the crowd you "disrupt the disruption." In addition, by sheer proximity, you continually prompt the students to *get on the ball.*

The nemesis of working the crowd during a lesson transition is a student who says to you, "May I ask you a question?" This student could be a future Rhodes Scholar or the biggest "clinger" in the classroom. It makes no difference. Your answer is always the same.

"As soon as we are back in our seats."

During a lesson transition, you have far more important jobs to do than instruction. If you want a quick lesson transition, you must work at it. A lesson transition is perhaps the most concentrated example of classroom management during the entire school day. Thinking of it as a "break" represents a classic rookie error.

All for One, and One for All

As the lesson transition nears completion, you head to the front of the room. Imagine, however, that, as you make a final check around the room, you see some crumpled paper on the floor over by the door. Most of the students are already seated, but one student is standing near the paper. As you point, you say:

"Class, there is a piece of paper over there on the floor."

Can you imagine the student who is standing near the paper saying,

"It's not mine."

Simply look at the student and shrug. After all, it is not your problem. What do you think several classmates seated nearby will say to the student standing near the paper?

"Pick it up! Pick it up!"

Welcome to "all for one, and one for all." You have just observed peer pressure in the form that it almost always takes in Responsibility Training – *urgent whispers.*

Wrapping Up the Transition

As the last student sits down, you say,

"Thank you class for doing such a good job of cleaning up and arranging your desks. Let's check the time. You saved one minute and seventeen seconds. Let's add that to our PAT."

You walk to the board and add a minute and seventeen seconds to the PAT. The students are all smiles.

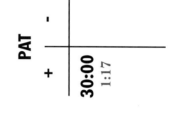

The teacher gives a Hurry-up Bonus for a quick lesson transition

The role into which you are consistently placed by Responsibility Training is *benevolent parent*. You give time, you protect time, and you congratulate the group for saving time. Your benevolence, however, is tempered by the next component of Responsibility Training, *time loss*.

Time Loss

The Lord Giveth, and the Lord Taketh Away

Our first bonus in Responsibility Training, the Hurry-up Bonus, provides us with our first view of the inner workings of discipline management as a system. The system is far more complex than the simple giving of bonuses.

The first complication with Hurry-up Bonuses results from the fact that *you can't win 'em all*. Some days, in spite of your best efforts, the Hurry-up Bonus bombs as the students run overtime. This can happen for legitimate reasons which may include any combination of the following:

- A storm front is blowing through.
- It is two days until the beginning of vacation.
- It is the full moon.

As you work the crowd during the lesson transition, you feel the time slipping away. You work the crowd and prompt the students with increased urgency, but to little avail. The students seem to be moving in slow motion.

With fifteen seconds left in the allotted time, you head to the front of the classroom. You stand calmly facing the students and look at the clock as the time runs out. Then, as you point to the clock, you say,

"Class, you are on your *own time* now."

Relax and wait for the last student to be seated. Then say,

"Thank you, class, for straightening up the room and getting back in your seats."

Then, after taking a second to look at the clock, walk to the board and record the time consumed under your PAT tally. The tally has two columns, one for time *gain* and one for time *loss*.

The tally in the example below would indicate that the students have saved time during two previous lesson transitions but have lost five seconds during this one. This example is actually quite representative of the proportion of time gain versus time loss in Responsibility Training.

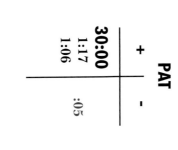

PAT	
+	**-**
30:00	
1:17	
1:06	:05

On rare occasions students lose some time due to dawdling.

As you can see, the system is *rigged* so that the students *come out ahead*. When they gain, they gain in minutes. But, if they lose, they only lose in seconds. Five seconds actually represents a rather large time loss. It usually takes only two or three seconds for students to get into their seats when half of their classmates are urgently whispering,

"*Sit down! Sit down!*"

The time loss component of Responsibility Training is both necessary and the bane of my existence. It is necessary because Responsibility Training *does not work consis-*

tently without it. And it is the bane of my existence because it *opens the door to abuse* by poorly trained or negativistic teachers.

Time Loss Produces Consistent Success

First, let's deal with Responsibility Training working *consistently.* Responsibility Training is *group management:* all for one, and one for all. Turning management over to the peer group has significant advantages:

- Kids will do things for their peer group that they would never do for you.

- You side-step the resentment that some students harbor toward adult authority.

However, without a time *loss* component within Responsibility Training, the peer group lets you down just when you need them. The *many* do not stand up for themselves as their time is being wasted by the *few.* They just sit there and let it happen.

This tendency of the many to act like sheep comes from the natural awkwardness of any student taking a public stand for righteousness. Imagine, for example, that during a typical five-minute lesson transition, some student were to stand up and say,

"Class, some of us are dawdling and wasting valuable learning time. I wish everyone would just hurry-up so that we could get back to work."

While voicing a noble sentiment, this "goodie-two-shoes" has just distinguished him or herself as being the biggest dweeb on the continent.

If you want students to enforce your classroom standards, you must give them a reason for doing so that does not make them look like a bunch of dweebs. Enlightened self-interest is the ticket. The time loss component of Responsibility Training gives the students a plausible vest-

ed interest in enforcing your standards. A student does not have to be a dweeb to say,

"Sit down! You're wasting our PAT."

Of course, you would not want students to become *overzealous* with rule enforcement so that they would get nasty. Nor would you want to make any student into a scapegoat.

Don't worry. There is much less of a tendency in that direction than you might think. Here are some of the reasons that overzealousness is all but nonexistent:

- **Students will not allow it.** They look at the overzealous student in an irked fashion and say something like, "Chill out."

- **You will not allow it.** You immediately set limits on it just like you would with any other form of disruption.

- **There is little reason for it to occur.** When the few can no longer abuse the many, you find that there is much less latent animosity between students that might surface at such times in the form of rude remarks.

Time Loss Opens the Door to Abuse

Next, let's deal with the fact that the time loss condition within Responsibility Training is the *bane of my existence.* Can you imagine a colleague who is a bit *negative* or *burned-out* eventually saying to the class,

"All right, class, it is only Wednesday, and you have already lost *half* of your PAT. If we continue like this, there will be *no* PAT this week!"

This teacher is obviously using Responsibility Training as a *weapon* by abusing the time loss condition. When used properly, time is lost in seconds rather than in minutes, and even then, time is lost only rarely. Furthermore, time loss typically self-eliminates in a matter of days or weeks so that thereafter it exists in the students' minds as a *potentiality* rather than as an actuality.

For teachers to take large amounts of PAT from the students, they must be:

- **Poorly Trained:** This can easily occur when a teacher hears about parts of this system second-hand – often from a well-intentioned colleague who has been to a workshop. Since the manipulation of PAT smacks of "instant cure," teachers are tempted to try it without other elements of the program being in place. When time loss is used for high-rate behaviors such as *talking to neighbors* and *out of seat* that are the proper domain of working the crowd and Limit Setting, excessive time loss is the natural outcome.

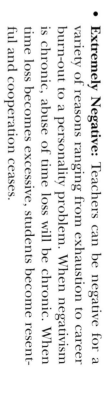

- **Extremely Negative:** Teachers can be negative for a variety of reasons ranging from exhaustion to career burn-out to a personality problem. When negativism is chronic, abuse of time loss will be chronic. When time loss becomes excessive, students become resentful and cooperation ceases.

Layers of Management

A Foundation for Successful Incentives

You consistently place yourself in a position to congratulate the group for its success because success was not left to chance. Each piece of behavior needed for an efficient lesson transition was carefully built and supervised.

The clean-up committee erased your boards properly because you had *trained* them to do so during the first month of school. And, they knew that, had they done a sloppy job, they would have done it over because you were *supervising* their work. The students moved their desks properly rather than dragging them across the room for the same reasons.

In addition, you systematically eliminated bootleg reinforcement as you worked the crowd. And, finally, as you worked the crowd, you set limits on any goofing off that you encountered.

The incentive of extra PAT for hustle was only *one* layer of management among *many* during the transition. Indeed, the incentive was not even the main one. Rather than saying that the students succeeded *because of the incentive*, it would be more accurate to say that the incentive succeeded

When time loss becomes excessive, students become resentful, and cooperation ceases.

because of the solid foundation of management upon which it was built.

A Slice of Life

To understand how discipline management works as a *system*, let's first list the four layers of our discipline management program.

1. Classroom Structure

2. Limit Setting

3. Responsibility Training

4. Backup System

The strategy for solving a problem is very simple:

- Extract as much management from Classroom Structure as you can before moving on to Limit Setting.

- Extract as much management from Limit Setting as you can before moving on to Responsibility Training.

- Extract as much management from Responsibility Training as you can before even considering the Backup System.

Think of discipline management as a four-layer cake. We would never serve a birthday cake by cutting off the top layer and serving it one layer at at time, would we? Rather, we would cut through all four layers to serve a slice of cake.

Similarly, we will never serve up one layer of our management system all by itself. Rather, think of every management dilemma as a "slice of life." The solution will potentially contain all four layers of the management "cake."

Management Deferred

By far, the greatest investment of time and energy in a well-managed classroom is in *Classroom Structure*. The

teacher will first rearrange the furniture in the room in order to *work the crowd*. In addition, the teacher will invest heavily in the *teaching of routines* early in the semester. During the teaching of a lesson, *working the crowd will be facilitated by additional elements of classroom structure which include *Say, See, Do Teaching* plus *Visual Instruction Plans* plus *Praise, Prompt, and Leave.*

Any management task that is not taken care of with Classroom Structure will be shifted to the next level, *Limit Setting.* Consequently, as we mentioned in chapter 19, "Adjusting As You Go," teachers who do not spend enough time teaching their classroom routines will find themselves constantly setting limits on noise and misbehavior during those routines.

Any management task that is not taken care of by Classroom Structure or Limit Setting will be shifted to the next level of management, *Responsibility Training.* Herein lies the problem.

If teachers get only a brief explanation of Responsibility Training without the rest of the program, they will have little choice but to use it as a "solo" management procedure. When used solo, Responsibility Training comes across as a cure-all. The natural tendency, then, is to use Responsibility Training, and especially *time loss,* to manage *everything* – talking to neighbors, out of seat, wandering around the classroom, dawdling, not having pencils – you name it!

Success with Incentives

Rather than saying that the students succeeded because of the incentive, it would be more accurate to say that the incentive succeeded because of the solid foundation of management upon which it was built.

The proper domain of Responsibility Training is relatively *narrow*. It builds behaviors such as hustling or showing up on time with books and pencils – those jobs for which Classroom Structure and Limit Setting are poorly suited.

If you were to ask Responsibility Training to bear the entire burden of discipline management, it would collapse under the weight of that burden. You would back yourself into continually *taking* time rather than *giving* it. As a result, the system would become a weapon rather than a gift, and its entire intent would be perverted.

Automatic Bonuses

Right Place, Right Time, Right Stuff

Automatic bonuses are used when you cannot measure the amount of time that the students have saved. Imagine, for example, that the students are in their seats ready to go when the bell rings. How much time did they save? You have no way of knowing. You can only measure time *loss*.

When the students are on time, *automatically* give them a bonus of a predetermined size. The size of the bonus is up to you, but one minute is the norm.

Automatic bonuses are most commonly given for students being at the *right place* at the *right time* with the *right stuff*. They are most useful in training students to begin class on time rather than wasting the first five minutes of the class period with "settling in."

Imagine, for example, that the students are in their seats ready to go when the bell rings. As always, they are in their seats for more reasons than one. You greeted the students at the door; the students had a Bell Work assignment, and you worked the crowd during Bell Work while setting limits on any goofing off. As a final layer of management, you provided an incentive.

Having laid the groundwork for the success of the incentive, you are now in a position to congratulate the students at the beginning of class with the daily "automatic bonus routine."

"Class, thank you for being in your seats. That is one minute. How about pencils? (The students hold up their pencils.) Good! That's two minutes. Let me see lab manuals. (The students hold them up.) Good! Three for three."

You then walk to the board and add three minutes to the bonus column of the PAT.

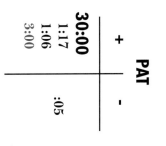

PAT

+	−
30:00	
1:17	:05
1:06	
3:00	

Daily automatic bonus routines eliminate the wasting of time during "settling in."

Taking Responsibility for Pencils

Now, let's imagine that, thirty seconds before the bell rings, a girl in your class discovers that she has no pencil. That pencil is worth a full minute of PAT.

She asks the students near her for a pencil, but nobody has an extra one. As you walk by, the student says,

"May I please borrow a pencil?"

You answer,

"I don't lend pencils."

You knew that was coming, didn't you? It is now fifteen seconds until the bell rings! What should the poor girl do? What if she said to the class,

"Hey, you guys! I need a pencil!"

In a class of thirty, twenty-nine other students have a vested interest in this girl having a pencil. She will get a pencil. When the whole class wants something to happen, it will happen.

The beautiful thing about this pencil routine, apart from the girl having a pencil, is that it is not *your* pencil. Even better, you do not care whether the person who loaned the pencil gets it back. It is *not your problem!* Group management makes it *their* problem. You are no longer caught in the middle.

Learning to Help Each Other

Some students are just forgetful. Imagine for a moment a boy in your class who often forgets things. He is a good kid, but just a little flakey. He forgets homework and deadlines and pencils and notebooks.

Think of responsible people, in contrast, as having "Post-It notes" all over their brains. When my kids were in school, my brain was buried under Post-It notes, as was my wife's.

"Bring refreshments to school for Brian's birthday party at 11:00 today."

"You have to chaperone Anne's field trip, and the bus leaves the school at 1:00."

"Dinner will be late this evening because Patrick has a basketball game after school."

Some people have never learned to bother with Post-It notes – flakey kids, for example. They don't "sweat the details." You can remind them a dozen times, but they will still forget and then say, "Nobody told me."

Switch perspectives for a moment, and imagine that you are a student who shares science class with the flakey kid. Your locker is next to his, and you remember (because you have a Post-It note on your brain) that today is lab day. As you grab your lab manual, you remember that last week the class failed to get its bonus minute because "Mr. Flake" forgot his manual. To make sure that it does not happen again, you say,

"Hey, Herb. Got your manual?"

When students have a vested interest in "taking care of business," they often take care of it when you are nowhere around. Neither Classroom Structure nor Limit Setting can do that.

Classroom management is much easier when you have some help. Responsibility Training gives everyone a vested interest in helping.

Bonus Contests

Contests Are Optional

When we first began experimenting with PAT bonuses at the high school level, some of our teachers posted the net PAT for each of their class periods on the board. They revised the total after each class period while keeping a

While bonus contests work nicely, I would say that less than half of the teachers I train actually use them. Those who don't say that they do not need them. However, bonus contests may give you some extra management leverage when you need it. It might help, for example, when you have one class period out of the day that is especially difficult to manage.

Cutoff Point Contests

An incentive system will be more powerful if everyone participates, and it will be less powerful if people drop out. One of the problems of having prizes based on *rank order* (first through fifth place, for example) is that fourth and fifth places tend to quit trying when they see that they cannot catch up. Soon, not trying becomes an expectation and a habit.

To eliminate this tendency, you can substitute *cutoff points* for rank order. The cutoff points would be the

separate record at their desks. We noticed that each class period consistently earned 5 to 8 minutes more of PAT per week than the classes of the teachers who did not post the PAT publicly.

As an experiment, we asked all of the teachers to post PAT for each class period. Sure enough, when the teachers who had not posted the PAT began to do so, their classes' net PAT immediately shot up by 5 to 8 minutes. It seemed that the class periods were competing with each other without even being aware of it.

To maximize the benefit, we instituted a formal contest in which bonus PAT was the prize. During a five period day, bonuses would be given as shown in the box above. Notice that even last place got a bonus minute. You can afford to err in the direction of generosity if PAT will be used for learning anyway.

PAT Bonus Contest Prizes

First Place	5 bonus minutes
Second Place	4 bonus minutes
Third Place	3 bonus minutes
Fourth Place	2 bonus minutes
Fifth Place	1 bonus minute

By including bonus points for rank order, everyone has a vested interest until the end of the contest.

PAT Bonus Cutoff Points

45 minutes of PAT earns	5 bonus minutes
42 minutes of PAT earns	4 bonus minutes
39 minutes of PAT earns	3 bonus minutes
36 minutes of PAT earns	2 bonus minutes
33 minutes of PAT earns	1 bonus minute

The beauty of cutoff points is that any class can earn extra minutes of PAT with just a little more effort.

rough equivalents of the time that might be earned by competing class periods, but evenly spaced. The example below would be for the five class periods of a teacher who gave each class period 30 minutes of PAT to start the week.

The beauty of cutoff points is that any class can earn extra minutes of PAT at any time with just a little more effort, regardless of what the other classes are doing. Since the class periods are not actually competing with each other, they could all get the "first place" bonus. This tends to eliminate the problem of dropping out.

Layering Bonuses

Teachers will often want to use a field trip or a big project of some kind for PAT. Since these activities require an extended PAT, teachers are tempted to save PAT for several days or weeks in order to accumulate the necessary time.

This extension of the time frame for Responsibility Training typically has disastrous results. Asking a fourth grade class to save PAT for a week is like asking them to wait for the rest of their lives. In a similar fashion, asking a high school class to save time for several weeks is asking for trouble.

You can have the class work for long-term goals without giving up the power of short-term goals by *layering bonuses*. Simply keep two sets of books side by side.

Imagine, for a moment, that you are a fourth grade teacher who would like to have the class earn time for a field trip. Keep two PAT tallies side by side at the board – one for the normal PAT that might occur at the end of the

You can have long-term goals without giving up your short-term incentives by keeping two bonus tallies on the board.

day, and one for the field trip. Whenever you add a Hurry-up Bonus or an Automatic Bonus to the daily total, add the same bonus to the field trip total. Only bonuses add to the field trip total, not the initial gift of PAT.

Individual Bonuses

What about Larry?

Can you imagine having one student in the class who might ruin bonuses for the group just to show that he or she can? Most teachers report that they have at least one such student. As always, let's call this student Larry.

Larry is the reason that group incentives have such a poor record in the research. With group incentives, you cannot give a reinforcer to anyone unless *everyone* has cooperated. Consequently, one student can always ruin it for the group, and there always seems to be one in every class.

Failsafe Mechanisms

Of course, we cannot allow Larry to ruin the incentive for the group if we want Responsibility Training to succeed. Preventing this will require a failsafe mechanism.

The following chapter will describe the failsafe mechanism needed to motivate Larry to join the group. That failsafe mechanism is called Omission Training. Larry's individualized program will, in turn, create a general pattern for dealing with students having special needs.

Eliminating Annoyances

Pencil Sharpening

While automatic bonuses help us with part of "pencil management," we are still left with the problem of sharpening pencils during class. The first step toward solving this problem is to inform your class that you do not allow pencil sharpening after the bell rings.

To deal with broken pencil leads, you need a canister of sharpened pencils on your desk. They should be short, grungy pencils. If you buy nice new pencils, break them in half, sharpen both ends and break off the eraser. The little pencils used to keep score at golf courses are perfect.

Next, instruct your students as follows:

"If you break your pencil lead during class and have no other pencil, hold your pencil in the air so I can see it. I will nod to you at which time you may leave your seat to exchange pencils at my desk. Leave your pencil on my desk, and take one out of the canister. You may get your own pencil back at the end of class when you return mine to the canister."

Typically, this is the end of the problem. Occasionally, however, students take advantage of the situation by killing time at your desk looking for the best pencil in the canister. First, try a little "heart-to-heart" talk with the group to see if the problem will go away without further sanctions. If the problem persists, you may need to put students on the clock when they get out of their seats to exchange pencils. When students see that you have the situation covered, they usually "shape up" without you ever having to actually take away time.

Hall Passes

Hall passes allow administrators to tell whether students should be out of class when they meet the students in the hall. There are many legitimate reasons for students being out of class. The use of hall passes only becomes a problem when students use them to go to the restroom.

The flim-flammery of using hall passes to go to the restroom becomes clear in the light of one biological fact: *An average three-year-old child can sleep through the night dry.* This means that teenagers who want a pass out of class in order to avoid wetting themselves might have a little brother or sister who last night "held it" for *eight hours* *while unconscious*. Does this sound as though the teacher is being taken for a ride?

You need to understand that every institution on the face of the earth has a toilet training program. There are only two options:

• When you gotta go, you gotta go.
• When you gotta go, do it on your own time during the breaks provided.

Option number one provides an incentive for using toileting as a means of getting out of work. Option number two removes that incentive.

The simplest solution is to eliminate the use of hall passes for going to the restroom altogether. Of course, any student with a note from a physician would be excepted. For the rest of the student body, the rule is, *Go to the bathroom during the breaks provided.*

If you feel as though you must have hall passes for going to the restroom, you could subtract the time that students are gone from the PAT. I have seen this work, but I can also imagine it blowing up in your face depending on the class. Whenever you use time loss to manage a problem, you put PAT at risk.

Elementary teachers, particularly at the primary level, will often show concern about eliminating hall passes for going to the restroom given their experience with such young children. These concerns are legitimate and point out the complexity of the issue. As always, management problems are best solved preventatively.

Let me share an observation. Primary teachers often bring their classes in from recess and march them right past the restrooms without stopping. These are frequently young teachers who lack experience with child rearing.

Anyone who has raised children knows how flakey young kids are about having to go to the bathroom. I would ask my six-year-old son when we were near the restrooms, "Do you have to go?" and he would say, "No." Five minutes later when we were nowhere near a restroom, he would be doing the one-legged dance. Soon parents learn not to ask. You just say, "Go in and *try!*"

Discipline from a Distance

Small Group Instruction

How do you manage goofing off in the classroom when you are *seated* during small group instruction? As soon as you sit down, you lose working the crowd, and the rate of disruption skyrockets. In addition, Limit Setting becomes extremely expensive since you have to stop instruction and stand up before you can even begin. As a result, students gamble like bandits. In chapter 19, "Adjusting As You Go," we called this, "yo-yoing the teacher."

Data taken during small group instruction showed that *talking to neighbors* and *out of seat* tripled as soon as the teacher sat down. Simultaneously, the percentage of time-on-task among those students *not* in the small group plunged by over half to 30 to 35 percent. This translated into the noise level that most teachers had learned to accept as the price of small group instruction.

Toilet Training

Every institution on the face of the earth has a toilet training program. There are only two options:

• When you gotta go, you gotta go.
• When you gotta go, do it on your own time during the breaks provided.

This dilemma of managing from a seated position produced the research that evolved into Responsibility Training. At the beginning, we gave the teachers a stopwatch to hold up as a warning cue when they saw a disruption on the far side of the classroom. If the disrupting students returned to work, no time was lost. If the disruption continued, the teacher started the watch and let it run until the students were back on task. Any time on the stopwatch was deducted from PAT.

The peer group immediately became involved in "shushing" disruptive students. In the research, disruptions were reduced by 80 percent, and time-on-task doubled during the first week. By the end of the second week, disruptions were down by 95 percent, and time-on-task was the same as when the teacher was working the crowd.

More importantly, time loss was small. By the end of the second week, time loss averaged about fifteen seconds during a one-hour class period. By the end of the third week, most of the stopwatches were in the drawer. After that, teachers only had to point to the wall clock when they caught the eye of a disruptor.

Subsequently we learned how to exploit bonuses through trial and error so that management was more a matter of giving than of taking. Yet, from a seated position, the original version provides an effective alternative to both noise and nagging.

To put it simply, time can be substituted for distance. Using the stopwatch from a seated position is like beam-

> **Never use time
> to manage
> a behavior
> that you could
> have managed with
> your body.**

ing your body across the room. It's like magic. "The wanderer" literally jumps into his seat to turn off the stopwatch.

Beware of More Abuse

The very magic of using Responsibility Training for *talking to neighbors* and *out of seat* when you are seated can be highly seductive. It can train even the best teachers to use time loss for high-rate disruption at other times *in lieu of working the crowd*. This can be disastrous.

It is important to *discriminate* the *change in ground rules* for the use of time loss that occurs when the teacher is *seated* during small group instruction as opposed to when the teacher is *mobile*. When you are mobile, you *never* use time loss for high-rate disruptions like talking to neighbors and out of seat. When you are seated, you *must* use time loss for these same high-rate disruptions.

Responsibility Training is robust enough to absorb time loss for high-rate disruptions if its use is limited to small group instruction *when the teacher is seated*. Problems occur only when *the teacher* "steps over the line" and uses time loss for the sake of convenience when *not seated*.

To help delineate the proper use of time loss in Responsibility Training, trainees learn the following rule:

> *Never use time to manage a behavior
> that you could have managed with your body.*

Open Field Settings

Physical education teachers sometimes find Limit Setting difficult due to sheer distance. When students are goofing off on the far side of the gym or playing field, the use of physical proximity for management may be impractical.

Teachers in open field settings usually find themselves substituting the time loss of Responsibility Training for the physical proximity of meaning business more often than teachers in regular classrooms. If used judiciously, this can work.

Responsibility Training can increase hustling and reduce "standing around" in such settings enough to create a sizable PAT by the end of the class period. I know physical education teachers whose kids hustle through the required assignments in order to get:

- a three-on-three basketball tournament
- access to gymnastics equipment
- access to the weight room

Simple versus Complex Incentive Systems

A Technological Breakthrough

For decades teachers have been using incentive systems to manage student behavior. Almost all of these incentive systems are simple applications of Grandma's Rule:

You have to finish your dinner before you get your dessert.

We have called them "simple" incentive systems because they have few parts: a *task*, a *reinforcer* for completing the task, and *accountability* to make sure that the task was completed properly. These incentive systems were discussed in chapter 9, "Creating Motivation." While such incentive systems work well for instruction, for discipline management they require a lot of work to get limited results.

Responsibility Training represents a technological breakthrough. By using time as a medium of exchange, the teacher can hold the *entire class* accountable for a *wide range of behaviors all day long* for no more effort than a PAT tally on the board.

Unlike simple incentive systems, this "high tech" incentive system has additional parts like bonuses and penalties. And, as we will see in the next chapter, it also has failsafe mechanisms to prevent Larry from ruining PAT for the group. Therefore, we will refer to Responsibility Training as a "complex" incentive system.

The Devil Is in the Details

The good news about Responsibility Training is that it is not so complex that you cannot learn it in a reasonable amount of time. The bad news is that it is not so simple that you can explain it to a colleague in twenty minutes.

As always in management, the devil is in the details. The success of Responsibility Training will come from the proper implementation of the nuts and bolts, not from some "grand idea" that is used out of context as a quick fix. For example, a teacher recently called to say,

"I did something just like Responsibility Training, but it didn't work. I gave them 5 points at the beginning of the hour and then took one point away every time somebody did something wrong. They lost all their points every day. The students complained and said that it wasn't fair."

Parallel Programs

Responsibility Training will probably be your primary structure for using incentives in the classroom, but it is not the "be all and end all" of incentive management. The main advantage of Responsibility Training is efficiency. It trains the students to do a lot of different things in the classroom with very little added work for the teacher.

If you are presently operating a simple incentive system that makes a valuable contribution to management, do not feel that you must discontinue it. Simply run it parallel to Responsibility Training.

For example, elementary teachers often have "responsibility charts" in their classrooms upon which students can earn stars or points for doing basic tasks during the day. You do not have to take down the responsibility chart just because you initiated PAT. The chart might provide valuable cues and added incentives that make students more mindful of getting certain jobs done.

Just let the two incentive systems run side by side. Eventually the cueing and reinforcing functions of the responsibility chart will be transferred to Responsibility Training so that the chart can come down, usually between semesters, without any loss of management leverage.

Push motivation is primitive and simple. It is coercion. Pull motivation is far more complex. You must know a thing or two about incentive management to give people a good reason for consistently choosing to do something.

Having a "thing" about incentives simply reveals naivete about management. If you do not learn to use *pull* motivation, you will be left with *push* motivation by default.

Push versus Pull Motivation

Many teachers, particularly at the secondary level, are not comfortable with incentive systems. They are not used to them, they don't use them, and they don't like them. Such teachers often fight the notion of using incentives in their classrooms. They relegate their use to the primary grades and Special Education.

However, as mentioned in chapter 9, "Creating Motivation," there are only two ways to manage motivation - push and pull. *Push* motivation makes demands and threatens punishment if the demands are not met. *Pull* motivation gives people a reason to choose to do something.

> ## Push versus Pull Motivation
> If you do not learn to use pull motivation, you will be left with push motivation by default.

Chapter Twenty Two

Turning Problem Students Around

What about Larry?

The Confrontation

Imagine a Hurry-up Bonus in which all of the students but Larry are in their seats ready to begin as the time runs out. You point to the clock and say,

"Class, you are on your own time now."

Larry turns to you and blurts,

"This whole thing is stupid! PAT is stupid too! This sucks!"

Do you have a student in your class who might respond in this way? If so, you have a lot of company.

Who Is Larry?

Before we make a plan for dealing with the confrontation, let's take a moment to think about Larry. Is Larry a happy child? Is Larry a popular child?

Hardly! What kind of kid would say to the class, in effect,

"I have the power to hurt everyone in the class by ruining PAT, and I am going to do it"?

Typically, Larry is angry and alienated. He takes it out on you, and he takes it out on his classmates. He does hurtful things, and he is often a bully. As a result, he tends to be unpopular with his classmates.

Preview

- Omission Training supplies problem students with an incentive for self-control by providing a reinforcer when they refrain from a behavior for an interval of time.

- Omission Training mated with Responsibility Training gives the teacher a powerful and flexible means of motivating the peer group to help the student with individual needs.

- If the student on Omission Training refrains from the problem behavior for a given amount of time, he or she earns bonus PAT for the group.

- Omission Training typically eliminates the problem behavior rapidly while making a hero out of an unpopular student.

- Omission Training is easy to use since it amounts to nothing more than a bonus clause added to Responsibility Training.

Would Larry like to be popular? Show me a child who would not.

Yet the anger gets in the way. He does not seem to know how to be popular. He keeps doing things that seem calculated to make the other students dislike him. He is his own worst enemy.

Your Immediate Response

Take a relaxing breath. Turn in a regal fashion. Take another relaxing breath. Give yourself a moment to think. Your demeanor signals to everyone that this is serious.

Walk slowly to Larry, and wait for a moment before saying anything. Allow your own calm to help Larry relax. What you then say is not what Larry expected to hear.

"Larry, if you think PAT is stupid, we may as well forget it. I would not expect you to work for something that you did not want. I know I wouldn't."

Larry was expecting much worse. Usually he signals relief by saying something inconsequential like, "Right."

It would seem that Larry does not value PAT as an incentive. The fact that you know better is beside the point for the moment.

Rather than being a "tactic," your words simply acknowledge the realities of the situation. You cannot make students like PAT any more than you can force them to cooperate.

Your Plan

If you can finesse the short-term situation, do so. If you stay calm and wait, Larry may take his seat for a lack of anything better to do. You can talk to Larry later.

Of course, you cannot guarantee the outcome of any situation. If Larry chooses to escalate, you will probably end up using your Backup System.

Let's assume for the moment that you successfully finesse the immediate situation. Before the day is over you must have a heart-to-heart talk with Larry. During this talk, you will implement Omission Training.

Omission Training

The general name given to an incentive system that *decreases* the rate of a behavior is *Omission Training*.

Omission Training

Incentives to Eliminate Behavior

As described earlier in the book, the basic strategy that underlies behavior management is quite simple. *Increase* the behaviors that you *do* want, and *decrease* the behaviors that you *do not* want. If you can do this, sooner or later you will be left with what you want.

Not too surprisingly, therefore, there are two basic kinds of incentive systems. One kind *increases* the rate of a behavior, and the other kind *decreases* the rate of a behavior. The vast majority of incentive systems used in classroom management, including Responsibility Training, are of the first kind. Yet, incentives to decrease behavior can be very helpful, especially when dealing with severe or chronic behavior problems.

The general name given to an incentive system that *decreases* the rate of a behavior is *Omission Training*. Omission Training has a unique structure.

The Structure of Omission Training

The structure of Omission Training is dictated by the simple fact that you cannot reinforce the *non-occurrence* of a behavior. It would sound stupid if you tried:

"I like the way you did not just hit him."

The recipient of this compliment might well conclude that you were losing it.

You can, however, reinforce someone for not doing something *for a given length of time*. You could, for example, reinforce a student for going *ten minutes* without interrupting or for going *twenty minutes* without getting out of his or her seat or for going *an entire class period* without hitting.

Omission Training plus Responsibility Training

While Omission Training is useful in providing a means other than the Backup System for eliminating problem behaviors, it becomes especially powerful when mated with Responsibility Training. This combination of management programs mobilizes the peer group to help both the teacher and the student with special needs.

For example, you could give the group a minute of bonus PAT if Larry could go ten minutes without making an inappropriate remark. This gives the peer group a vested interest in supporting Larry's efforts and ignoring his provocations. Cheers typically erupt as the PAT is posted on the board.

As you can see, Omission Training within a group context goes beyond simply changing a behavior. It makes Larry a hero with you as his cheerleader. And, it gives you "the power of the peer group"

A Vested Interest in Helping

While Omission Training is useful for eliminating problem behaviors, it becomes especially powerful when mated with Responsibility Training. This combination gives the peer group a vested interest in supporting Larry's efforts to improve while ignoring his provocations.

---

while involving the class in helping a child they usually dislike.

In addition to helping Larry, you can also reinforce the *entire class* for omitting a behavior. You could, for example, give the group a minute of bonus PAT if *no one* interrupted for a given amount of time. This can help you deal with a problem behavior that is brief but scattered, and, therefore, difficult to deal with using Limit Setting.

The Heart-to-Heart Talk

Find a quiet place where you will not be interrupted for the next twenty minutes. Heart-to-heart talks usually require plenty of "wait time." Of course, you will impart your own style to this conversation. The following dialogue is only intended to map out the terrain. The heart-to-heart talk has four parts.

Enough Is Enough

"Larry, that scene in front of the classroom this morning in which you told me that PAT was stupid – that is what we call in education 'unacceptable behavior.' And I will make you a promise: if one of us has to go, it will be you.

"Right now, we are looking at the Backup System. As I explained on the third day of school, it goes from a verbal warning to the state penitentiary and everything in between. Its purpose is to raise the price of a behavior so high that you are no longer willing to pay for it. It is not supposed to be fun.

"Between where we stand right now and the Backup System lies another option. It is a lot more enjoyable than the Backup System.

"Let me explain it to you. Then, if you want to do it, we will. And, if you don't, we won't."

Acknowledging Your Own Responsibility

"This morning when you said that PAT was stupid, my first thought was that I had thoroughly failed in explaining PAT. So, let me try again.

"First of all, you do not have to do what the rest of the group is doing during PAT. It is always possible to do your own thing as long as it is constructive. It is even possible that everyone in the class might do a different activity during PAT. The only thing that must be the same for everyone is the *duration* of PAT.

"So, let's sit down with a pad of paper and make a list of things that *you* would like to do during PAT. The boundaries are as always: It must be something that *you want*, and it must be something that *I can live with*."

This phase of program building is known as "brainstorming a reinforcement menu." It marks a change of direction in the conversation from "enough is enough" to becoming a partner with Larry in seeking enjoyment. If the two of you can pinpoint some PAT activities that Larry really wants, you have the basis of a win-win solution to the problem.

As you brainstorm PATs with Larry, remain flexible without giving up your focus on learning. You will never accept just "kicking back" as a PAT. But management is *the art of the possible.* If the most achievement-oriented activity that Larry lists is reading his motorcycle magazines, you may want to put it on the list even though you might expect more from some other students. After all, those magazines represent fairly challenging reading.

Estimate a Time Frame for Omission Training

How long can Larry behave himself during a typical day? When in doubt, shorten your estimate. You want Larry to *succeed every day*.

The most common time frame in regular classrooms is half a class period (25 minutes). Even on days when Larry gets into trouble, he will probably give you at least half a class period without getting into trouble. Be conservative. If 25 minutes seems like a lot to ask, shorten it to something that is "doable."

Explain the Mechanics to Larry

Brainstorming a reinforcement menu usually puts Larry in a different frame of mind than he had at the beginning of the heart-to-heart talk. Estimating the time frame gives you the final piece of the puzzle. Now, it is time to explain what you have in mind to Larry.

"You can do any of the items on our list during PAT. That is, you could if you had PAT. But, unfortunately, you don't. You said it was stupid, and I said, 'Then, let's forget it.' And you said, 'Right.'

"Kidding aside, I do want you to have PAT. But I also want to relax and enjoy teaching when I come to work. And that little 'altercation' we had this morning was hardly enjoyable.

"That is to say, while I want you to have PAT, I want something in return. I want something that you have given me *every day* that you have been in my class since school began, even on days in which you got into trouble. I want you to give me *half a class period* of appropriate behavior. Just cool it for 25 minutes.

"Think of it as a gesture that says, 'I will meet you halfway.' If you meet me halfway, I will meet you *more* than halfway. I will give you back your PAT, but that is not all. I will give you your PAT *plus a minute*. But it is not just *your* minute. It belongs to the *entire class*."

Always rehearse your announcement of the program to the class with Larry beforehand so that there is no embar-

rassment when the time comes. Typically with older students, the less said the better.

The next day you begin the program. As soon as Larry earns his first bonus minute, announce it just as you rehearsed.

"Class, let me have your attention. Larry and I have devised a program that we are implementing today,

and Larry is doing a great job. As a result, Larry has just earned a bonus minute of PAT *for the entire class.* I will put a circle around it so that you can see how many minutes he earns for the group. You might say that this minute is a gift from Larry to all of you."

Walk to the board to post the minute on the PAT tally. Draw a circle around the bonus minute and all other minutes that Larry subsequently earns for the class. Then say,

"Let's hear it for Larry. (Lead the group in giving Larry applause.) Come on, class! Let's not be a bunch of ingrates. Let's hear it for Larry! (You can always get a class to applaud if you try.)

"Okay, Larry, let's see if we can get another minute before the period is over."

As the class period comes to an end, say to the group,

"Class, let me have your attention. Larry has just earned a *second* minute for the group. Larry, you are doing a great job. Let me post your bonus minute on the board.

"Class, you are all two minutes richer thanks to Larry. Let's hear it for Larry." (Once again, lead the group in applause.)

Let us return to our conversation with Larry for a moment. There is one more detail of the program that needs to be explained to him.

Larry becomes a hero by earning time for the group.

"There is one more part to this program, Larry, that I need to show you. It is a kitchen timer.

"If anybody ruins this program, it will probably be me, not you. I will get busy teaching and forget about keeping track of the minutes. As I see you walking out of the room, I will think, 'Oh no! I forgot all about Larry's minutes.'

"So that I do not have to be a clock-watcher, I will use this kitchen timer. I will set it to 25 minutes and forget it. When 25 minutes is up, it will ring, and we will both know that you have earned another bonus minute."

In fact, the class quickly learns that the sound of the kitchen timer signals a bonus minute for them as well. Within a day or two, cheers erupt before you even make the announcement.

One final detail needs to be explained to Larry.

"With this program you can only earn time for the group. You can no longer lose time.

As you can see, Larry could not lose time for the group if he wanted to. Since Larry showed a weakness for playing the bully, we have simply removed the temptation.

A Bridge to Healing

Making Larry Popular
As we mentioned earlier, Larry is typically neither happy nor popular. But he would like to be. He just doesn't seem to know how.

Getting the Class Involved

For the price of a heart-to-heart talk and a few marks on the PAT tally, you have rearranged the group dynamics of the entire class to support Larry's growth.

Unless you have some powerful means of changing the group's perception of Larry from the outset, Larry's classmates will put his improvements on extinction while continuing to treat him as an outcast.

"Consequently, if you should get into trouble in class, you will deal with me personally. After you rejoin the group, I will reset the kitchen timer so that you can immediately begin earning bonus PAT. If the period should end before you have earned the next minute, I will carry all of your time forward to the next day so that you *never lose time*."

Over the years these negative emotions can produce serious deficits in social skills. Larry is not very good at getting along with people because he has not spent much time trying. Omission Training serves as a "pump primer" for helping Larry learn to get along with people by setting him up for success from the very beginning.

If I needed a behavioral program to make an unpopular child popular, I would immediately pick Omission Training. I have seen it bring an outcast child into the middle of the class sociogram in two weeks!

Changing Perceptions of Larry
The peer group is in the habit of noticing what Larry does *wrong* and failing to notice what he does *right*. Unless you have some powerful way of causing the peer group to look at Larry differently, they will continue to expect the worst and fail to notice Larry's improved behavior.

Omission Training focuses the peer group's attention on Larry's new behavior and helps them see Larry through new eyes. Without the theatrical aspect of Omission Training plus the bonus PAT that the class shares, the peer group might be so slow to notice Larry's improvement that they actually put his new behavior on extinction. Rather than let that happen, we will make a hero out of Larry in order to get quick results.

In Omission Training, we allow the normal hunger of young people for peer approval to serve a constructive end. And we give the peer group an opportunity to experience being part of the healing process.

It Is Cheap

In addition to Omission Training being powerful, it is *cheap*. For the price of a heart-to-heart talk and a few marks on the PAT tally, you have rearranged the group dynamics of the entire class to support Larry's growth.

It is actually cheaper to institute Responsibility Training just so you can institute Omission Training than it is to institute a traditional individualized B-Mod program. And it is far more powerful since it delivers "the power of the peer group."

The Life Span of Omission Training

How Often Do You Need It?

Upon learning about Omission Training, most trainees envision two or three students in each class period who would need it. They assume that every "Larry" will be a

candidate. This misperception must be corrected before we can get an accurate picture of the implementation of Omission Training.

It is impossible for you to assess your need for Omission Training until you are properly implementing Classroom Structure, Limit Setting, and Responsibility Training. Only then can you count the problems that are left over.

Typically, the tally is zero. Proper Classroom Structure plus Limit Setting plus Responsibility Training should give you far more management leverage than you have ever experienced.

My biggest problem with Omission Training is that it is so seldom needed that, by the time it is finally called for, many trainees have forgotten about it and have unnecessarily gone to their Backup System. While a sudden blow-up may force you to use your Backup System, Omission Training almost always provides a cheaper and more pleasant way of resolving a repetitive problem.

Won't Others Want It?

During a workshop, someone will always ask, "Won't other students want Omission Training if it makes them into heroes?" As logical as this seems, I have no memory of it ever happening.

The explanation probably has to do with the fact that Omission Training is so seldom used and then, only for problems of marked severity. To put it bluntly, the student

---

How Often Do You Need Omission Training?

It is impossible to assess your need for Omission Training until you are implementing Classroom Structure, Limit Setting, and Responsibility Training. Only then can you count the problems that are left over.

Typically, the tally is zero.

who receives Omission Training is "way out there." He or she is so deviant that no classmate would want to be put in the same category. Consequently, while other students appreciate the extra bonus minutes, they are quite happy to let someone else get the "glory."

How Long Do You Let It Run?

Students who need Omission Training are severely damaged. Consequently, after you set up an Omission Training program for these students, let it run for a long while. You need to allow time for healing to take place.

At the special education facility, we would typically allow Omission Training to run for six to eight weeks before we even considered eliminating it. During that time, we would look for "soft signs" of healing. In addition to improvement in Larry's behavior, we would look for signs of acceptance by the peer group such as:

- being included in games and activities just like the other students
- taking a seat in the lunchroom and having students sit near him before all of the other seats were taken
- walking down the hall in animated conversation with classmates

When it seemed as though the target student was part of the social fabric of the class, we would consider eliminating the Omission Training program. But we were very conservative. If you are in doubt, let it run a little longer.

Eliminating Omission Training

Fading Procedures

The easiest way to eliminate Omission Training is through a simple fading procedure. The two most common methods are:

Let Omission Training run until you see Larry accepted as a valued member of the peer group.

- gradually extending the time frame
- fading critical features

Of the two, I would choose the second, fading critical features. Extending the time frame can backfire since the student might feel as though you are constantly changing the rules.

Fading Critical Features

The fading of critical features is a simple three-step process. Discuss it with the student beforehand as follows:

Step 1: Fade the schedule of reinforcement.

"I keep setting the kitchen timer, and you keep getting the bonus minutes. You have gotten all of your bonus minutes for so long that I am beginning to wonder why I bother setting the timer.

"Would you mind if I just announced to the class that you had earned two bonus minutes at the *end* of every class period? Then I could forget the timer."

Rarely does the student object to this alteration in procedure. By the time the program has been running for over a month, chances are that Larry has also noticed that the kitchen timer has become superfluous. Besides, he is still earning the same number of bonus minutes for the group, and he is still receiving public recognition, although only once at the end of the class period.

Step 2: Eliminate the contingency of reinforcement.

"You know, Larry, I am beginning to think that it is silly to wait until the end of the period to give you your minutes. I am usually busy with other things then. I have almost forgotten it several times.

"Why don't I just give you your bonus minutes at the *beginning* of the class period so that I won't forget? You will get the same number of minutes, and I will announce it just as I always do."

Step 3: Eliminate the program.

The arrangement described in step 2 can run indefinitely. There is no pressing need to eliminate the program, particularly if you are worried that the student might revert to his or her old habits.

If you decide that the program has finally become "excess baggage," the easiest time to eliminate it is to simply drop it at the end of the semester. Have a simple ceremony in which both you and the class recognize Larry's achievement, and then begin the new semester without the program.

When Fading Fails

Fading any management program is a calculated gamble. You won't win them all. Consequently, as you progress with the fading program described above, you must be very attentive to signs of failure.

The main sign of failure is a gradual reemergence of the problem behavior. Seeing the old problem reemerge tells you that fading was premature.

The cure is to simply reverse the fading procedure. Reinstitute the last step that was faded and wait. Typically, you only need to go back one step, although you can go back to the original program if the reemergence of the problem behavior is sudden. If you have to reverse course, remain where you have reestablished success for a long time before you risk going forward with the fading procedure again.

All or Nothing

If Larry can deprive the class of its bonus, Larry is not only in control of the class, but he also puts the rest of the students on an *extinction program* for cooperation.

Protecting Automatic Bonuses

All or Nothing

Imagine an automatic bonus in which all of the students get a minute of PAT for being in their seats when the bell rings. Today when the bell rings, everybody is seated but Larry.

Obviously, you cannot give the class its bonus minute. Group management is "all for one, and one for all."

But imagine that this problem occurs again the next day. Now, the class has failed to get its bonus *twice in a row.* Are you beginning to get a sinking feeling of powerlessness? What if it happens a *third* time?

Early in our discussion of Responsibility Training, I said that I wanted perfection, not just improvement. The reason I gave was purely *practical.* What is the practical difference between a teacher having two students who show up without pencils as opposed to four? In either case, the teacher ends up dealing with pencils at the beginning of each class period. The overall hassle of pencil management has not been appreciably reduced.

Now, let me give you the *technical* reason for seeking perfection. If Larry can deprive the class of its Automatic Bonus, Larry is not only in control of the class, but he has also placed the rest of the students on an *extinction program* for cooperation. This is a management disaster!

You must have cooperation by *everyone,* or the entire notion of Automatic Bonuses collapses. That is why group management has such a poor track record in the research literature. It promises great efficiency and power, but there is usually at least one Larry in the class who will wreck it.

Failsafe Mechanisms

We need a failsafe mechanism to keep Larry from ruining Automatic Bonuses for the group. I will give you two versions.

- Cutting Larry out of the herd
- Cutting Larry out of the herd plus Omission Training

Cutting Larry out of the herd might sound like this:

"Class, as you can see, Larry was not in his seat when the bell rang again today, which means that you will not get your bonus minute. However, this is the third time it has happened in the past two weeks.

"When a problem occurs for a third time, it is time for me to do something about it and make a change. We need to have a talk.

"First, class, let me add to your PAT tally the three minutes that Larry has cost you over the past two weeks because he was not in his seat. This gift from me is meant to signify to you that Larry's not being in his seat is now my problem, not yours.

> ## An Alternative to the Backup System
>
> When a student consistently blocks the teacher's management objectives, the resulting exasperation naturally leads the teacher's mind toward the Backup System.
>
> A "mini" Omission Training program is an excellent alternative. For very little effort, the teacher can substitute a positive approach to management for one which is adversarial by nature.

"Next, let me address everyone in the class with the exception of Larry. In the future, if you are in your seats when the bell rings, you will get your bonus minute.

"Larry, if you are not in your seat when the bell rings, you will deal with me. Any questions?"

While cutting Larry out of the herd protects the PAT from abuse by Larry, you still end up with the cost of dealing with Larry. You can usually save yourself that cost by adding Omission Training to the program. Simply add the following paragraph to the explanation given above.

"If, however, Larry is in his seat when the bell rings, you will *all* get a *second* bonus minute. So, class, while Larry can no longer cost you time, he can give you time if we all choose to work together. Class, Larry, let's see if we can't take care of this problem the easy way."

Turning the Tables

When a student consistently blocks the teacher's management objectives, the resulting exasperation naturally leads the teacher's mind toward the Backup System. But, the Backup System is costly and prone to failure.

The Omission Training program described above is an excellent alternative. For very little effort, you have protected the many against the abuse by the few. And, you have substituted a positive approach to management for the Backup System which is adversarial by nature.

Of course, the Backup System is still there if you need to use it. But, if you use Omission Training as the "carrot," you can use the Backup System as the "stick" without having to go to the trouble of actually delivering the "stick."

Using a "mini" Omission Training program to preempt the use of the Backup System is a general strategy that can often solve management dilemmas caused by highly oppositional students. I refer to this strategy as "turning the tables" since it so efficiently turns a negative management situation into a positive one.

Piggybacking

Beyond Discipline Management

Using Omission Training in conjunction with Responsibility Training to get the peer group involved in problem solving is a general notion that can be stretched well beyond the bounds of discipline management. You might also use it for motivation.

You can make a kid a hero for doing anything you want. For example, you can make a kid a hero for participating in a group discussion. You can make a kid a hero for completing an assignment. And you can get the peer group to support the kid's efforts just by adding a bonus clause to Responsibility Training. I call this process "piggybacking."

An Example of Motivation

A fourth grade teacher that I trained several years ago had a student with an unblemished academic record. He

You can make a kid a hero for anything you want.

had never turned in a complete assignment in all of his years of formal education. Yet, the student was bright.

The teacher decided to use the peer group to gain some leverage over motivation. She said to her "do-nothing" student during Guided Practice of a math assignment,

"I want you to show me that you can do these math problems. I know that you understand the material. But today I will give you an added reason to try. For each math problem that you complete, I will announce to the class that I am adding a bonus minute to our PAT. I will be back soon to see how you are doing."

The teacher was very attentive to the student using Praise, Prompt, and Leave to its fullest to get the student through the first problem. The teacher's announcement to the class was greeted with cheers as the minute was added to the PAT tally. Soon, the student was hooked on hero status. Eventually, the schedule of reinforcement was thinned so that bonus minutes were earned for doing larger and larger amounts of work.

The good news is that, within two weeks, the student was turning in all assignments. The bad news is that, the following year, this student's teacher would not continue the program because she believed that all incentives were bribes. The student immediately reverted to his old pattern and did no work.

Recounting this experience allows me to add a note of balance to our understanding of Omission Training and

piggybacking. It works like magic, but, of course, we know that there is no magic in behavior management. You cannot expect a brief experience with a successful program to change the habits of a lifetime. You can, however, expect years of effective management to change a child's life.

Helping Substitute Teachers

Placing your Responsibility Training program in the hands of substitute teachers is a bad idea. Since you will not have time to train substitutes adequately, they will be forced to "wing it." As a result, they will typically overuse the penalty portion of the program as was discussed in earlier chapters. You are liable to return to find that your class has lost all of its PAT through the end of the year.

You can, however, give substitute teachers a bit of help by supplying them with a simplified "bonus only" version of the program. A "bonus only" program is relatively failsafe and amounts to nothing more than a little piggybacking.

Tell the students before you leave that the substitute will keep a list of the names of all of the cooperative students. When you return, each name on the list will be worth three bonus minutes.

Or, you could have the substitute teacher give the students a "cooperation score" of 0, 1, 2 or 3 at the end of each assignment. All of these scores will be added when you return. The total will represent the number of bonus minutes of PAT that the class earns for cooperating with the substitute while you were gone.

> ## Making a Difference
>
> You cannot expect a brief experience with a successful program to change the habits of a lifetime. You can, however, expect years of effective management to change a child's life.

Realistically, this use of incentives is weak compared to the strength of the "bootleg reinforcement" for goofing off that will be supplied by the peer group if the substitute is unable to control the class. But if the substitute has some management skills, a little extra incentive power can make his or her day in your classroom more pleasant.

Overview

While Omission Training is not magic, it is as close to magic as you will ever get in behavior management. It all but eliminated office referrals at the regional Special Education Center where we developed Responsibility Training.

In regular classrooms Omission Training typically serves as the alternative to the Backup System in all but the most difficult of situations. Consequently, Omission Training has tremendous power to save the child who might otherwise be a casualty of discipline management.

> **While**
> **Omission Training**
> **is not magic,**
> **it is as close as**
> **you will ever get**
> **in behavior**
> **management.**

Chapter Twenty Three

Initiating Preferred Activity Time

Two for the Price of One

You'd Do It Anyway

The fifth grade students had just taken their seats to begin the school day when their teacher made the following announcement.

"Class, before we start the day, I want to point out the art materials on the project table over by the window. The art project will be your PAT this afternoon.

"As always, I have set aside twenty minutes at the end of the day. You know, however, that once you start a project like this, you always wish you had more time. Well, you can have more time. All of the bonus PAT that you earn today will be added to the art project."

The students did not know that, had their teacher never heard of PAT, they would have done the art project anyway. They only knew that all of their hustle throughout the day translated into art.

By using learning as a PAT, you get "two for the price of one." You give the students a special enrichment activity which they enjoy while getting motivation for free.

Self-Contained versus Departmentalized

Teachers in self-contained classrooms have more potential PATs during a school day than they can use. They have art and

Preview

- When you use curriculum enrichment for PAT, you get "two for the price of one." You give the students a special learning activity while getting motivation for free.

- One of the best motivational hooks in education is team competition. You can teach anything by playing team games.

- The best game rules create the most time-on-task. One of the most effective ways to reduce "standing on the sidelines" is to have teams play defense as well as offense.

- When the team on offense misses a question, give the other team a chance to field the question for extra points. This creates peer pressure among the students on defense to look up the answer as soon as they hear the question.

- Additional PATs can be found in the appendix entitled "PAT Ideas."

music and reading stories to the class to say nothing of special projects. Add to this all of the curriculum enrichment activities that are available for the units being studied, and they have quite a list. Rather than spending a lot of time planning PAT, these teachers need only pick the best activity of the day and call it PAT.

PAT only becomes a potential headache in a departmentalized setting. Art and music now belong to other departments, and recess is just a memory. Of course, these teachers will often use curriculum enrichment for PAT just like their colleagues in self-contained classrooms. But their choices are more limited since they only have their students for one subject.

With fewer "freebies" lying around, these teachers will more often have to build PATs from scratch. If you teach economics, you will repeatedly have to ask yourself, *How do we have fun with economics?* The answer had better be cheap. I cannot grant you extra planning time.

Team Competition

A Motivational Hook

Apart from curriculum enrichment activities, *team competition* is perhaps the most reliable and easy to use motivational "hook" in education. Anything can be taught in the form of a team game, and team games make terrific PATs.

The power of team competition hit me one day while I was working at juvenile hall. As I walked into one of the classrooms to make an observation, I was met with,

"All right! Seventeen to fifteen! We've got 'em!"

"Josh is up. Josh, the next word is 'mosquito.'"

"You can do it. You can do it."

"Mosquito, M-O-S-Q-U-I-T-O."

"Yes! We rule! Eighteen to fifteen!"

Slowly it dawned on me that I was watching a bunch of kids in juvenile hall going ape over spelling. Spelling!

At the time of my visit to "juvy," I was in a quandary about PAT. My high school teachers were telling me that they did not have time to mess with it. It was too much trouble.

The classroom at juvenile hall caused a lightbulb to go on in my head. I tried to remember playing games in school when I was a kid.

I clearly remember my fourth grade teacher, Mrs. Franklin, playing a team game. It was raining, and we could not go out for afternoon recess. She divided the class in half, and we spent twenty minutes playing math baseball. She did it on the spur of the moment, and we loved it.

The strange thing about my memory of math baseball is that we only did it once. I remember wishing that we could do it again, but we never did. We would have gladly worked for the opportunity to play academic baseball over and over if we had only been given the chance.

Team competition is the most reliable motivational 'hook' in education.

Game Rules

The realization that you can make lessons into team games caused me to study team game rules. Did you know that there really aren't that many different games in the world? Did you know that the rules to baseball, football, basketball, hangman, and Jeopardy are all the same?

With a half-dozen sets of rules you can generate hundreds of PATs, and you won't need any planning time. You can do it on the spur of the moment!

Let me tell you what makes the best team games – *time-on-task*. Kids hate to sit and watch. They love to play. The more they play, the more they learn.

Academic Baseball

More Playing Time

Let's begin with the rules for academic baseball. I played it as a kid, and you probably did too. Studying the rules for baseball will teach us a lot about game rules in general.

In baseball, your team is up roughly half of the time, and the other team is up roughly half of the time. If PAT lasts 20 minutes, your team will only be up for about 10 minutes. By having innings in which teams takes turns at bat, you *halve the length of everybody's PAT.*

How can we improve the rules of the game so that kids spend more time playing and less time on the sidelines? The answer is *defense*. Make the students play defense, and they will be engaged in playing when the other team is up at bat.

Playing Defense

We will play the game with questions at four levels of difficulty; singles, doubles, triples, and home runs. These questions usually come right

The kids at juvenile hall were going ape over a team game that taught spelling.

off the top of your head. If you want to simplify the game, make every question worth a run.

Lay out *two diamonds* on the floor with small pieces of masking tape as bases. Have the students get out of their seats to "run the bases." They have fun strutting their stuff, and you don't have to keep track of who is on base.

Divide the room into two teams. On the team that is "up" first, pick a student and say,

"Batter up! Do you want a single, double, triple or home run?"

The student picks a level of difficulty, and you *pitch* a question. If the student gets a *hit* by answering the question correctly within ten seconds, he or she is on base. Mild showing off as the student rounds the bases is usually greeted with hoots and cheers from teammates.

If, however, the student *misses* the question, you turn to the other team and say,

"Fly ball!"

Repeat the question and then wait before calling on anyone. This brings us to our next element of team game structure. Do you play this game open-book or closed-book?

Aha! If you play the game open-book, the team on defense can start looking up the answer as soon as they hear the question. As a result, the team on defense frantically flips through books, lab manuals, and notes to find the answer while the student who is "up" attempts to answer the question. There is actually peer pressure to look up the answer since dropping a fly ball means that a teammate was simply too lazy to look up the answer.

There is a certain contagion to looking up the answer that fills the room. Since kids hate to sit on the sidelines

with nothing to do, the students on the team that is "at bat" usually start looking up the answer as well.

After you say, "Fly ball!" wait at least five seconds or until the rustling of book pages dies down. Then, call on a student.

Usually, teachers train the students not to raise their hands and go "Ooh, ooh, ooh" since it becomes tiring after a while. In addition, by calling on whomever you please, you can distribute questions more effectively while assuring that the weaker students get questions that they have a good chance of answering.

Scoring

If students on defense answer the question correctly, they *catch* the fly ball and make an out on the other team. If, however, they miss the question and *drop* the fly ball, the batter is on base with an error, and all runners advance one base.

Normally in baseball, the team with the most runs wins, but not in *this* game. In this game the final score for each team is calculated as *runs minus outs*. Catching a fly ball nullifies a run. In the final score it is the equivalent of hitting a solo home run. Defense is serious business.

Baseball Becomes "Double-Diamond Baseball"

Alternate questions between the teams. Consequently, a team would be up for one question and then on defense for the following question. By alternating questions between teams, each team has the same number of at-bats, and the dramatic tension is maximized since everyone can see who is ahead at any moment and what difficulty of question is needed to score.

Alternating the questions in this fashion eliminates innings. Rather, you have two games running side-by-side like a race. It is a race to see which team can get around the bases more often before time runs out.

The generic name for this set of rules is Ping-Pong since the play continually alternates back and forth between the teams. Since you have two baseball diamonds on the floor, however, we have gotten into the habit of referring to this version of academic baseball as "Double-Diamond Baseball."

Baseball Becomes Football

To change baseball to football, draw two gridirons on the board, one for each team. Begin the game by saying to a student,

"Ten, twenty, thirty, or forty yard question. What will it be?"

Questions alternate between the teams as they move their footballs down their respective gridirons.

If a student misses a question, turn to the team on defense, and say,

"Sack!"

If the student you call on answers the question correctly, he or she throws the other team for a ten-yard loss.

An alternative way of structuring academic football is to pit one team against another on a *single gridiron* as in the real game of football. Secondary students often prefer this variant. Start on the fifty-yard line. Rather than using the Ping-Pong format, each team gets three downs to score. Three downs to score forces the students to use the long yardage questions.

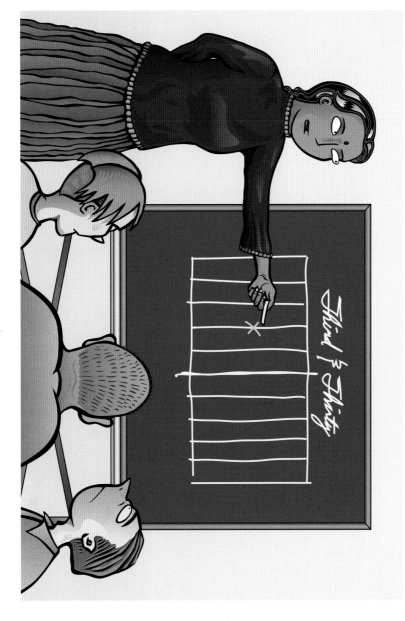

Academic baseball becomes academic football with the change of seasons.

If a ten-yard question is missed, the teacher says, "*Sack!*" as in the previous example. A correct answer throws the offense for a ten-yard loss. If, however, a twenty-, thirty- or forty-yard question is missed, the teacher says, "*Interception!*" A correct answer gains possession of the ball at the line of scrimmage.

Of course, teachers can elaborate this basic format to suit their pleasure. You could have extra point questions after a touchdown. You could have difficult "Hail Mary" questions when more than forty yards are desperately needed. I have even seen teachers have a classroom Super Bowl complete with a satirical coin-toss ceremony. One teacher played football so often that she made a felt board for the gridiron with a felt football to make changes in field position easy.

Football Becomes Basketball

Think of football as simply a "path game" like the preschoolers' "Candyland." In such games the players move down the "squares" of the path in order to reach a "goal." A gridiron is simply a path with ten squares.

Once you envision games played on courts or fields as path games, you can play basketball or soccer just as easily as you can football. By answering more difficult questions, you can move down the path several squares at a time in order to score more quickly.

Basketball is simply a path game that requires seven "moves" in order to score, whereas football requires ten moves to score. In basketball, if the team with the ball misses the question and the team on defense answers it, they "steal the ball." The game then switches directions.

Hangman

"What'll it be? One, two, three, or four body parts?"

To use the Ping-Pong format, draw two gallows on the board, and alternate the questions between the teams.

Add fingers and toes to make enough body parts so that the game lasts longer.

Jeopardy

"Pick a ten, twenty, thirty, or forty point question. The category is . . ."

All games from television make great PATs. Like *Jeopardy*, *Who Wants To Be A Millionaire?* and *Twenty-One* can be used to review factual information. However, some older game shows such as *What's My Line?* and *To Tell the*

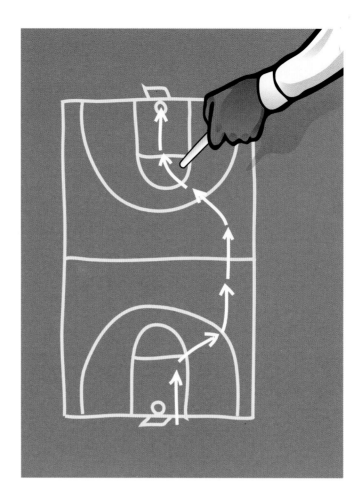

Basketball is simply a path game that requires seven "moves" in order to score.

Truth are great for history. Students love impersonating historical figures and attempting to fake each other out.

Generating Questions

While teachers typically come up with questions on the spur of the moment, you can involve the students in the writing of questions. You could say, for example,

"Class, as you know, our test on chapter 7 is Thursday. I want to give you some class time to prepare for the test. But, I am going to have you prepare in the following fashion.

"Take out four pieces of paper, and number them one through four, placing the number in the upper right-hand corner. Write a single, double, triple, and home run question corresponding to the number on the paper.

"As you write these questions, look through chapter 7 for those things that are most important. Imagine that you are a teacher writing test questions.

"In fact, I will use some of your questions on the test. You may get to answer your own question on Thursday. In addition, I will use them during PAT.

"Don't make the singles too easy because the other team might get that question. And, don't make the home runs too hard because you might get that question.

"Below the question, write the answer. I want complete sen-

tences. Beneath the answer, write the page number where the information can be found.

"You have the rest of the period to write your questions and answers. I will be coming around to see how you are doing."

In addition to structuring a good review activity, you end up with a stack of singles, doubles, triples, and home runs. Save the questions for your unit test review. *Jeopardy* is an excellent review game since the stacks of questions from different chapters supply your *Jeopardy* categories.

Academic Volleyball

Perfect for Vocabulary

In volleyball, your team can only score when *you have the serve*. When you have the serve, you can score points *in succession*. If, however, you miss, the service goes to the other team. Then, they can score points in succession until they miss.

You would not want to use questions that require explanations for answers. A team could be on defense a long time if the other team were to run up a string of points. For such questions, baseball would be a much better choice.

For volleyball, the questions must come "fast and furious" with quick answers to keep the game from dragging. The quick pace of questions makes volleyball ideal for vocabulary. Volleyball, therefore, is often used by foreign language and biology teachers.

The Rules

Divide the room into two teams, and say,

"I will begin by giving a word to one of the teams. Then, I will point to a person on that team. You will have *one second* to give me the first letter of the word.

Then, I will point to another person on that same team, and he or she will have *one second* to give me the next letter of the word.

"If someone misses, the word will come over to the other team. I will point to someone on that team, and he or she must pick up where the other team left off. The second team will keep the word as long as they spell it correctly. If they miss a letter, the word comes back to the first team. The team that gives me the last letter of the word gets the point and the next word.

"Ready? Here we go! The first word is 'photosynthesis.'"

Point to a student, and you are off and running. Drive the pace of the game so that students must be on their toes. You are a high-energy game show host.

For younger students whose attention spans are short, you can reduce the burden on memory and attention as follows. Give the word to the entire class, and have them write it down. Then, as the word is being spelled, everyone can follow along to keep track.

Keep 'em Honest

Perfect for Math

What kind of game rules work for math? The whole class could fall asleep while the person who is "up" attempted to solve a quadratic equation.

The game described below was described earlier in chapter 10, "Providing Accountability," as a method of work check. However, work check takes place in the form of a contest that can serve as a PAT.

To review, divide the class into two teams. Pair each member of Team A with a member of Team B, and have the pairs place their desks side by side. Write a math prob-

lem on the board, and give each problem a time limit as follows:

"All right, class, you have two minutes for this next problem. (Write the equation on the board.) Ready? Go!"

Give the students a warning as time runs out.

"Class, you have fifteen seconds."

Keep 'em Honest Work Check

When time runs out, go through the following routine:

"Time! Exchange papers.

"The answer is…

"Check them and return them.

"How many got it right on Team A?

"How many got it right on Team B?

"The score is now ___ to ___

"Class, you have three minutes for the next problem.

Would people on Team A let people on Team B have extra time to work on the problem? Hardly! They'll say, "I'll take that!" and grab the paper.

Would anybody on Team A cheat for anybody on Team B? Not likely!

Did You Know?

With a half-dozen sets of rules, you can generate hundreds of PAT games.

Did you know that the rules for baseball, football, basketball, hangman, and Jeopardy are all the same?

Television Game Formats

Television games must be of high interest or they wouldn't be successful. Be on the lookout for ones that you can adapt to your classrooms.

Speed Games

Family Feud

When you call on the first person who has his or her hand up, you have a *speed game*. An example of a speed game on television is *Family Feud* in which the first team to hit the buzzer gets to answer the question.

College Bowl

College Bowl is a hybrid of a four-level/Ping-Pong format and a speed game. On the TV version, two universities were represented by four students each. Questions at four levels of difficulty were given during 10, 20, 30, and 40 point rounds.

To start the game, Team A would be given a 10 point question. The team would huddle, and the captain would shout out their answer. If they got it right, they would get 10 points. But, if they missed it, the same question would go to Team B. Then, Team B would get their own 10 point

keeps the other team honest. With every additional problem the score mounts and the tension builds.

Of course, you could give the class the same math problems on a worksheet. But, that would be a drag; and *you* would have to grade them.

The whole check routine takes seconds, and each team keeps the other team honest. With every additional problem the score mounts and the tension builds.

After the papers are returned, would students on Team B let their counterparts on Team A hold up their hands if they did not get it right? What do you think?

The whole check routine takes seconds, and each team

question. If they missed it, the same question would go to Team A.

The final part of the 10 point round was a toss-up question. This was the speed part of the game. The moderator would read a question, and the first person to "buzz in" answered the question. If that person answered the question correctly, he or she earned an extra 10 points for his or her team. But, if that player got it wrong, the other team could *huddle* before answering – a penalty for *buzzing in* before being sure of the answer.

This game format does not work well for large teams. Too many students become passive while the smarties dominate. Teachers commonly use their cooperative learning groups as teams with College Bowl. Having stacks of questions prepared in advance makes it easier to use this format. Since you cannot moderate several games simultaneously, have students moderate by simply pulling questions off of the appropriate stack.

PAT in the Elementary Grades

Using Curriculum as PAT

Debra Johnson, a first grade teacher from Dunlap, Tennessee, can honestly say that, after she learned to exploit PAT, she never taught another spelling lesson. Yet, at the end of one semester, all of her students passed the spelling achievement test at the second grade level, and some went as far as the fourth grade level.

How did she do it? Debra played spelling games for PAT two or three times a week. She posted lists of spelling words so that the students could prepare for Spelling Baseball. Soon, the students asked for harder words so that they could hit triples and home runs.

Spelling was not the only lesson she taught through PATs.

"We also did math, vocabulary, art, reading, journal writing, story telling and sharing. One of their favorite activities was reading from their journals. Soon I began to see every lesson as a potential PAT."

How Much PAT?

Finding the correct time for PAT was a matter of trial and error, reported Ms. Johnson. At the beginning she tried one a day, but her first graders could not "hold it together" that long.

"It all fell into place when I did three PATs a day. It was a match for their maturity level."

Debra gave the class fifteen minutes as a gift, but she was always able to bring PAT up to 30 minutes with bonuses. That meant one hour and 30 minutes of PAT a day! When asked if she lost anything by having so much PAT, she said,

"I didn't give up *anything*. In fact, we saved enough time to do learning activities that I had not been able to fit into my schedule."

"At one point they earned so much additional time that I had to put it into a savings account. They spent it to watch Reading Rainbow and the Magic School Bus."

Key to Success

When asked for the most important ingredient of a successful PAT, Debra told us,

"Teacher involvement is the key. It does not work as well if you just turn the kids loose. You must be there enjoying it with them and structuring it."

Interestingly, teachers at the secondary level have also reported that their participation made the difference.

PAT for Research

Using PAT to Do Reports

The fourth grade class of Ann Owen in East Noble, Indiana frequently earned more time than it could use during its daily PAT. Ann put the unused time into a special account so that the class could eventually earn an entire day of PAT. The class used that day to present group reports on Great Britain.

From Monday through Thursday on the week of the presentations, the regular PAT was used to get ready for the big day. The class used video tapes, books, magazines, encyclopedias, and the internet to aid in their research.

The presentations showed that the students had learned about Say, See, Do Teaching by watching Ann. The geography group had everyone make maps of Great Britain. They then supplied stickers so that classmates could mark key areas and cities. The Games Group brought pancakes and skillets to reenact the famous Leeds Pancake Relay that celebrates Shrove Tuesday. Another group made transparencies showing the evolution of the Union Jack and what each part represents. They then passed out materials so that each classmate could design a flag of his or her own.

Cost and Benefit

When asked what all of this cost her, Ann said, "It was just another lesson. We would have had group presentations anyway."

When asked what the class gained, Anne said, "They owned the activity. They were responsible for earning the time and for making the most of it. They were successful, and they felt it."

PAT in Middle School

Using PAT for Foreign Language

Dale Crum of Arvada Middle School in Jefferson County, Colorado uses PAT with his Spanish classes.

"Most of our PATs are games. One of their favorites is basketball. Each of two teams sends a member to the board, and when I say a word in English, the first one to write it properly in Spanish wins. The winner gets to shoot a Nerf basketball at the trash can with more difficult shots earning more points

"Another game they love is Pictionary. Each team sends a person to the board, and I secretly give them a word in Spanish. They have to draw a picture of it while each team tries to guess the word. The kids get excited as they call out words, but there is a penalty for using English."

Scheduling PAT

Dale uses different schedules of PAT for his seventh and eighth grade classes. According to Dale,

"The eighth graders have PAT once a week. I start them out with 15 minutes on Monday, and by Friday they have earned over a half-hour. They love Fridays.

> If a group of your colleagues shares one PAT a week, you will all have more ideas than you have time to use.

"A couple of my seventh grade classes can be squirrely, and they could not wait until Friday if their lives depended on it. For them we have PAT at the end of each 50 minute class period. I tell them, 'Earn it today.' We play learning games that review the material I taught that day."

PAT in High School

Using PAT for Science

Annette Patterson in Artesia, New Mexico uses a game she calls "Tag Team" in all of her science classes from Basic Science through Chemistry. *Tag Team* combines large motor activity with review to create a high level of excitement.

"First, I divide the class into four teams and line them up. Then, I name a category of information. It could be the attributes that distinguish birds from other animals or the signs and chemical symbols for earth elements.

"Once I name the category, the first member of each team races to the board to write down an example of that category. Then they race back to hand the chalk to the next person in line who races to the board. Each round of the game lasts one minute. The team with the most correct answers wins. Since repeats don't count, everybody pays close attention."

Everybody Likes to Play

Annette finds that the advanced students look forward to PAT just as much as her Basic Science students.

"When I first started with PAT, I was afraid that the older college-bound students would not go for it. I couldn't have been more wrong. I guess kids just like to play."

Getting Started

Anxiety and Avoidance

"I teach Kindergarten, and the kids can't tell time."

"Our high school kids are too cool for PAT."

"I don't know what to use for English."

"I just don't have time for it."

"If we played games, my kids would go wild."

Comments like these occur during every workshop and reflect the anxiety that we all feel about starting something new. A voice inside says, "What if I try this, and it bombs miserably?"

Those who give it a try invariably report, with a sense of wonder, "It works!" As Annette Patterson said, "I guess kids just like to play."

Assessing Maturity Realistically

Many secondary teachers scare themselves out of doing PAT by imagining that teenagers are more mature than they really are. The teacher who said, "Our high school kids are just too cool for PAT," had convinced himself that his students were seventeen going on twenty-five.

It would be more accurate to think of the students as seventeen coming from seven. Any game that the students have ever enjoyed playing, they still enjoy playing. I have seen high school classes work up a sweat playing "Steal the Bacon" just like fourth grade classes. One of the most commonly chosen games in seventh grade is "Heads Up Seven Up." Until I saw it repeatedly, I wouldn't have believed it.

A Little Help From Your Friends

Make a PAT Bank

Coming up with PAT ideas will be easier with a little help from your friends. Every member of the faculty has great PAT ideas. If your colleagues were to take turns sharing one PAT a week, you would have more ideas than you had time to use.

Create a PAT Bank at your school site. Have faculty members write up their favorite PATs on 4x6 cards and keep them in a file box. Also, collect books of PAT ideas, and keep them in a central location.

There are books of games for teaching almost anything, but they are often in print for only a short time. Have everyone sort through their boxes of old materials to find long-lost treasures.

One faculty at a middle school in Polk County, Florida required copies of a favorite PAT as the admission for an end of the year teacher luncheon. In August, each teacher received these ideas in a PAT book to begin the school year.

Any game that students have ever enjoyed, they still enjoy.

A Little Help from the Appendix

The Appendix entitled "PAT Ideas" at the end of this book contains enough PAT games to keep you going for a long time. We have included protocols for games that work for both a broad age span and a wide range of curriculum areas.

A Little Help from www.fredjones.com

Additional information on Preferred Activity Time is provided on our web site. Look for:

- More PATs
- Links to publishers' web sites for books of games
- Lists of web sites where you can find computer games
- Links to web sites where step-by-step individual PATs are available
- Examples of when and how other teachers use PAT
- New postings that you send to us

The **www.fredjones.com** web site is updated continuously. Bookmark our web site and check back frequently for new ideas.

We invite you to send games, ideas, and comments to:

info@fredjones.com

Section Eight

Using
the Backup System

Chapter Twenty Four

Dealing with Typical Classroom Crises

Preview

- The Backup System is a hierarchy of consequences for dealing with severe or repetitive discipline problems.

- Once a student is sent to the office, management becomes expensive because it consumes the time of at least two professionals and often requires meetings and paperwork.

- It is far cheaper to nip the problem in the bud. But what, exactly, do you do when such a nasty problem first occurs in the classroom?

- Most teachers enter the profession without a clear answer to this question. Consequently, when the time comes, they must "wing it."

- Small backup response options provide strategies for nipping problems "in the bud." These responses are "in the bud." These responses are low-key and private. Yet they clearly communicate to the student that "enough is enough."

Beyond Limit Setting

What the...?

As you turn from writing a sentence on the board, you see something fly across the room.

"What the....?"

Your head quickly follows the trajectory back to its source. You catch Larry as his body comes around. He gives you his innocent look.

Your brainstem shouts out, "Why you little..."

Meanwhile, your cortex whispers, "Slow down. Take a relaxing breath. Turn in a regal fashion."

What Next?

Larry is trying to disappear, but he knows he's been busted. Your lesson has come to a halt. Everybody can tell that this is serious.

As you take another relaxing breath, you size up the situation. You have time to think: "I can't just go on teaching after something like that. Should I send him to the office? He's just sitting there innocently now."

Do You Have a Plan?

In your training to be a teacher, did you ever receive a clear answer to the following question? Exactly what do you do when a student pulls some stunt in your classroom that causes you to say to yourself, *I never want to see that in here again?*

I have asked that question to thousands of teachers in dozens of locations, and almost never does a hand go up. This should teach us something. There is no plan. Our profession does not have any straightforward, generally understood way of dealing with one of the most predictable discipline management dilemmas that might occur in the classroom.

With no plan of action, we are left to devise some kind of plan on our own. We read a book. We ask the teacher down the hall. We search our memories. We beg, borrow, and steal and finally we "wing it."

What do you think the odds are that thousands of young teachers will all come up with a good plan during their first year on the job? And, once they come up with a plan, what do you think the odds are that they will ever change it?

The Structure of the Backup System

A Hierarchy of Consequences

The Backup System is a hierarchy of consequences arranged in a stair step fashion from small to large. The logic of the Backup System was discussed briefly at the beginning of chapter 13, "Understanding Brat Behavior." This logic is timeless – *the punishment fits the crime*. The bigger the crime, the bigger the punishment.

The objective of the Backup System is to suppress the unacceptable behavior so that it does not reappear. This is done by raising the price of a behavior to the point where the student is no longer willing to pay for it. As you go up the Backup System, unfortunately, the program becomes more expensive for everyone involved.

Certain of the milder consequences are under the teacher's control *within the classroom*. Common examples that you may remember from your childhood include keeping a student in from recess, talking to a student after class, or keeping a student after school.

The remainder of consequences at the school site occur *outside of the classroom* where they are referred to as "The

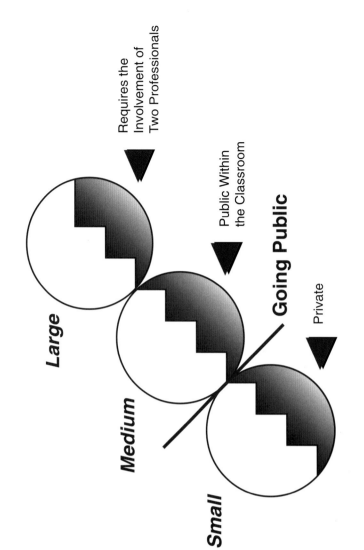

Large

Medium

Small

Going Public

Requires the Involvement of Two Professionals

Public Within the Classroom

Private

*As you go up the Backup System,
the program becomes more expensive for everyone involved.*

School Discipline Code." These, too, have not changed much since you were a kid and include being sent to the office, detention, in-school suspension, and out-of-school suspension.

Beyond the school district, the Backup System is administered by the juvenile justice system and the criminal justice system. It is a rare high school administrator who has not had some dealings with juvenile hall.

Problems with the School Discipline Code

We had some fun with the School Discipline Code at the beginning of chapter 13 with our "mock freshman assembly." As we all know, the same 5 percent of the student body, the "Larrys," produce 90-95 percent of the office referrals for as long as they are in school. Year after year, we ask our school discipline system to "put the lid on." And, year after year, we are left frustrated, muttering to ourselves,

It should work!

Why doesn't it?

What do we have to do to make it work?

No matter how many times we convene a task force to revise the School Discipline Code, nothing ever changes. For one thing, as I mentioned earlier, there is nothing that you can legally do to Larry that every educator has not known about since his or her first day on the job. And, secondly, many of the things that we do try, like kicking Larry out of class or out of school, backfire by reinforcing him for giving us a hard time.

Levels to the Game

The diagram on the opposite page is a schematic of the "hierarchy of consequences" with consequences divided into three sections, *small, medium, and large*. The three levels of the Backup System can be described as follows:

• **Large** – Large backup responses require help from outside of the classroom. Sending a student to the office, assigning detention, or suspending a student are the most common examples.

Large backup options are expensive because they consume the time of at least two professionals and often require meetings after school and extensive paperwork. In addition, by the time you send a student to the office, you have already paid a high price in terms of stress.

Since large backup responses can serve as stress reducers just by getting rid of Larry for a while, they have a tendency to become addictive. A certain percentage of teachers on any faculty will repeatedly "bounce" students to the office just to make them disappear.

• **Medium** – Medium backup responses occur within the classroom. Their defining characteristic, apart from being under the teacher's control, is that they are *public*.

Most of the classroom sanctions that we remember from childhood come under this category. There is nothing private about having your name put on the board, being sent to time-out or being kept after class for a talk with the teacher.

Medium backup responses tend to be cheaper than large ones because they consume the time of only one professional while rarely requiring extra meetings or paperwork. However, a hidden cost of these sanctions can be the revenge of an embarrassed student who was antagonistic to begin with.

• **Small** – Small backup responses provide teachers with a clear idea of what to do the *first time* they see a problem that they never want to see again. They are your first line of defense.

Small backup responses are *private*. They are *subtle*. The rest of the class usually does not even know that they occurred. Consequently, small backup responses avoid the potential for revenge from an embarrassed student.

It is the job of small backup responses to "nip problems in the bud." They say to the student, in effect,

You are entering the Backup System. A word to the wise. Stop what you are doing now while it is still cheap. The price will only go up from here.

If the student takes the teacher seriously and stops goofing off, management is cheap for everyone. As you can see, however, it all hinges on the student taking the teacher seriously.

Classroom versus School Site Discipline Management
While it is important for a teacher to understand the Backup System in its totality, most of the Backup System occurs outside of the teacher's classroom. Rather than being part of classroom management, it falls under the heading of school-site management.

School-site management covers anything that happens outside of your door. It includes the management of noise in the halls, litter and graffiti, and rowdiness during assemblies, in the lunch room, on the school grounds, and at the bus dock.

Effective school-site management has been described in detail in the books, *Positive Classroom Discipline* and *Positive Classroom Instruction*. Relevant chapters will be posted on our web site **www.fredjones.com** so that you may read them at will. Since this book describes the skills of *classroom* management, our discussion of the backup system will focus upon sanctions that teachers can use by themselves within the classroom to keep small problems from becoming large.

Using Small Backup Responses

Entering the Backup System
You will typically enter the Backup System for one of two reasons:

- A sudden obnoxious incident
- A repeat disruptor

While obnoxious incidents are plain to see, it would be worth our while to spend some time with *repeat disruptors*. As I mentioned in chapter 19, "Adjusting As You Go," some kids come from homes in which the parents never follow through after saying "no." These children learn to simply pause when they are told to stop *until the parent looks away*. Then, they continue doing as they please.

When you see the this pattern a few times, a red flag should go up in your brain that says, *We may have a repeater.* When you conclude that you do, it is time to go to the Backup System. There is no point in playing this game all year.

After you have used the Backup System to make the point that "no means no," you can probably fade your consequences back to Limit Setting. Until you make that point in no uncertain terms, repeaters assume that you are a "weenie" like mom and dad.

Camouflage and Containment
During training I do a demonstration in which I say to the trainees,

"I am going to model working the crowd. It is a boring demonstration because working the crowd is never dramatic.

"Watch carefully though, because, when I am done, I will ask you a question. Do not guess at the answer. If you know the answer, raise your hand."

As I work the crowd, I interact briefly with a series of students just as any teacher might during Guided Practice. Then, I say to the group,

"Raise your hand if you know who is in trouble."

No hands go up — not even the hands of those sitting next to the person who is "in trouble." Then I say,

"Let me tell you why you do not know who is in trouble. Because, I don't *want* you to know. It is none of your business.

"Will the people who received corrective feedback on a math problem please raise your hands (two hands go up). Will the people whose work I checked please raise your hands (two more hands go up). Now, will the person who is in trouble please raise your hand."

Some mild laughter ripples through the group as those sitting next to the person "in trouble" realize that they were unaware of it.

"One of the things that we learn from this demonstration is that, when you are working the crowd, the students cannot tell *corrective feedback* from *work check* from your *Backup System*. They all look the same.

"When you are working the crowd, you talk to students from close range. You typically lean over to whisper so as not to pull other students off task. Consequently, it is a private communication."

As with meaning business, *working the crowd* provides the camouflage that allows your Backup System to be invisible. When discipline management is invisible, you have a greater ability to keep small problems small.

Just a Warning?

What I said to the student "in trouble" was:

"This is the second time I have had to deal with this talking, and I want it to stop. If I see any more talking, we will have a little conversation of our

As with meaning business, working the crowd provides the camouflage that allows your Backup System to be invisible.

own after class. For right now, all I really care about is getting some of this work done."

This is a verbal warning. The specific words are not critical. You will ad-lib something of this general nature when the time comes.

But there are warnings, and then, there are warnings. I could have admonished the disruptive student in front of the class, or I could have written the student's name on the board. Both are types of warnings commonly used by teachers. But they would have been *public events*.

Imagine that you are sixteen years old in a high school class full of your friends, and the teacher calls you down in front of your peer group. How would you feel toward that teacher? Would you get even?

If you were the teacher, that student's "getting even" would be your next discipline problem. Isn't it a little self-defeating to have the "solution" to one discipline problem be the cause of the next one?

Keep It Private

As I mentioned in an earlier chapter, there is no such thing as a win-lose situation at this level of discipline management. It is win-win or lose-lose. If you make students look foolish in front of their peer group, they will make you look foolish in front of the same peer group.

If, on the other hand, you are protective of the students, even when they are out of line, they will probably cut you some slack when you need it. At the very least, they will have no reason for revenge.

If the warning is a public event, it is a *medium* backup response that unavoidably involves the peer group. If the warning is private, it is a *small* backup response that does not involve the peer group. It would be far more protective of the student and far less risky for you to keep the warning as private as possible.

The Function of Small Backup Responses

A *Word to the Wise*

Small Backup responses are a series of two or three messages, arranged in order of increasing explicitness. As mentioned earlier, they say to the student,

"You are entering the Backup System. A word to the wise…"

The objective of these communications is to get the student to fold in the poker game before the price gets high for everyone.

Goofing off in the classroom is typically a penny-ante game. Kids are rarely in it for big risks and high stakes. Usually they are just in it for a diversion in the midst of work. Most of the time the students will fold before the price gets too high if you give them a chance to do so gracefully. Of course, all bets are off if you embarrass them or back them into a corner.

An *Invitation to Fold*

Small backup responses are *communications*, not sanctions. They are "promissory notes." Their objective is to:

- inform students that they are entering the Backup System (i.e., that you have had about enough of their foolishness)

- invite students to fold (i.e., to cool it before you are forced to deliver consequences with real price tags attached)

You are making an offer that the student would be foolish to refuse. Most of the time, unless students have a big chip on their shoulders, they will make the pragmatic choice and keep "the price of doing business" low.

The backup response options listed below are arranged from most private (smallest) to most explicit (largest). Most of them have been around for ever, and you may be able to add an item or two of your own to the list. The two or three that you choose may differ depending on the student and the situation.

Small Backup Options

Pre-Warning

A pre-warning clearly communicates that "enough is enough" without specifying consequences. This gives you time to observe the situation, and it gives the student time to think. A fourth grade teacher from Memphis, a "natural" if I ever saw one, described her pre-warning to me. She said,

"Students know perfectly well when they are 'stepping over the line.' Rather than letting it slide, I will confront that person privately with my most serious demeanor. I will look the student in the eye and say, 'If I see any more of this behavior whatsoever, I am going to have to start planing what to do.'

"Their eyes get big. The student knows that I am serious. Rarely do I ever have to 'start planing' what to do."

A pre-warning often elicits a short burst of nervous laughter from students. Due to the teacher's manner, students know that it is a serious matter. But when they process the words, they realize to their relief that they are not really "in trouble" yet.

A pre-warning is frequently all that you need. It serves as a "wake-up call" to students who are too busy "goofing off" to realize that they are being inappropriate. If the problem continues, you can always go to an explicit warning.

Warning

Warnings have already been discussed in detail. A warning describes the consequence to the student if you "see this behavior one more time." A warning is *never* a bluff.

Pulling the Card

Imagine that you have a 3-by-5 card file on your desk containing each student's name, address, and home phone. Having students fill out these cards is not a bad Bell Work activity on the first day of school.

Imagine, further, that you have given a warning to a student, let's call him Larry as usual. You look up to see Larry doing "it" again. You catch his eye as you take a relaxing breath. He gives you his best "oops, sorry" look.

Slowly, without calling any attention to yourself, walk to your desk and casually pick up the card file. Leaf through it, and pull out Larry's card as you look at him. Lay the card on the corner of your desk face up. Look at Larry again with your best Queen Victoria face as you place the card file back on your desk. Then return to what you were doing, giving Larry one final look.

Obviously, you are communicating with Larry. He would have to be pretty dense not to realize whose name, address and home phone number is sitting face-up on the corner of your desk.

Students will usually fold before the price gets too high, if they can do so gracefully.

You have literally "rolled one more card" in the poker game, and now Larry must decide whether to raise or fold. Hopefully, he will "cool it" and keep the price of poker cheap for everyone.

A Note in the Grade Book

Having already interacted with the disruptive student once, you look up to see the problem reoccur. You catch the student's eye.

Walk slowly to your desk, and, making eye contact with the disruptor, sit down and pick up your grade book. Write a note concerning the incident in the appropriate place, and give the student another look. Stand slowly, lay the grade book down on your desk, and return to what you were doing. With a permanent record of the behavior in the grade book, poker is getting more expensive.

Once again, the student must make a decision to raise or fold. As always with small backup responses, you are attempting to communicate as subtly as possible that folding would be a very wise thing to do.

A Letter on the Desk

A letter on the desk is your last stop before medium and large backup responses. It is not frequently done, but it has saved a few teachers from needing more expensive sanctions.

Having already given the disruptive student two opportunities to fold (your choice as to the options used),

you decide to give small backup responses one more shot (a judgement call). You catch the student's eye and then go to your desk where you sit down and begin to write.

Write a brief letter home. It takes less than a minute to write since it only contains five sentences which cover the following points:

You have literally "rolled one more card" in the poker game, and now Larry must decide whether to raise or fold.

- Dear _____, today in class I have had to deal with (briefly describe the problem behavior).
- I need your help.
- If we work together now, we can prevent this from becoming a "real" problem.
- I will call you tomorrow at which time we can make a plan.
- Thank you for your help.

Sign the letter, and put it in an envelope. Address the envelope, but don't waste a stamp yet. Take the letter and a piece of tape to the student's desk. Lean over and tape the letter on the desk, and whisper to the student as privately as possible,

"This is a letter home to your parents describing exactly what I have had to put up with in here today. If I see *no more* of this behavior before the end of the (day, for young students, or week, for older students), then, with my permission and in front of my eyes, you may tear up this letter and throw it away.

"If, however, I see *any* more of this behavior, I will send the letter home even if I have to hand-deliver it. Do I make myself clear?

"For now, all I really care about is getting some of this work done. Let's see if we can keep life simple."

The letter on the desk is what you might call a visual prompt. It can serve as a continual reminder to be wise.

I am sometimes asked, "What would you do if the student just tore up the letter and threw it on the floor?" This question is almost always asked in a tone that says, "These little sanctions won't work with some of my students."

To put small backup responses into perspective, let me emphasize again that the critical variable in a well imple-mented Backup System is *never* your success. The only critical variable is the price paid by the student. As I have mentioned, you cannot guarantee any outcome because you are only half of the equation. The ultimate price is determined by the student. If the student forces you to deliver stiffer sanctions, then deliver them.

Medium Backup Options

Medium backup responses include those public classroom sanctions that are familiar to us from our own schooling. Some, such as public warnings and reprimands, tend to be counter-productive because they generate resentment. Others, such as time-out, can serve the teacher well by providing an unequivocal means of saying "no" that is nonadversarial.

Because medium backup responses are familiar to us, it is easy to assume that we understand them. As always in the implementation of classroom management procedures, however, the devil is in the details. This section describes the details of some of the more common and useful procedures in order to maximize their success rate.

Heart-to-Heart Talk

When a problem reoccurs in class, my first instinct is to have a talk with the student to find out what is going on. Have the student do most of the talking.

"Jennifer, tell me, what was going on in class today between you and Michelle?"

Good clinicians are masters of wait time, and they are masters of making the other person do all of the work.

"What are we going to have to do to resolve this problem?"

Sometimes it is possible to have this conversation privately during class time. But, usually it will be after class.

Time-Out in the Classroom

Time-out has served as an alternative to more punitive sanctions in behavior management during recent decades. Time-out, however, is a prime example of a detailed procedure that is often used casually – "Like benching a kid, right?" Well, not exactly.

For starters, time-out should have the following elements:

- Two time-out areas should be prepared in the classroom since problems often involve two students. These need to be visually isolated so that the students in time-out cannot entertain each other or the rest of the class.

- Time-out should be considered an extension of meaning business with the same body language and the same withering boredom in response to any wheedling or arguing.

- Time-out should be relatively brief, usually not in excess of five minutes.

- Time-out should be boring. It is time away from desirable activity. There should be no "bootleg" sources of entertainment available in the time-out area.

The first problem with using time-out hits you as soon as you try to find two visually isolated areas in the classroom. It is hard enough to find just one.

The second problem in using time-out is the natural resistance of young people to being bored. If they would just sit in time-out quietly and be repentant, the whole thing would be so simple. But, instead, students who are squirrely in class tend to be squirrely in time-out.

Time-Out in a Colleague's Classroom

If a student continues to disrupt after being sent to time-out, you might consider time-out in a colleague's classroom. It often produces more reliable results than dealing with the office, and it sends the message that the teachers can handle serious problems themselves. The fine points of time-out in a colleague's classroom are as follows:

- The colleague to which the student is sent must thoroughly understand the program, approve of it and feel free to reciprocate should he or she need to.

- Time-out in a colleague's classroom should last for the remainder of the period or for at least 20 minutes.

- The student should be delivered to the colleague's classroom with a folder of work.

- The student must do the work in the folder during the entire time that he or she is in time-out. Academic help from the teacher should be brief and matter-of-fact.

- The student cannot join in any classroom games or activities. Usually he or she sits facing the wall so as not to be distracted or entertained.

- Finally, the student should be separated from his or her peer group *by as many years as possible.*

This last condition is perhaps the *most important* of all since it almost guarantees that the student will not want to repeat the experience. Yet, it is the condition that is *most commonly violated.* It is far easier for a fifth grade teacher to send Larry

The Key to Success

The key to success with a Backup System is not the size of the negative sanction.

Rather, the key to success is *the person who is using the Backup System.*

to the fifth grade class across the hall than to deliver him to a first grade class in another wing of the building.

If, however, you put Larry in an adjoining fifth grade classroom, he will probably have a grand old time showing off for his friends. The failure of time-out in one classroom has simply been exported to another classroom.

But put a fifth grader in a first grade classroom, and he or she will feel like "a fish out of water." Or, at the high school, send the goof-off from freshman life science to physics where he or she will not get the time of day.

Staying After School

This option can be difficult to implement due to problems with bus transportation. But, where practicable, it can be powerful.

Keeping students after school to complete their work can be just as useful as keeping students who disrupt. Students who just "twiddle their thumbs" in class soon learn that completing assignments is not an option. Rather, it is "pay me now, or pay me later."

The key procedural element to keeping a student after school is that he or she do schoolwork rather than playing games or being the teacher's "little helper." It is not supposed to be reinforcing.

You must be particularly wary of the possibility of *reinforcement errors* in this time of latchkey children. Sometimes just being with someone after school is preferable to being with no one.

Keeping students after school can be costly to any teacher who has other obligations at the end of the school day. One cheap solution is to keep the student for only five or ten minutes after dismissal. This provides time for some values clarification, while Larry's buddies go off and leave him.

Why Do Classroom Backup Responses Work?

Traditional Logic

The traditional logic of the Backup System is that *the punishment should fit the crime* as a means of suppressing crime. It seems logical. It should work.

Unfortunately, our experience tells us otherwise. The same group of "Larrys" produce the vast majority of the office referrals for as long as they are in school.

In addition, we know that some teachers send students to the office several times a day and have no classroom control, whereas other teachers rarely raise their voices and almost never need to send a student to the office. Why does the Backup System seem to fail those teachers who use it the most while helping those teachers who use it the least?

The Key to Success

The key to success with a Backup System is *not* the size of the negative sanction as logic might dictate. Rather, the key to success is *the person who is using the Backup System*.

If, from the first day of school your students learned that *you say what you mean, and you mean what you say*, and that *no means no* regardless of the circumstances, then, when you say "enough is enough" with your small backup responses, it means something. If, on the other hand, you are not perceived as meaning business, you can make any threat you want, and the kids will test you further just to see what happens. Weenies get no respect.

Chapter Twenty Five

Exploiting the Management System

The Management System

Beyond a Bag of Tricks

The term "bag of tricks" accurately describes our traditional approach to classroom management. Over the course of our careers we try a little of this and a little of that in the hope that things will get better.

Every year a new crop of fads and buzz words arrive on the scene to add to our bag of tricks. Yet we know from experience that this approach will not take us anywhere that we have not already been. As a profession, we have had no "game plan."

Good News

The good news is that the methods described in this book provide that missing game plan. They represent a clear window into the world of the exceptional teacher. They are both high-tech and down-to-earth. They define working smart instead of working hard.

Discipline or Instruction?

Over the years I often found it difficult to get educators to focus on instruction as part of successful discipline management. They would express the desire for "just a discipline program," adding that discipline was the main source of teacher complaints.

Yet, educators know that good discipline and good instruction go together in the classrooms of highly effective teachers. The question is, *how* do they go together?

Preview

- A management system differs from a bag of tricks by providing a full range of effective procedures that can easily be exploited in solving classroom management problems.

- The management system described in this book is organized into three levels based upon cost; interpersonal skills, incentive systems, and the Backup System, with the Backup System being the most expensive.

- The more effective teachers become at management, the less they will use the Backup System and the more they will rely on their interpersonal skills.

- In general, the more difficult the management problem, the more reinforcement-oriented is the cure. Only a management system organized in this fashion can avoid the tendency of alienated students to "raise the ante" when confronted by the Backup System.

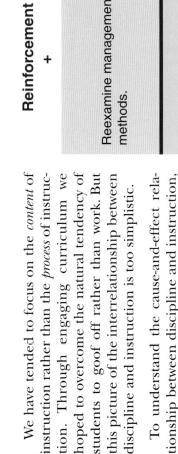

We have tended to focus on the *content* of instruction rather than the *process* of instruction. Through engaging curriculum we hoped to overcome the natural tendency of students to goof off rather than work. But this picture of the interrelationship between discipline and instruction is too simplistic.

To understand the cause-and-effect relationship between discipline and instruction, we must delve deeply into the social dynamics of the classroom. For example, we cannot even work the crowd, a precondition of effective discipline management, until we wean the helpless handraisers. And, we cannot wean the helpless handraisers until we create mastery by integrating the verbal, visual and physical modalities of learning in the teaching of a lesson.

Since everything in the classroom is interconnected, we must manage discipline and instruction simultaneously. And, to solve management problems quickly, our choices must be organized so that we may review them at a glance.

Three Levels of Management

The figure to the right organizes the management system into a *decision ladder*. As you can see, our management options are arranged along two paths: positive and negative, carrot and stick. Furthermore, they are arranged from inexpensive to expensive moving from bottom to top. In problem solving we would move systematically up the decision ladder in order to resolve the dilemma as inexpensively as possible.

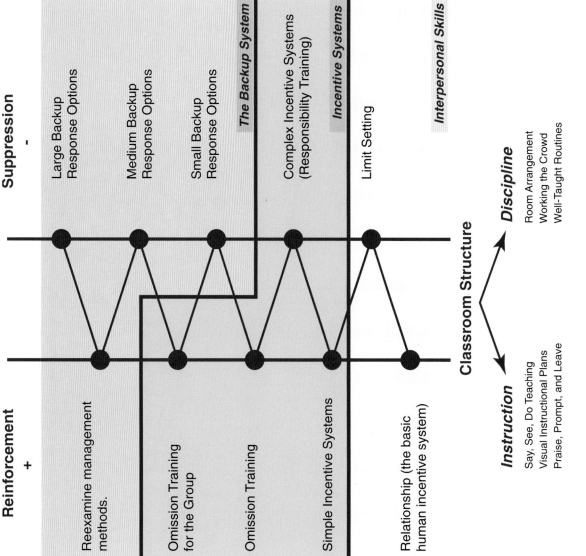

Reinforcement +

Suppression −

Reexamine management methods.

Large Backup Response Options

Omission Training for the Group

Medium Backup Response Options

Omission Training

Small Backup Response Options

The Backup System

Simple Incentive Systems

Complex Incentive Systems (Responsibility Training)

Incentive Systems

Relationship (the basic human incentive system)

Limit Setting

Classroom Structure

Interpersonal Skills

Instruction

Say, See, Do Teaching
Visual Instructional Plans
Praise, Prompt, and Leave

Discipline

Room Arrangement
Working the Crowd
Well-Taught Routines

To solve problems, go up the Decision Ladder.

The decision ladder is divided into three levels of management:

- **Interpersonal Skills:** This level of management describes the skills that have traditionally defined the natural teacher. This is the least expensive level of management since implementation requires skills rather than complicated programs, and since those skills reduce your stress and work load.

- **Incentive Systems:** Incentive systems provide motivation. As part of *instruction*, they provide motivation for working hard and being conscientious. As part of *discipline*, they provide motivation for cooperating with both the teacher and with classmates in carrying out classroom routines.

  Incentive systems add an element of cost to management since they require recordkeeping and the giving of reinforcers. However, more sophisticated incentive systems minimize these costs. Responsibility Training, for example, trains the entire class to cooperate in a wide range of management situations at almost no additional cost to the teacher.

- **The Backup System:** The purpose of the Backup System is to communicate that "no means no" to students who exhibit severe or repetitive disruptive behaviors. While the greater part of the Backup System is contained in the School Discipline Code, some of the most important sanctions are delivered invisibly by the teacher in the classroom.

These sanctions can keep small problems from becoming large by nipping them in the bud. However, for these inexpensive sanctions to work, the students must already perceive the teacher as meaning business.

Interpersonal Skills

Structure and Instruction

As you can see on the decision ladder to the left, Classroom Structure is the ground upon which effective management stands. Classroom Structure, however, is far more than room arrangement, rules, and routines.

Classroom Structure includes the process of instruction itself. It includes Say, See, Do Teaching so that students are fully engaged in learning by doing. It includes the use of Visual Instruction Plans (VIPs) so that the steps of learning are crystal clear. And, it also includes Praise, Prompt and Leave as an indispensable tool in making helpless handraisers into independent learners.

Effective teachers invest most of their classroom management effort at the level of Classroom Structure. Any element of Classroom Structure that is omitted or overlooked by the teacher will become a problem that requires Limit Setting.

Relationship Building

The first item on the positive side of the decision ladder is relationship building. While this could be subsumed under the heading of Classroom Structure, I have placed

Classroom Structure is the ground upon which effective management stands.

it as a separate item on the positive side of the ladder to remind us that all other aspects of management rest upon the goodwill that teachers establish with their students.

Relationship building is not just a matter of being nice. It is a *program*. It requires an investment of time and energy for both planning and implementation. It begins with an ice-breaking activity during the first period of the school year and never lets up.

Limit Setting

Since Limit Setting says "no" to an unacceptable behavior, we cross over to the negative side of the decision ladder. However, setting limits must not be adversarial or it will continually undermine our relationships with our students. Staying calm and using effective body language in Limit Setting allows teachers to say "no" to unacceptable behavior without producing alienation or embarrassment.

Most of the time-honored ways of saying "no," like nagging, threatening, and punishing, have the opposite effect on relationships. By the end of the school year, teachers and students in classrooms characterized by such methods are usually glad to be rid of each other.

Incentive Systems

Simple Incentives

Simple incentive systems represent a straightforward application of Grandma's Rule: *You have to finish your dinner before you get your dessert.* For dessert, we cross over to the positive side of the decision ladder.

Incentives for work productivity are of this type. As soon as you finish the assignment correctly, you may work on your project. Traditional incentive systems for discipline management such as the point systems and star charts common to elementary classrooms are also simple in design.

However, in discipline management these systems tend to be a lot of work for what you get. Complex record-keeping and the giving of reinforcers produce some improvement but no cure. To make the use of incentives cost-effective in broad areas of discipline management, complex incentive systems are required.

Complex Incentives

Complex incentive systems have more parts than simple incentive systems, most notably, bonuses and penalties. Responsibility Training represents the state of the art in complex incentive systems for discipline management.

We place complex incentives on the negative side of the decision ladder because they contain penalties. However, when used properly, complex incentive systems are overwhelmingly positive in nature.

Omission Training

If more management leverage is needed, probably because Larry chooses to ruin PAT, we go to the positive side of the decision ladder for Omission Training. Omission Training is a bonus-only management program. Larry can no longer lose PAT for the group.

Omission Training delivers the power of the peer group in order to turn Larry around. It is extremely cost-effective because it delivers that power for no more work than a heart-to-heart talk and a bonus clause added to PAT. Yet it rearranges the social dynamics of the classroom so that Larry is now a hero rather than an outcast.

Omission Training for the Group

As you can see by looking at the decision ladder, Omission Training for the group typically occurs after you have gone to small backup responses for repeated infractions. If you find that you are using small backup responses too often, you can give the group bonus PAT for avoiding the Backup System.

The Backup System

Small Backup Responses

Small backup responses take us to the negative side of the decision ladder. Small backup responses represent a series of communications that say, in effect, "A word to the wise..." If the student takes a hint and cools it for the rest of the period, the communication has done its job. However, the likelihood of that happening is a direct function of the degree to which the student already takes the teacher seriously.

Medium Backup Responses

Medium backup responses are also on the negative side of the decision ladder because they represent the penalties that teachers have traditionally used in the classroom. In the overall scheme of discipline management at the school site, sanctions such as sending a child to time-out or keeping them after class are viewed as small consequences, the kinds of things a teacher might do upon first encountering a problem.

As you can see from the decision ladder, however, medium backup responses are near the top. Teachers have a great many management options that they can and should employ before even considering a medium backup response.

There are serious reasons for avoiding medium backup responses. For one thing, they are expensive. Simply setting up a parent conference can cause the teacher several phone calls, to say nothing of time after school for the conference *if* the parent shows up. Even time-out can be a pain if the student in time-out chooses to disrupt further.

Large Backup Responses

Large backup responses are typically contained in the School Discipline Code. When it comes to large backup responses, there is nothing new under the sun.

Reexamine

On the decision ladder between medium and large backup responses is an option entitled "reexamine." A sudden crisis can take even the most effective teacher into large backup responses. Yet, under normal circumstances, effective teachers rarely send students to the office. Frequent reliance upon large backup responses should serve as a signal for us to get together with colleagues who understand the management system and reexamine what we are doing.

Using The Decision Ladder

The Region of Finesse

The figure on the following page shows the decision ladder with the contributions of this program outlined in red. The elements of discipline management unique to this program comprise most of the teacher's choices between Classroom Structure and the Backup System. This is the region of management in which finesse solves problems before they become expensive.

A Matter of Balance

Effective discipline management typically deals with *pairs* of behavior. You systematically strengthen the behaviors you want while weakening the behaviors that you do not want. If you simply suppress problem behavior without systematically building appropriate behavior, one problem might well be replaced by another problem.

Discipline management, therefore, should be viewed as the differential reinforcement of appropriate behavior rather than as simple suppression. It is *discrimination training* in which students are given both a good reason to stop *that* and a good reason to start *this.*

Consequently, as we move up the decision ladder in problem solving, we continually move back and forth

Suppression

-

Large Backup Response Options

Medium Backup Response Options

Small Backup Response Options

Complex Incentive Systems (Responsibility Training)

Limit Setting

Reinforcement

+

Reexamine management methods.

Omission Training for the Group

Omission Training

Simple Incentive Systems

Relationship (the basic human incentive system)

Classroom Structure

Discipline

Room Arrangement
Working the Crowd
Well-Taught Routines

Instruction

Say, See, Do Teaching
Visual Instructional Plans
Praise, Prompt, and Leave

Discipline management can be nonadversarial if you have the right tools.

between positive and negative. If Limit Setting isn't working, rather than upping the ante on the negative side, cross over and consider incentives. If the penalty component of Responsibility Training is not working, cross over and try Omission Training.

Looking at the decision ladder, you might characterize this program as "everything you can possibly do to avoid the Backup System." The larger the negative sanction, the more difficult it becomes to offset it with a positive sanction. Thus, the higher up you go in the Backup System, the more unbalanced discipline management becomes.

Understanding this characteristic of the Backup System should cause us to be very cautious concerning its use. You may be forced to go to the Backup System on occasion to deal with a crises, but you would not want to go there very often. In training we say, "You may have to visit, but you wouldn't want to live there."

Working Up and Down the Decision Ladder

As you attempt to solve a problem, you move in a step wise fashion from the bottom of the decision ladder to the top. The more effectively you exploit each step of the management system, the less likely it becomes that you will need to move further up.

Over the long run, as the management system becomes established in your classroom, you will work your way *down* the decision ladder. While you may need to use the Backup System early on with repeaters in

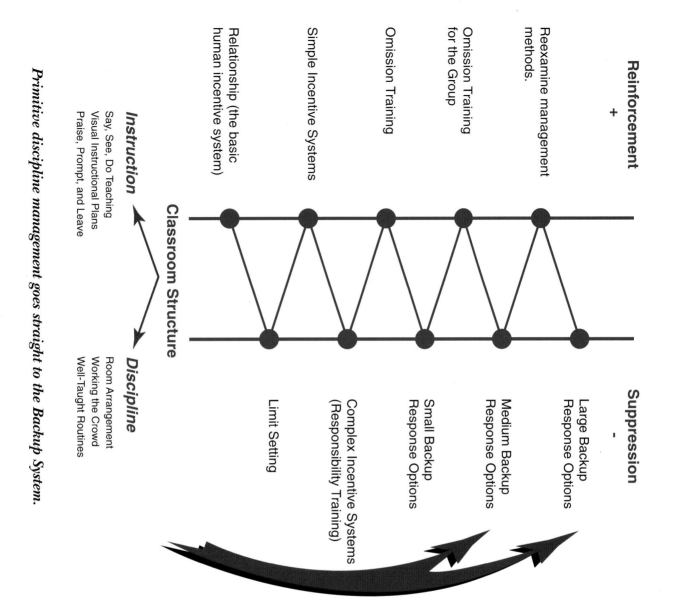

Reinforcement
+

Reexamine management
methods.

Omission Training
for the Group

Omission Training

Relationship (the basic
human incentive system)

Simple Incentive Systems

Classroom Structure

Instruction

Say, See, Do Teaching
Visual Instructional Plans
Praise, Prompt, and Leave

Suppression
−

Large Backup
Response Options

Medium Backup
Response Options

Small Backup
Response Options

Complex Incentive Systems
(Responsibility Training)

Limit Setting

Discipline

Room Arrangement
Working the Crowd
Well-Taught Routines

Primitive discipline management goes straight to the Backup System.

---

order to get their attention, eventually meaning business will get the same result.

When you watch highly effective teachers in the classroom, it becomes apparent that almost all of their discipline management is at the level of interpersonal skills. The more expensive parts of the management system have self-eliminated, leaving the teacher free to teach.

Primitive Discipline Management

Three Strikes

The figure to the left represents discipline management as it is all too frequently done. It goes from Classroom Structure directly to the Backup System with only a few reprimands in between. Sometimes it is no more than a name on the board and a few check marks followed by a trip to the office. Call it "three strikes and you're out."

I will refer to such a simplified approach to discipline management as "primitive discipline." Primitive discipline is a fight-flight reflex in institutional form. It lacks any of the finesse that might make discipline management invisible or cause it to self-eliminate over time.

Leapfrogging to the Backup System

It is natural when we are upset to leapfrog up the negative side of the decision ladder. At such times we may be dealing with truly outrageous behavior that requires a strong and immediate response. When we are angry, we reach for our largest sanctions. But we pay a high price for upset, especially when we have only a limited range of options. It can easily degenerate into a war of wills.

Turning Common Sense Upside Down

Positive Sanctions for Negative Behavior

The figure on this page presents the major discipline management procedures analyzed in terms of positive and negative consequences. The procedures are Limit Setting, Responsibility Training and Omission Training.

Limit Setting, in conjunction with working the crowd, is the most cost-effective way of dealing with the typical, high-rate disruptions like talking to neighbors. Yet, as we mentioned earlier, Limit Setting falls squarely into the negative column. It is a gentle and nonadversarial form of suppression, but it nevertheless says "no" in a convincing fashion.

Next comes Responsibility Training, which is a hybrid of bonus and penalty. It is used for more difficult management situations – dawdling, coming to class without materials, wasting time with pencil sharpening and hall passes, and management from a seated position.

Beneath Responsibility Training comes Omission Training, which is a bonus-only management program. Omission Training is used for our most difficult management situations – angry, alienated students who say to the teacher, "You can't make me."

Common Sense Revisited

The common sense of discipline management, of course, holds that the punishment must fit the crime. The bigger the crime, the bigger the punishment.

As you can see from the figure on this page, our management system turns common sense upside down. The more difficult and oppositional a student's behavior

becomes, the more *reinforcement oriented* is the cure. With the most angry and oppositional students, the management program has no penalty component whatsoever. Why would our system be constructed in this fashion?

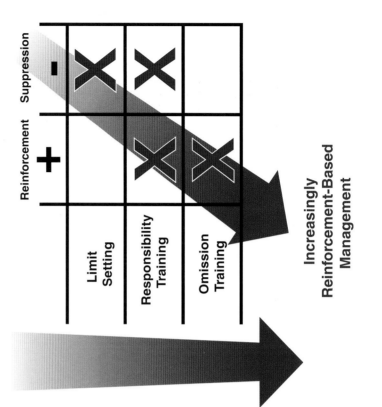

The more provocative the student, the more positive the response.

The Only Game in Town

I would like to say that I designed the management system in this fashion from the outset for the salutary effect it would have on alienated young people. But, I did not.

Rather, I simply worked with highly effective teachers until we had solved most of their everyday problems. Only after years of work did it become increasingly clear that positive management could be much more powerful and flexible than negative management.

Contrast the options available to educators in their school discipline codes with the homes that some of our students come from. Some students come from highly abusive environments. These young people are understandably angry, and they take that anger out on their teachers.

To counter this acting out, we have a Backup System that says, *If we see that behavior one more time, we will...* Now, imagine yourself facing an angry student, and finish the sentence. You'll *what?*

Many of these students grew up on physical abuse. Do you expect them to be intimidated by the mild sanctions that are permitted by law in your school discipline code? Do you really expect them to "fold" on the threat of detention or a day off of school?

The management system described in this book treats more oppositional behavior with more positive consequences because, in the final analysis, it is the only game in town. If we do not have the skill and finesse to get Larry to cooperate, we are faced with an endless war of attrition.

Appendix

PAT Ideas

Planning Your PATs

Exploiting Team Competition

You can quickly turn any lesson into a PAT by making it a team game. This appendix describes team game formats that are useful in a wide range of subject areas and with a wide range of age levels.

In addition to these team games, any game show format used on TV will work. Teachers commonly use Jeopardy, Family Feud, Twenty-One, Concentration, What's My Line?, Who Wants to Be a Millionaire?, To Tell the Truth, and College Bowl.

Developing a PAT Bank

Every teacher has good ideas for PAT. If teachers at a school site were to share one PAT a week, they would soon have a PAT bank. As we mentioned earlier, one middle school in Polk County, Florida had a faculty luncheon in which each teacher brought copies of a PAT as a ticket of admission. They received enough ideas to make a book.

Most PATs could be thought of as high-interest lesson formats. As the faculty's repertoire grows, the notion of having fun with learning increasingly permeates teaching.

See Our Web Site

Teachers who have been through our workshops often send us PAT ideas. We will post new PATs on our web site. We hope that you will be a frequent visitor as well as a contributor to **www.fredjones.com**.

Double-Diamond Baseball (Grades 1-12)

Subject Area: Math, History, Foreign Languages, Science, Vocabulary Development, Spelling, etc.

Objective: Test review.

Materials and Preparation:

- The teacher or students prepare questions in four degrees of difficulty; single, double, triple, home run.

- Two baseball diamonds will be needed in order to use a Ping-Pong game format. Mark the bases on the floor.

Student Grouping: 2 teams

The Play

1. The batter is asked by the pitcher to pick the level of difficulty of their question – single, double, triple, or home run.

2. The pitcher selects and asks a question from the single, double, triple or home run stack. If, however, the teacher is "pitcher" and does not have stacks of questions already prepared, he or she can just ask questions "off the top of their head."

3. If the student answers correctly, the student walks to the appropriate base and other runners advance the same number of bases.

4. If the question is answered incorrectly, a "fly ball" is called, and the question goes to a player of the team that is "in the field."

   - When you say "fly ball," wait before calling on a student so that everyone in the field must dig for the answer.

   - If the player in the field answers the question correctly, the fly ball has been caught and the batter is out.

   - If the outfielder misses the question, the fly ball has been dropped, and the batter goes to first base on an error. All runners advance one base on an error.

5. When using the Ping-Pong game format, the questions alternate between teams. So, the second question goes to the team that was in the field (i.e., playing defense) during the previous question. The Ping-Pong format guarantees that both teams

get to bat an equal number of times, that everybody plays all of the time, and that both teams are continually engaged in scoring runs.

6. The "Ping-Pong" format does away with innings. In order to make outs meaningful, compute the final score as runs minus outs.

Diagram of Scoring

Fine Points:

TEAM #1 _____   TEAM #2 _____

SCORE   SCORE

Runs _____   Runs _____

-Outs _____   -Outs _____

Total _____   Total _____

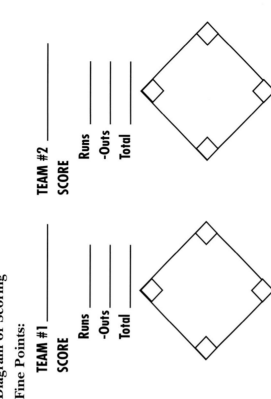

- Most 4-Level games follow a Ping-Pong format with the question going to the opposite team if missed. It is best to play such games open book. You will find the players on defense digging for the answer as soon as it is asked. Since kids hate doing nothing, you will usually find the rest of the students on the team that is "at bat" digging for the answer as well.

- Football is similar except that the defense can "sack the quarterback" for a ten-yard loss when the student picks a 10-yard question, or they can intercept a 20, 30 or 40-yard pass play.

- If you have any questions about rules, turn it over to the students. They will make sure the rules are fair. And, speaking of keeping things fair – a perennial preoccupation with teenagers – how do you choose teams fairly?

Pick four students of roughly equal scholastic ability to be captains. They do not need to be fast students. In fact this is a nice chance to honor some of your slower students. Give them your class list and say:

"I want you to take this class list to the table in the back of the room and make equal teams for me. Horse-trade until they are equal because you will have to live with them."

If you wish to add a further guarantee of fair play, say to the students:

"It is your job to choose and trade until the teams are equal. After you give me equal teams, you will draw lots to see which team you will captain."

Fingerprint (Grades K-12)

Subject Area: Math, Social Sciences, Foreign Languages, Science, History, Reading, etc.

Objective: Reinforce skills and information – fast recall.

Materials and Preparation: Write at random on the chalkboard answers to questions like those to be covered on the upcoming test.

Student Grouping: 2 teams, equally balanced.

The Play

1. Have the two teams line up single file about 20 feet away from the chalkboard.
2. Announce the question. The first person in line for each team runs up to the board and touches the appropriate answer. A team player may only touch one answer.
3. The first person who touches the right answer earns a point for the team.
4. The winning team has the most points at the end of PAT.

Comments or Variations
Running to the board and spotting the answer may be a real equalizer for those students who are not fast with the answer. This game may be used from kindergarten to high school.

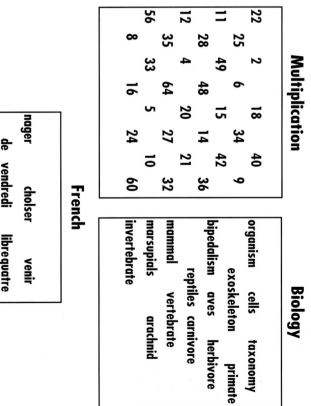

Multiplication

22	2	18	34	40
11	25	6	15	9
12	28	49	14	42
56	35	4	20	36
8	33	64	27	21
		5	10	32
		16	24	60

Biology

organism	cells	taxonomy
bipedalism	exoskeleton	primate
mammal	reptiles	carnivore	herbivore
invertebrate	marsupials	aves	arachnid
	vertebrate	

French

nager	cholser	venir
grand	de	librequatre
donner	vivant	apprendre
jeter	avoir	il	les devoirs
	sur	entendreaider

Alphabet Search (Grades 2-12)

Subject Area: All subjects.

Objective: To aid the students in recalling information given over a long period of time.

Materials and Preparation: Paper and pencils.

Student Grouping: 2 teams with a recorder on each team.

The Play

The teams, using the alphabet as a base, will find as many words as possible related to the subject matter. At the end of the allotted time, the team members will turn their papers in to their recorder for tabulation.

Students eventually begin to make mental notes of new words presented in the curriculum to use during Alphabet Search.

Scoring: 1 point is given for each word 10 bonus points if all 26 letters have accompanying words.

Sample:

Primary	History
Can you find a word that starts with...?	American Revolution

A = apple	A = Crispus Attucks, Ethan Allen
B = ball, bat, Bill	B = Britain, Boston Massacre
C = cat	C = Continental Congress
D = dog	D = Delaware River
E =	E =
F = fun	F = Benjamin Franklin
G = go, give, girl	G = Guerrilla Warfare
H =	H = Patrick Henry, Nathan Hall
I = ice	I =
J =	J = Thomas Jefferson

Caboose (Grades 4-9)

Subject Area: English, Science, Foreign Language, History.

Objective: To encourage vocabulary enrichment in a specific subject area while emphasizing spelling.

Materials and Preparation: None.

Student Grouping: Two or more teams.

The Play

1. The first student says a word in a particular category. i.e., The category is animals. The word is dog.

2. The first student on the second team must give a noun beginning with the last letter of the previous word (dog). i.e.,goose

3. Points are given for each correct word.

4. Think up words that have last letters that are difficult to use.

5. Words may not be used again.

6. The team with the most points wins.

Comments or Variations

This game is great for science, foreign language and history vocabulary development.

Cut Throat (Grades 3-12)

Subject Area: English, Math, Foreign Language, History.

Objective: Review of specific information.

Materials and Preparation: Chalkboard space, chalk, prepared questions or problems.

Student Grouping: Divide the class into 4 equal teams and have teams count off.

The Play

1. The teacher picks two members of each team to go to the board to write the answer a specific question or to translate a passage as in a foreign language course.

2. Each pair of students at the board may collaborate with each

other and with the seated team members. One of the students acts as writer, the other student as the runner.

3. Caution students not to get too loud or the other team may hear them.

Scoring:

First chalk in tray – 2,000 points

Second chalk in tray – 1,500 points

Third chalk in tray – 1,000 points

Fourth chalk in tray – 500 points

Further Play

Now the class plays Cut Throat! Imagine a passage that each team has translated into French. Each team's translation is written on the board. The teacher takes each team's translation in turn and has the other teams critique it.

When an error is found, the teacher subtracts a given number of points from that team's score. Consequently, teams can hack away at each other's scores by finding errors – a fiendishly enjoyable activity. Teachers can assign different values to different kinds of errors as they see fit. As an option, teachers can also assess penalty points for an incorrect critique. This prevents students from guessing. Allowing team members to collaborate in the critique adds a strong element of cooperative learning.

This fast-moving game with high scores allows for punctuation and spelling review for English, computation for math, history answers in complete sentences, or dictation for a foreign language.

California Countdown (Grades 4-12)

Subject Area: All subjects.

Objective: Test review and teamwork.

Materials and Preparation: Prepare two types of questions appropriate to the subject area, "Toss-Up" questions and "Bonus" questions. "Toss-Up" questions should require accuracy and speed. They may reflect your tests' true/false questions, fill-in, multiple choice and short answer. "Bonus" questions, since they may be answered by the total team, may require lengthy answers involving cause and effect and detailed explanations.

Student Groupings: 2 teams, each with a captain.

The Play

1. Ask a "Toss-Up" question. The first hand up on either team is allowed to answer the question.

2. An incorrect answer costs the team 5 points, and a student from the other team gets a chance to answer the question.

3. If answered correctly, the team gets 10 points and a chance at a "Bonus" question.

4. A "Bonus" question may be answered by the team's captain after discussion with the team. A correct answer is worth 20 points. There is no penalty for an incorrect answer.

Scoring

- 10 points for a correctly answered "Toss-Up" question
- 5 points penalty for incorrect answer to "Toss-Up" question
- 20 points for correctly answered "Bonus" question

Comments or Variations

Student enthusiasm for this variant of College Bowl is unbelievable. After students become familiar with the appropriate types of questions, have each student write 4 good "Toss-Up" and 4 "Bonus" questions with answers and reference page numbers if necessary.

Chalkboard Relays (Grades 4-12)

Subject Area: English, Math, Foreign Languages, Science, Social Science, Reading.

Objective: Fast recall and categorizing in the subject area.

Materials and Preparation: Chalkboard space, chalk, categories.

Student Grouping: The class is divided into 4 equal teams.

The Play

1. Four different categories are written on the board (example: noun, verb, adjective, adverb).
2. The teams are lined up across from the chalkboard.
3. At a given signal, the first student in each line writes one word under the team's category title. He or she then hands the chalk to the next student in line and is seated.
4. The next student writes a word in the same manner and the race continues until a line is completely seated.
5. The scores are tallied and the teams rotate and line up in front of the category to their right.
6. The play continues until each team has a chance against each category. Words may not be repeated.

Scoring

- First team seated – 100 points
- Second team seated – 90 points
- Third team seated – 80 points
- Fourth team seated – 70 points
- Plus 10 points per correct word

Comments or Variation

Math Relays: Students race to list multiples of a number.

Foreign Language Relays: Students race with parts of speech or words that begin with a certain letter.

Science Relays: Students race to list items of such categories as plants, minerals, insects, etc.

Social Science Relays: Students race to list items of such categories as famous places, rivers, mountains, cities, etc.

Reading Relays: Students race to list items of such categories as starting sounds, prefixes, suffixes, compound words, etc.

Tic Tac Dough (Grades 4-12)

Subject Area: All subjects.

Objective: Test review and teamwork.

Materials and Preparation:

1. Numbers 1-9 are assigned to all students.
2. Each student writes four questions and answers on four separate slips of paper with the student's "number" on the back. Therefore, all of the questions by the same student have the same number.
3. The questions are turned in and put into nine stacks according to their number.

Student Grouping: 2 equal teams.

The Play

1. The first student on Team A selects a number off the Tic Tac Dough board which is written on the chalkboard.
2. The teacher selects and asks a question out of the same number stack that the student has selected.
3. Anyone on Team A can give the person who selected the question the answer. However, the person who is "it" must say the answer.
4. If his/her answer is correct, an "X" or "O" is put in the numbered square that he/she selected. Then it's Team B's turn.
5. If the answer is incorrect, Team A loses their turn, and Team B is up.
6. Once an "X" or "O" is placed in a particular square, questions from that numbered stack may not be used for the rest of that game.

Diagram Of Tic Tac Dough Board

1	7	3
6	9	5
4	2	8

Around the World (Grades 1-12)

Subject Area: All subjects.

Objective: Fast recall of important information or calculations.

Materials and Preparation: A list of questions or problems for review.

Student Grouping: Total class.

The Play

1. The first student stands beside the seat of the second student.

2. The teacher asks a question and shows a flashcard to both of the students at once.

3. The first to answer correctly wins and gets to stand beside the seat of the next student in line.

4. The student who misses sits down.

5. The play continues as students rotate around the room.

6. At the end of the playing time, have the students count the number of seats they have moved during the game.

7. The two students who have moved the most stand and face each other for one last question or problem.

Comments or Variation

Math Around the World: Flash cards or math facts such as multiplication, fractions, metrics and word problems may be used.

English Around the World: Questions concerning comprehension of recently assigned materials, parts of speech, authors, etc.

Science Around the World: Questions concerning classification, adaptations, bone identification, etc.

History Around the World: Quotations, famous people, great events, governmental structure, cause and effect, etc.

Foreign Language Around the World: Flashcards for vocabulary reinforcement showing nouns and verbs (dog, tree, apple, run, swim, talk).

Home Economics Around the World: Utensils and their uses, sewing machine parts, nutrition facts.

Add It (Grades 2-10)

Subject Area: Math.

Objective: Quick addition review.

Materials and Preparation: Paper and pencils.

Student Grouping: Total class.

The Play

1. The teacher announces any number and an addend. For example: 7 and 4

2. The students write and add the two numbers and continue to add the same addend to the new sum until the teacher calls stop at the end of one minute.

Example: 7

$$\begin{array}{r} 7 \\ +4 \\ \hline 11 \\ +4 \\ \hline 15 \\ +4 \\ \hline 19 \\ +4 \\ \hline 23 \end{array}$$

3. Class stands and a volunteer begins reading problems and answers aloud, slowly.

4. As students no longer have the answers, they are seated.

5. The student left standing is the winner.

Comments or Variation

This is an easy, quick game that the students love. The time period may be varied, and it may be used with subtraction.

Comprehension (Grades 3-12)

Subject Area: Literature, Health, History, Biology, etc.

Objective: To increase comprehension and review important points of an assignment.

Materials: Paper and pencils.

Student Grouping: Divide the class into 4 equal groups.

The Play

1. Each group writes 10 questions and answers about what they have read (assigned reading, chapter or unit). The first hand to go up from another group gets to answer the question.

2. A group member asks a question to the whole class. The first hand to go up from another group gets to answer the question.

3. If that person answers correctly, he or she gets a point for his or her team. If the answer is incorrect, the teacher chooses someone from another team to get a try at the question.

4. If no one can answer the question, the team who asked it gets a point, but they must be able to defend or prove their answer.

5. The play continues with each team taking turns asking questions.

6. The game is over when time is up or when all the questions have been asked.

7. The team with the highest score wins.

Comments or Variation

When creating the questions, your students will review the material. During the game the students will also be reviewing important information. These two reviewing sessions add up to a lot of learning and fun. You'll be amazed at the tough questions your students will ask and answer.

Popcorn Balloon Game (Grades 3-8)

Subject Area: Math.

Objective: Multiplication review for a popcorn party.

Materials: Pencils, balloon, ditto, popcorn kernels, popcorn popper, paper plates.

Student Grouping: Divide the class into small groups (6) and have each group sit close together for sharing.

The Play

1. Each group will have:

   a. one paper plate with a handful of unpopped popcorn kernels.

   b. one paper plate with a star drawn in the middle.

   c. a ditto and pencil for each student.

2. Each student is directed to fill the 9 balloons on his ditto with numbers 1-12, one number per balloon.

3. The teacher calls out a number. (Example: 15) and each student thinks of the factor of the number (Example: 3x5=15).

4. If the student has the balloons #3 and #5, he puts a popcorn kernel in each balloon.

5. The teacher calls time after 30 seconds and asks the students the factors of the number.

6. Every student who put a kernel on the factors of the number may take those kernels and only those kernels and place them on the star paper plate. The star paper plate now contains the beginning of the popcorn to be popped for the party.

7. Dittos are cleared of kernels and the teacher calls another number.

8. The popcorn balloon game is over when PAT is up or when you have enough popcorn for a party.

9. Watch out for numbers like:

   24 = 8x3x1, 6x4x1, 3x2x4x1, 3x2x2x2x1, 12x2x1, 6x2x2x1

   = 22 possible kernels

   36 = 6x6x1, 3x2x6x1, 9x4x1, 12x3x1, 3x4x3x1, 3x2x2x3x1

   = 22 possible kernels

Unscramble Me (Grades 2-12)

Subject Area: All subjects.

Objective: To emphasize spelling across the curriculum.

Materials and Preparation: List of vocabulary or important words appropriate for curriculum area scrambled on ditto, chalkboard, overhead, or opaque projector.

Student Grouping: Individuals or pairs.

The Play

1. The students are given or shown the list of important words scrambled and are challenged to unscramble them within a given time period. The students enjoy making up these lists themselves. Be sure they include the answer sheet.
2. A point is given for every word successfully unscrambled.

Example:

Where in the world?		*Math*	
Livbiao	Bolivia	Cainfrot	Fraction
Turieb	Beirut	Repnect	Percent
Salnep	_____	Cuerde	_____

Stump the Panel (Grades 3-12)

Subject Area: English, Reading, Science, History, Foreign Language, Social Science.

Objective: Unit or chapter review.

Materials and Preparation: Students prepare questions from the unit or chapter.

Student Grouping: Total class.

The Play

1. Select or ask for five volunteers to be on the panel.
2. The class tries to stump the panel by asking questions from the unit.
3. The panel member selected is given 30 seconds to answer the question.
4. If the panel member can correctly answer the question, they remain on the panel.
5. If the panel member is stumped, the person who asked the question may answer it and become the new panel member.

The Moon (Grades 3-12)

Subject Area: Math.

Objective: Addition review and probability.

Materials and Preparation: Dice plus paper and pencil for score keeping. However, this may be played with the entire class at once with an overhead projector.

Student Grouping: 2-5 players.

The Play

1. The object of the game is to have the highest score after 10 turns or to be the first player to reach 100.
2. The players take turns rolling the dice.
3. Each player may roll as many times as they want adding up the numbers rolled. If the player rolls a one, he or she loses all points accumulated during that turn. If the player rolls a one on both of the dice, he or she loses everything and starts over with zero.
4. If the player stops his or her turn before throwing a one, then he or she passes the dice to the next player and records the total score for that turn.
5. The only time a one doesn't cause a loss of points is when it appears during your first roll of the turn. You get to roll again.

The teacher rolls until a one appears during each turn. Students may stop at any time and add the score.

Diagram: Possible Scoreboard

	JAMES	CATHY	BRIAN	LYNNE	ERIC
1.	14	13	29	21	31
2.	$\frac{14}{28}$	$\frac{19}{32}$	$\frac{0}{29}$	$\frac{14}{35}$	$\frac{0}{31}$
3.	$\frac{23}{31}$	$\frac{0}{32}$	$\frac{31}{60}$	$\frac{0}{35}$	$\frac{0}{31}$
4.	–	–	–	–	–
5.	–	–	–	–	–

Dictionary (Grades 4-12)

Subject Area: Language Arts and Vocabulary Development.

Objective: To increase dictionary appreciation and vocabulary development.

Materials and Preparation: 1 dictionary per group, paper and pencils.

Student Grouping: Small groups of 5-8 students.

The Play

1. One student in each small group starts as "Dictionary Person."
2. One "Dictionary Person" finds a word in the dictionary that he/she feels the rest of the group doesn't know and announces the word to the group. If someone knows the word, the "Dictionary Person" keeps trying until he/she finds a word that is unknown to all.
3. Each person writes the word on the top of a piece of paper, creates a definition for it and signs his or her name.
4. The "Dictionary Person" writes the word and real definition on a piece of paper. The definition may be shortened and paraphrased.
5. All newly created definitions and the real definition are turned into the "Dictionary Person" to read over silently in order for them to become familiar with the wording of each definition.
6. The "Dictionary Person" numbers the definitions and reads them aloud to the group.
7. Each person writes the number of the definition they feel is the real definition on a scratch piece of paper.
8. The "Dictionary Person" calls for the votes and tallies each person's score. Peals of laughter may be heard when players discover whose definition they voted for.
9. The dictionary is now passed to the left and the play starts again. The game is over when every player has been "Dictionary Person."

Scoring

1. A player may earn 2 points each time someone votes for his/her definition.
2. A player may earn 1 point if he/she votes for the "real" definition.
3. The "Dictionary Person," if no one votes for the real definition, gives 1 point to each person in the group.

Example: Round 1

BILL	SANDY	JUAN	PEARL	FRED
	2	**1**	**6**	**1**
(Dictionary Person – no points earned)	(1 person voted for Sandy's definition)	(Juan guessed the real definition)	(3 people voted for Pearl's definition)	(Fred guessed the real definition)

Comments or Variation

This is a very popular game with everyone. The students become fascinated with new words in their treasure chest, the dictionary!

Imagination (Grades 4-12)

Subject Area: English and Art.

Objective: Enjoy the combination of work, play and art.

Materials and Preparation: Scratch and drawing paper, pencils, crayons, and/or marking pens.

The Play

1. Using your students' imagination, have them literally picture a statement like, "My father is playing bridge." You can imagine a river with the father being the bridge.

2. Together your students can think of many interesting statements.

Examples:

We gave my room a coat of paint.

My brother has a hoarse throat.

We took the bus home.

She said her baby was a little dear.

She has bare feet.

The teacher got fired.

3. Let each student choose a statement and illustrate it.

You may want to use the pictures on pages 117 and 305 in this book as examples of how an artist might use imagination.

Oh, What a Story! (Grades 4-12)

Subject Area: English, Creative Writing.

Objective: Experience in group creative writing.

Materials and Preparation: Paper and pencils.

Student Grouping: 5 or 6 groups of equal size. As time passes, the size of the groups may shrink or expand for variety.

The Play

1. Each student begins by writing a story for one minute on a topic of his or her choice.

2. When time is up, the teacher says, "Stop!"

3. Each story is passed to another member in the group who reads and continues the story until "Stop" is called.

4. Repeat this process until stories pass through the entire group, allowing more time as stories get longer.

5. The last person or the person who started can conclude the story.

6. Some or all of the stories may be read to the class by the students.

Web Site

www.fredjones.com

Beyond the Book

Tools for Teaching presents Dr. Jones' work in training teachers over a period of three decades. While *Tools for Teaching* describes the basic skills of classroom management, describing these skills is only the beginning of a process of mastery and successful implementation.

Mastery of skills requires training. It requires a thorough understanding of the nature and intent of the skills, coaching in their fine points, sharing of classroom experiences and effective problem solving. Successful implementation requires that teachers and administrators work together over an extended period of time until these new procedures are fully internalized into the school culture.

At Fredric H. Jones and Associates we are committed to helping teachers master the skills of classroom manage-

ment. For new teachers these are survival skills and will determine to a large degree whether promising young teachers stay in the profession. For more experienced teachers these skills can be the difference between professional fulfillment and burnout. Our web site is an important part of our reaching out to educators in an effort to help them succeed.

Levels of the Game

Mastering the skills of classroom management represents a process of growth and change that should last as long as a teacher's career. Yet, there is no simple template for this process. Rather, each school site and each school district will develop a program of professional development that meets its current needs. We provide resources that will help educators develop an effective staff development plan. Resources include:

The Book

It is not uncommon for teachers to successfully implement major elements of *Tools for Teaching* on their own. More and more school districts are providing copies of *Tools for Teaching* as a basic component of their new teacher induction programs.

Study Group Activity Guide

As mentioned earlier (page v), the *Study Group Activity Guide* structures twelve 45-minute after school meetings in which teachers share ideas, solve problems, and practice the tools for teaching. Each meeting includes reading assignments and focus questions, performance checklists, and skill building activities. Skill building activities include the practice of discreet management skills and the coaching of participants through more complex management scenarios. As a free download, the *Study Group Activity Guide* in conjunction with *Tools for Teaching* provides a strong basis for professional growth regardless of local budgetary limitations.

Tools for Teaching Conferences

Three day training conferences are held throughout North America in which teachers are trained in the skills of classroom management. While individual teachers often attend these conferences for the sake of their own professional growth, school sites and school districts commonly send teams to these conferences to serve as trainers when they return. A workshop calendar is posted on our web site.

The Video Toolbox

The *Video Toolbox* brings a *Tools for Teaching Conference* to your school site. It is designed to parallel the *Study Group Activity Guide* providing each of the twelve after school meetings with a video component. The *Video Toolbox* is indispensible in bringing the fine points of implementation to teachers and is a vital resource for school site training teams.

Tools for Teaching Web Connection

The internet allows us to provide a range of services to educators that extend beyond a training program in *Tools for Teaching*. The following list gives you a brief idea of what you might find:

Preferred Activity Bank

- PAT ideas from teachers in the field
- links to publishers of learning games and activities
- links to other web sites that feature learning games and activities

Omission Training Stories – how teachers have used *Tools for Teaching* and especially Omission Training to turn around their most unlikely candidates for student of the year

Applications of Bell Work – Bell Work activities that eliminate waisted time at the beginning of class

Tips for Substitute Teachers – how to get *Tools for Teaching* up and running *fast*

Message Board – a place for teachers to share their ideas and experiences with colleagues worldwide

College Report Page – resources for college students with a report to write. Due to the popularity of the textbooks by C.M. Charles, Robert Tauber, and Charles Wolfgang, all of whom include sections on Dr. Jones, many students need a little help in getting focused.

Index

About the Authors

I have been working with teachers regarding classroom management for over thirty years now. I began my career as a clinical psychologist, receiving my Ph.D. from UCLA. My first job was director of the ward for autistic children at the UCLA Medical Center where I succeeded Ivar Lovaas. He had trained the staff beautifully, and they in turn trained me. It was at this time in 1969-70 that I began working in classrooms for emotionally disturbed children. There I came across two natural teachers who could make these "handicapped" students eat out of the palms of their hands. This story is recounted in Chapter 1, "Learning from the 'Natural' Teachers."

From 1972-78 I was on the faculties of both the University of Rochester and the University of Rochester Medical Center. There I was part of a large program-project grant from the National Institute of Mental Health to study "high-risk" families – families with one parent having a severe psychological disability. Soon after I arrived in Rochester, I began working with the regional Board of Cooperative Educational Services to help with severe behavioral problems in their classrooms. Working in classrooms with highly capable teachers and graduate students became my career "hobby." By 1978, it became clear to me that I was having much more fun with my hobby than with the high-risk research. In 1978, I cancelled a final site visit for a Career Development Award from NIMH and resigned from the university. I have been a consultant ever since, training teachers and writing.

Jo Lynne and I met at the University of Kansas in 1961 where she was getting a degree in education. We married two years later and have been working together ever since studying classrooms and raising a family.

Patrick (below left) received his bachelor's degree from The Colorado College and his masters in education from the University of California at Santa Cruz.

Brian (below right) received his bachelor's degree from Kenyon College before doing post-graduate work at The San Francisco Art Institute.

Fredric H. Jones & Associates, Inc.
103 Quarry Lane
Santa Cruz, CA 95060
tel: (831) 425-8222   fax (831) 426-8222
www.fredjones.com